grog

Dearest Victoria,

Wishing you the very
happiest of birthdays.
I hope it is a day
full of fun and some
of this ↑
　　　Love Caroline.

grog

A BOTTLED HISTORY OF AUSTRALIA'S FIRST 30 YEARS

TOM GILLING

hachette
AUSTRALIA

Aboriginal and Torres Strait Islander people are advised that this publication contains names and images of people who have passed away.

hachette
AUSTRALIA

Published in Australia and New Zealand in 2016
by Hachette Australia
(an imprint of Hachette Australia Pty Limited)
Level 17, 207 Kent Street, Sydney NSW 2000
www.hachette.com.au

Copyright © Tom Gilling, 2016

National Library of Australia
Cataloguing-in-Publication data

Gilling, Tom, author.
Grog: A bottled history of Australia's first 30 years/Tom Gilling.

ISBN: 978 0 7336 3401 7 (paperback)

Liquor industry – Australia – History.
Australia – History – 1788–1851.

381.4566310994

Cover design by Luke Causby/Blue Cork
Cover images courtesy of Dreamstime.com
Typeset in 12/19 pt Bembo by Bookhouse, Sydney
Printed and bound in Australia by McPherson's Printing Group

For Rosemary

Contents

Author's note

Figures for the composition of the First Fleet are notoriously unreliable. The numbers quoted by officers who sailed with the fleet rarely tally. Where primary sources contradict each other, I have followed the numbers used by Mollie Gillen in her book *The Founders of Australia: A Biographical Dictionary of the First Fleet.* The spelling of convicts' names is another source of disagreement, long past any hope of resolution.

Introduction

Exactly ten years after the First Fleet sailed into Botany Bay, David Collins published his *Account of the English Colony in New South Wales*. Collins's book was not the first account of the colony to hit the English market – Governor Arthur Phillip had published his version in 1789 and Captain Watkin Tench of the marines had published two volumes by 1793 – but it was the most sensational.

As deputy judge advocate (he was also described, confusingly, as judge advocate), Collins knew all about the darker side of the government's social experiment. He realised that many of the convicts were incorrigible, and that a good number of the marines sent out to guard them were not much better. He reported the disgraceful behaviour he observed, and had no doubt that grog was largely to blame for it.

The word 'drunkenness', which did not appear at all in the hundreds of pages written by Phillip and Tench, peppered Collins's narrative of the colony's first years. The convicts had hardly disembarked when Collins was lamenting their eagerness to get drunk on spirits smuggled ashore at night by the sailors. Next he bemoaned the 'affrays and disorders' committed by drunken marines. After that it was the settlers, whose homes were 'nothing else but porterhouses, where rioting and drunkenness prevailed as long as the means remained'.

So it went on, a catalogue of alcohol-fuelled crime and debauchery.

Nor was Collins alone in concluding that alcohol was at the heart of all the colony's problems. '[V]ice of almost every kind prevails,' wrote Richard Atkins, Collins's successor as deputy judge advocate and himself a notorious pisspot. 'Gaming, whoring, and drunkenness stalk in broad day without the least check. Religion is laughed at, the Saboth profaned . . . neither civil or religious rites are observed.'

In a sermon published in London under the title 'An address to the inhabitants of the colonies established in New South Wales and Norfolk Island', the colony's first chaplain, Richard Johnson, railed against the convicts' propensity 'to steal, to break the sabbath, to be guilty of uncleanness, drunkenness, and other abominations'.

Johnson's successor, Samuel Marsden, reported Sydney to be a place of 'drunkenness, gaming and debaucheries'.

The perception of perpetual drunkenness continued to be reflected back from London in the form of royal instructions to incoming governors to control the liquor trade and stamp out illegal distilling.

The colony's reputation for intoxication stuck for another 150 years, regularly revived by writers such as Manning Clark and Robert Hughes. In his 1986 blockbuster *The Fatal Shore*, Hughes declared that between 1790 and 1820 'nearly all the men and most of the women were addicted to rum'.

If everybody had been as drunk as Hughes suggests, the colony would scarcely have been able to feed itself, let alone grow surpluses and prosper. Yet comments like Hughes's, rooted in the scathing observations of early chroniclers such as David Collins, testify to the appeal of this founding myth of European settlement.

Recognising the failure of his predecessors' attempts to control the rum trade, Governor Lachlan Macquarie declared in 1810 that 'it would be good and sound policy to sanction the free importation of *good* spirits'. Within a few years, grog was showing signs of becoming respectable – or as respectable as it ever would be. A strict licence system was in place to keep publicans (many of whom were women) honest, or honest enough.

Among the ex-convict landlords was a man named James Squires (or Squire), a chicken thief from Kingston upon Thames who turned himself into a successful brewer. By the time he died in 1822, Squires was one of the colony's most respected citizens, renowned for making beer 'of an excellent quality'. His funeral was said to be the largest Sydney had ever seen.

Over three decades of supposedly incorrigible drunkenness, the men and women of New South Wales transformed the colony from a squalid and starving convict settlement into a prosperous trading port with fashionable Georgian street names and a monumental two-storey hospital built by private contractors in exchange for a monopoly on rum.

The story of grog is the story of Australia (and perhaps vice versa). This is how it all began.

1

A great many casks

As the 11 ships of the First Fleet loitered off the Isle of Wight, a corpse floated alongside the *Lady Penrhyn*, a transport packed with 109 female convicts. The corpse, 'sew'd up in a hammock', was noticed by Arthur Bowes Smyth, the *Lady Penrhyn*'s 36-year-old surgeon, who considered the incident interesting enough to write about it that night in his journal. Another corpse bobbed past a few days afterwards. A fortnight later, gazing over the choppy waters of the English Channel towards the Lizard, Smyth saw, 'A great many Casks of Geneva [Dutch gin] floating on the water of which the Fishburn pick'd up 35 & the Scarborough 25. A Lugger from Falmouth came alongside, all Hands in her very drunk.' Bodies and booze: between them, they hinted at what lay ahead for Britain's far-flung penal colony.

In eighteenth-century England, death – and particularly the risk of death – was never far away. While strolling around the churchyard at Stokes Bay, not far from Portsmouth, Smyth observed a 'prodigious number of tomb stones'. Three days later, he reported the death of an infant named Hugh Sandlyn, whose mother was a convict. The same day, a boat belonging to another convict ship, the *Alexander*, overturned, tipping the first mate and five sailors into the sea. (Fortunately, they survived.)

Before the fleet had even set sail, disease swept through two of the transports, including the *Lady Penrhyn*, killing 11 convicts and an unknown number of sailors and marines. Smyth himself was the unwitting beneficiary of one death. His cabin on the *Lady Penrhyn* had previously belonged to the third mate, Jenkinson, who 'died of a putrid fever the night before I came on board'.

Although he practised as a surgeon and midwife, Smyth had no formal training in medicine. In that respect, he was not very different from the motley cast of soldiers and stocking weavers and buckle makers who, in the years to come, would have to reinvent themselves as farmers, builders and brewers in the new colony.

After coming down from London on the Portsmouth mail coach, Smyth boarded the *Lady Penrhyn* on 22 March 1787. By then, third mate Jenkinson's cabin had been freshly painted and fumigated. Smyth found the fleet 'in hourly expectation of the arrival of Governor Phillip'. But it would be another seven weeks before Phillip and the fleet were ready to embark. During that time, Smyth and his colleagues, and the convicts already on board the transports, could do nothing but wait.

On 19 April word reached Portsmouth 'that Governor Phillip's business is at last all finally settled & he may be expected at the Mother Bank on Saturday next'. There was no sign of Phillip the following Saturday or the one after that, but on 7 May rumours began to circulate that 'Governor Phillip is come down'. The next day Smyth noted gloomily, 'Governor expected on board but did not come.' It was not until 9 May, nearly four months after the first convicts had shuffled aboard the transports, that Smyth was finally able to report, 'The Governor came on board the *Sirius* this forenoon.'

Phillip had spent those four months battling with the Navy Board and the Treasury to have the fleet fitted out as he wanted.

Britain had more than half a century's experience of shipping its felons overseas, but none of it boded well for the nearly 800 convicts hunkered in the darkness between decks on the six transport ships of the First Fleet.

In the decade before the American Revolution, Britain had employed private contractors to ship around a thousand convicts a year to America. In 1778 one of the major contractors, Duncan Campbell, told a House of Commons committee on transportation that 'upon an average 10 is considered a moderate loss out of 100'; after seven years, it was expected that a seventh of all convicts would have died either in gaol or on board.

Crossing the Atlantic took just six weeks, but the Home Office estimated that it would take much longer – eight months – for the First Fleet to reach Botany Bay. The voyage would have been arduous enough for men and women who had set out from England fit and healthy, but the convicts assigned to the First Fleet were anything but. Culled from disease-ridden county prisons and from overcrowded hulks anchored in the River Thames, many were in a wretched condition before they embarked.

David Collins, the future deputy judge advocate, was not alone in predicting that before the fleet had been a month at sea, one of the six transports would have to be converted into a hospital ship. The *Bath Chronicle* speculated that 'the first land that two thirds of [the convicts] will reach will be the bottom of the sea, there to make their final deposit in the bosom of the great deep'.

These dire prophecies did not reckon on the character or capabilities of Arthur Phillip. Born in 1738, Phillip had been at sea since the age of 16. During the Seven Years' War, he had seen active service against the French and Spanish Navies before retiring on half-pay to manage his properties in Hampshire. Later, with the Admiralty's permission, he served in the Portuguese Navy while working secretly for the British Government, gathering valuable information about Spanish and Portuguese activities in America. This intelligence work brought him to the attention of influential political figures who saw in Phillip a reliable, conscientious and practical man with the personality and skills needed to carry out the government's plan to establish a penal settlement at Botany Bay.

On seeing the pitiful state of the female convicts, Phillip protested furiously to Evan Nepean, the wily and capable under-secretary at the Home Office. He railed at the magistrates who had sent the women aboard the *Lady Penrhyn* 'almost naked', and so feeble and filthy that a fever had broken out on the ship before they could be adequately clothed.

Weak and malnourished, the convicts had little chance of lasting the voyage out unless Phillip could build them up during the months the fleet lay idle in the English Channel. Writing to the home secretary, Lord Sydney, Phillip pleaded for orders to be given enabling him to supply both marines and convicts with fresh meat and vegetables while they remained at Spithead. At the same time, he asked for 'a small quantity of wine' to give to those already sick.

Although his immediate concern was the convicts' health, Phillip was already thinking ahead to what they would need when they reached New South Wales. The food and equipment allocated to the settlement struck him as hopelessly inadequate for a colony that would have to be self-sustaining for months, perhaps years. 'The number of scythes (only six), of razors (only five dozen), and the quantity of buck and small shot (only two hundred lb.), now ordered, is very insufficient,' he told Nepean.

Phillip's demands for more and better provisions were so relentless that the navy's procurement system could not cope. In the end, an exasperated Navy Board abandoned its own rules and advised Captain George Teer, the agent for transports at Deptford naval docks, to give Phillip anything he asked for 'without waiting for our further orders'.

As governor of the new colony, Phillip understood all too well that he would get the blame if the scheme went bad. His great worry was that hundreds would die before the fleet reached Botany Bay and that he would be held responsible for deficiencies in the fitting out and victualling (that is, supplying provisions) of the ships. Chief among his concerns was the failure to provide antiscorbutics to fend off scurvy, the disease caused by lack of vitamin C that had killed thousands of British sailors.

Reminding Lord Sydney that the contracts for the fleet had been drawn up and signed 'before I ever saw the Navy Board on this business', Phillip also protested about the absence of flour from the marines' rations, contrary to the navy's usual practice. Phillip was convinced that if salt meat were to be issued 'without any proportion of flour . . . the scurvy must prove fatal to the greatest part' of the marines and convicts. The blunt fact, he warned Sydney, was that the fleet was being sent 'to the extremity of the globe' as if it were being sent to America – a six-week passage.

'I have only one fear,' Phillip confided to Sydney, 'that it may be said hereafter the officer who took charge of the expedition should have known that it was more than probable he lost half the garrison and convicts, crowded and victualled in such a manner for so long a voyage. And the public . . . may impute to my ignorance or inattention what I have never been consulted in, and which never coincided with my ideas.'

An outbreak of typhus on board the *Alexander* confirmed Phillip's worst fears. Writing to Nepean at the Home Office, he demanded the Royal Navy supply lighters to take off the convicts while the ship was cleaned and smoked, and repeated his request for antiscorbutics. At the same time, he protested that the fresh meat he had asked for on behalf of all the convicts had not arrived; only the sick were receiving fresh meat. He also reminded Nepean that wine 'at the discretion of the surgeon' was necessary for the sick, as the convicts were not allowed anything more than water.

If decisive action were not taken to stop disease spreading through the rest of the fleet, Phillip warned, 'it may be too late . . . and we may expect to see the seamen belonging to the transports run from the ships to avoid a jail distemper, and may be refused entrance into a foreign port'.

Typhus, however, was not the only disease the seamen and marines of the First Fleet risked catching from the convicts. 'This day Lieut. Johnston . . . issued orders to keep the Women from the Sailors,' Arthur Bowes Smyth noted in his journal in the first week of April.

Johnston's orders had little effect. At ten o'clock on the night of 19 April, Johnston and Lieutenant William Collins went down into the women's berths and took a roll call. They found five female convicts missing; four were found with sailors and one was caught with the second mate. All five were segregated and put in irons, while Johnston wrote to the commander of the marines, Major Ross, asking for the second mate to be removed from the ship.

The gender imbalance among the convicts on the First Fleet – approximately 580 male and 190 female convicts were embarked at Portsmouth – raised concerns that, unless more women were brought to the colony, the infant settlement would be unable to regenerate itself. Those concerns were aggravated by the fear of venereal disease running riot aboard the transports. In a long document outlining his plans for the social development of the colony, Phillip had stated his determination to leave behind any convicts suffering from such diseases.

Later, in an anguished letter to Nepean, Phillip lamented the 'many venereal complaints' on board the *Lady Penrhyn* that 'must spread in spite of every precaution I may take hereafter'.

Draconian measures to prevent infection would continue after the fleet arrived in Botany Bay. The Norfolk Island regulations posted in December 1791 declared that anyone found concealing a venereal disorder from the surgeon would be flogged and put on short rations for six months.

After the convicts themselves and the ships' crews, the largest group aboard the First Fleet was the detachment of marines, some of them accompanied by wives and children. In recognition of the hardships they were expected to face, the Admiralty had called for volunteers. All but two of the 212 men who signed up to form the garrison at Botany Bay did so by choice. But those who enlisted under the illusion that their primary role was to be military would soon realise their mistake.

The official objective of the marine corps, as outlined by Lord Sydney in 1786, had been to form a military establishment on shore 'not only for the protection of the settlement, if required, against the natives, but for the preservation of good order'. In practice, the primary role of the marines, both during the voyage and after the fleet landed in New South Wales, would be that of gaolers.

While the convicts had been largely docile as the fleet waited off the Isle of Wight – the commander of the marine corps, Major Ross, described them as 'perfectly satisfied and obedient' – the fear of a convict uprising was ever-present. Less than four years earlier, on 16 August 1783, a British ship, the *Swift*, had sailed for America with 143 convicts. The American Revolution had put an end to the transportation of British convicts across the Atlantic, so the men on the *Swift* were falsely described on the ship's manifest as indentured servants. Near Rye on the Sussex coast, some of the convicts rose against the crew and escaped after running the ship aground. Their freedom was short-lived. The mutineers were all recaptured and charged with the capital offence of 'returning before expiry . . . being at large within the kingdom'. Six men judged to be ringleaders of the mutiny were executed; the rest had their death sentences commuted to transportation and were sent back to the hulks.

A year later, another transport, the *Mercury*, sailed for America laden with 179 convicts. Off the Devon coast, a group of them mutinied. Some made it to dry land but others were drowned in rough seas. All the survivors were eventually recaptured and returned to the hulks to await transportation.

Among the convicts on the First Fleet were a number of the mutineers from the *Swift* and the *Mercury*, including a forger and thief named Thomas Barrett, who would feature prominently (if briefly) in the court proceedings of the new colony.

The transport ships had been modified to resist any attempted mutiny by the convicts. Philip Gidley King, second lieutenant on the *Sirius*, detailed the security measures in his journal. Thick wooden bulkheads filled with nails ran between decks. These had been bored with holes to allow the marines to fire 'in case of irregularities'. The hatches, secured with crossbars, bolts and locks, were nailed in place. Behind the mainmast on the upper deck, a metre-high barricade 'armed with pointed prongs of Iron' prevented any connection between the marines and sailors on one side and the convicts on the other. Guards were placed at the various hatchways and an armed marine was permanently stationed on the quarterdeck of each transport 'in order to prevent any improper behaviour of the Convicts, as well as to guard [against] any surprize'.

The marines were sailing to Botany Bay as free men and volunteers, yet their rations and living conditions were scarcely better than those of the convicts they were guarding, and the punishments they suffered were often harsher – a grievance that would be felt even more strongly once they reached New South Wales.

The outbreaks of 'gaol fever' and dysentery on the transports claimed the lives of several marines. 'Since the time of their first embarkation,' Major Ross wrote in a letter to the Admiralty secretary Sir Philip Stephens, 'no less than one serjeant, one drummer, and fourteen privates have been sent sick on shore from [the *Alexander*], some of whom . . . are since dead.'

As far as Ross was concerned, the quarters allocated to the marines were so unhealthy that sickness was inevitable. Berthed on a deck directly below the sailors, the marines on board the *Alexander* had to breathe the putrid air drifting from the hatchway that led from the seamen's quarters. If soldiers were falling sick and dying even before the ships left England, how many more would succumb once the fleet lay becalmed in the morbid heat and humidity of the tropics?

If the marines' accommodation was inadequate, their rations were even worse. In his plaintive letter to Stephens, Major Ross recounted 'a scene of distress that I was witness to yesterday when visiting the transports at the Motherbank. In one of them I found a marine, his wife, and two children living upon a ration and a half of provisions.' Ross felt doubly betrayed since he had previously given his word to the marines under his command that their wives and children would be properly looked after.

In the course of the eight-month voyage to Botany Bay, Ross would develop a burning antipathy towards Governor Phillip, but during the weeks before the fleet set sail he needed Phillip's help to right an even more egregious wrong than putrid living quarters and short rations: the government was planning to rob the marines of their grog.

The daily ration for the marines on the First Fleet, which had barely changed in a century, included half a pint of rum and one gallon of beer, matter-of-factly described by Captain Watkin Tench as 'the usual quantity of beer allowed in the navy'. According to navy regulations, the same ration was due to every man on the ship, from the captain down to the cabin boy.

The Royal Navy had a long history of technical and administrative innovation, but provisioning for a voyage into the Southern Ocean was at the outer limits of its expertise. While constant development continued to reduce the spoilage of food shipped in casks, seamen and marines bitterly resented the monotony of the diet. At a gallon per man per day, the supply of beer didn't last long, and in any case it soon spoilt. After a few weeks even the water began to go bad; wine or vinegar sometimes had to be tipped in to mask the smell. With little else to look forward to, it was no wonder that British sailors came to depend on their daily rum ration.

The origins of the sailors' rum ration went back to England's capture of Jamaica from the Spanish in 1655. Before that, the navy doled out French brandy. Using rum from Jamaica, Trinidad and other Caribbean islands, the Royal Navy began to manufacture its own exclusive blend. Long after the beer had soured or been drunk away, rum enabled sailors and marines – many of whom had been press-ganged into service – to forget the hardships of life at sea.

Until 1740 it was issued neat: a quarter of a pint twice a day. During that time drunkenness became an endemic problem on Royal Navy ships, made worse by the tendency of lighter drinkers to make extra money by selling their allowance to old hands who thought nothing of drinking two or three times the standard allowance.

On 21 August 1740 at Port Royal, Jamaica, Vice Admiral Edward Vernon – nicknamed 'Old Grog' on account of the coarse grogram cloak he liked to wear – issued his notorious 'Order to Captains No. 349', which noted the 'fatal Effects' on morals as well as health of the 'pernicious Custom' of sailors downing their daily rum allowance in one go. Vernon's solution was for the daily allowance of half a pint per man:

> to be mixed with a quart of water . . . in one Scuttled Butt
> kept for that purpose, and to be done upon Deck, and in the
> presence of the Lieutenant of the Watch, who is to see that
> the men are not defrauded of their allowance of Rum . . . and
> let those that are good husband men receive extra lime juice
> and sugar that it be made more palatable to them.

The new concoction, referred to as 'grog' after its inventor, did not go down well with the sailors but – thanks to the lime juice – may have helped reduce the toll caused by scurvy. While the proportion of water to spirits was set by Vernon at four to one, in practice it was up to the ship's captain to decide how much rum went into the mix. John Nicol, a cooper by trade who spent a quarter of a century at sea, witnessed a mutiny on the *Defiance*, a 74-gun warship lying at anchor near Leith in Scotland, when the captain issued his crew with 'five-water grog' instead of the less diluted 'three-water' they were expecting. 'The weather was cold,' recalled Nicol. 'The spirit thus reduced was, as the mutineers called it, as thin as muslin and quite unfit to keep out the cold.'

For the marines sailing with the First Fleet, a bigger problem loomed over the horizon than the amount of water in the grog. According to the terms and conditions of their service, once they arrived in New South Wales they faced having their allowance cut off altogether. In a letter to the Lords of the Admiralty dated 31 August 1786, Lord Sydney promised that the marines would be 'properly victualled by a commissary immediately after their landing'. While the meaning appeared clear enough, the wording of Sydney's letter left considerable doubt as to who would be picking up the tab: the government or the marines themselves.

In November the Lords of the Admiralty replied to Sydney's letter, noting that while on board His Majesty's ships, the marines were victualled on the same terms as the seamen, without any deduction from their pay, and asking him to clarify whether this arrangement would continue after the marines had gone ashore at Botany Bay.

Nepean, who was under pressure to control costs as far as possible, added to the confusion by advising the Navy Board that both marines and convicts should 'after their landing [in New South Wales] be victualled in the same manner as the troops serving in the West India islands, *excepting only the allowance of spirits*'.

Nepean's advice was relayed to Phillip, who was assured that the government had no intention of allowing the marines in New South Wales to be 'constantly supplied' with wine or spirits. The argument now threatened to scupper the whole colonial enterprise. As the final provisions were being taken on board, the marines on the *Scarborough* wrote a desperate petition to their commanding officer, explaining that they had 'voluntarily entered on a dangerous expedition replete with numberless difficulties' and were 'sorely aggrieved' to discover that the government was planning to withdraw their liquor allowance after their arrival in New South Wales, a 'moderate distribution of the above-ment'd article being indispensably requisite for the preservation of our lives'. Reminding Major Ross of the 'calamities' they expected to encounter in the new colony, they begged him to use his influence to remove the uneasiness they felt at the awful prospect of being denied 'one of the principal necessaries of life, without which . . . we cannot expect to survive'.

Equally affronted and alarmed, the marines on the *Charlotte* urged the Admiralty to consider the hardships that 'being thus deprived of our grog' would subject them to on an 'island' where it would otherwise be impossible to procure liquor. The marines on the *Alexander* took it even harder, threatening to un-volunteer if their grog were taken away.

Governor Phillip and Major Ross both tried to intervene on the soldiers' behalf. The day after the marines on the *Scarborough* submitted their petition, Phillip wrote to Nepean warning of the 'very disagreeable consequences' he anticipated from the marine garrison at Botany Bay 'if they have not the same allowance of spirits . . . as the marines and seamen are allowed on board'.

It was as close to an ultimatum as Phillip could deliver, and it worked. Two days later, Nepean sheepishly informed him that Lord Sydney, 'wishing . . . to remove every possible cause of dissatisfaction', had recommended that the Lords of the Treasury authorise him to buy enough wine and spirits en route to Botany Bay to keep the marines happy for three years after landing, 'at the expiration of which time it must be understood that no further supplies of that sort will be allowed'.

There was a strict cap on the government's generosity: Phillip was allowed to buy as much spirits or wine as he could get for £200. But the backdown was enough to avert open mutiny by the marine corps – or at least to postpone it for a few years.

By the time the First Fleet sailed from Portsmouth, Phillip had got most of what he had asked for. Arthur Bowes Smyth remarked in his journal that 'few Marines going out of England on Service were ever so amply provided for as these convicts are'.

As well as the 747,000 nails, 8000 fish hooks, 127 dozen combs, 589 women's petticoats and 448 barrels of flour, room was found in the ships for a piano, a printing press, some puppies and kittens, and a small cask of raisins. According to Captain Teer, the hardworking agent for transports at Deptford, the 'Provisions and accommodations' of the convict transports were 'better than any [other] Set of Transports I have ever had any directions in'.

All this made it impossible for Phillip to find room for a last-minute consignment of grog. 'No spirits can be received at present on board any of the ships,' he told Nepean, 'but the greatest economy will be used in purchasing as much as the ships can stow when in the Brazil.'

By early May the fleet was almost ready to depart. On the morning of Thursday, 10 May Phillip signalled to the remaining ten captains to prepare to sail the following morning. Smyth, on the *Lady Penrhyn*, reported, 'An order sent on board all the Ships for All Dogs to be sent on Shore.'

The weather turned bad that afternoon and, instead of sailing, the fleet spent the next day 'very busy in compleating their Bread & Water'. On Saturday an order was given that no man would be allowed to leave his ship – an order that apparently did not apply to Smyth, who 'Went in the Afternoon with Capts. Campbell & Sever to Ryde & return'd abt. 9 o'Clock'.

On Sunday Phillip got the breeze he was after. By now he was so anxious to depart that he left some desperately needed women's clothes behind. He would not even wait for the fresh bread he had ordered to come out of the oven, settling instead for a batch he described as 'good, tho' coarse', which could be loaded at once.

Under a blue sky, and with a brisk easterly wind filling its sails, the First Fleet slid along the English coast, accompanied by the *Hyaena*, which had orders from the Admiralty to see the fleet '100 leagues to the westward'.

Among the 582 male convicts was 33-year-old James Squires. On 11 April 1785 Squires had been found guilty at the Surrey Lent Assizes of stealing '4 cocks, 5 hens & divers other goods & chattals the property of John Stacey'. He was sentenced to be transported for seven years. This was not his first brush with the law. In 1774 Squires had been arrested for highway robbery after escaping from a ransacked house, thereby avoiding the more serious charge of stealing. Sentenced to be transported to America for seven years, he chose to do his time in the army and was able to return to Kingston upon Thames as a free man, having served just two years. In 1776 Squires married a woman named Martha Quinton. A year later Squires and Martha took up lodgings in a house near the river. A son, John, was born on 16 August 1778; a daughter, Sarah, two years later on 23 August; and another son, James, on 2 May 1783.

Although Squires appears to have had a lawful occupation as the manager of an inn, the income was not enough for him to be able to support his wife and three children, and he fell back into crime. Stealing John Stacey's chickens seems to have been an act of desperation; Stacey lived in the same street and Squires must have been an obvious suspect. His arrest and conviction brought the family's destruction. Since it was almost impossible for the wife of a transported convict to accompany him, Squires sailed to New South Wales without his family. Neither his wife nor his three children would ever see him again.

It was not only the convicts who were separated from their families. While the detachment of marines was accompanied by a party of 46 wives and children, the majority of soldiers embarked alone. As the fleet passed Plymouth, Lieutenant Ralph Clark scribbled plaintively in his journal, 'Oh my God all my hopes are over of Seeing my beloved wife and Son.'

2

I never lived so poor in my life

Strolling the crowded deck of the slow-sailing *Charlotte*, Captain Watkin Tench noticed that the convicts' faces 'indicated a high degree of satisfaction, though in some, the pang of being severed, perhaps for ever from their native land, could not be wholly suppressed'. Tench observed a few of the women shedding tears but 'after this the accent of sorrow was no longer heard'; genial skies and a change of scene put an end to the convicts' discontent and replaced it, according to Tench, with 'cheerfulness and acquiescence in a lot, now not to be altered'.

While the government's critics were eager to denounce the Botany Bay scheme as 'big with folly, impolicy, and ruin', Tench was convinced from the beginning of its 'humane and benevolent intention'. The 'high degree of satisfaction' he observed in the convicts reflected his own feelings as much as theirs.

But not everyone was as satisfied as Watkin Tench. The English coast was scarcely out of sight when the sailors on the *Friendship* went on strike for an extra half a pound of beef a day. The agent in charge of provisioning the fleet was hastily summoned on board to find out what the matter was. After being assured that the crews of the other transports were all receiving the same amount of beef, the men on the *Friendship* 'agreed to goe to work again . . . but if any Ship in the fleet gives ther Ships Company more they are to expect the same'.

According to Lieutenant Clark, it was lust, not hunger, that caused the sailors to strike. 'I never met with a parcel of more discontent fellows in my life,' he wrote, 'the[y] only want more Provisions to give it to the damed whores the Convict Women of whome the[y] are very fond Since they brock throu the Bulk head and had connection with them.'

Industrial peace restored, the fleet sailed on. Acting on 'favourable representations' made by some of his officers, Phillip agreed to the removal of the convicts' fetters. Tench felt 'great pleasure in being able to extend this humane order to the whole of those under my charge, without a single exception'.

Tench's benevolent attitude to the convicts was not shared by all his brother officers. 'This lenient step towards making those unhappy wretches comfortable was very ill received in the *Scarborough*,' reported First Lieutenant William Bradley. Clark was equally unhappy:

'Capt Merideth and Self don't think is [safe] for so great a number to be out of irons at once.'

The captains of the six transport ships must have had serious misgivings at the sight of convicts wandering the decks without fetters, since each captain was liable to a penalty of £40 for every convict who escaped. After protesting to Phillip, the captain of the *Friendship* was told to let the convicts out of their shackles 'when we think proper and on the [smallest] falt to put them in again'.

As the fleet made its way into the Atlantic Ocean, it became clear that some of the ships were better sailers than others. Ten of the 11 ships under Phillip's command were six years old or less, and a large amount of money had been spent adapting and outfitting them for the long voyage to Botany Bay. From the deck of the flagship *Sirius*, however, the first impressions of the colony's deputy judge advocate, David Collins, were damning: 'At our outset we had the mortification to find that two of our convoy were very heavy sailers, and likely to be the occasion of much delay.' The *Charlotte* had to be taken in tow by the *Hyaena*, while the *Lady Penrhyn* was soon falling far behind.

As Phillip struggled to hold his fleet together, the first escape attempt was discovered. A plot was said to have been hatched among the convicts on the *Scarborough* to mutiny and take possession of the ship. The mutiny was thwarted when one of the convicts turned informer and betrayed his friends. Two alleged ringleaders were taken onto the *Sirius*, where the boatswain's mate gave each of them two dozen lashes before they were transferred in irons to the *Prince of Wales*.

The so-called ringleaders 'stedfastly denied the existence of any such design as was imputed to them'. John White, the surgeon-general, called it a 'futile scheme' and noted that, after they had been punished, the 'ringleaders . . . behaved very well'. Tench, the eternal optimist, made no mention of the incident.

On 3 June, exactly three weeks after leaving the Mother Bank, the fleet reached Tenerife. Tench found little to admire on the Spanish-governed island. 'Excepting the Peak,' he wrote, 'the eye receives little pleasure from the general face of the country, which is sterile and uninviting to the last degree.'

David Collins was more impressed. A sucker for a tall story, he was taken in by the Canary Islanders' tales of a homeland so benign that no venomous creature could survive there, 'several toads, adders, and other poisonous reptiles, which had been brought thither for proof, having died almost immediately after their arrival'.

Governor Phillip was told of 'a miraculous tree', solitary and perpetually shrouded in mist, that grew on the neighbouring island of Ferro and was able to supply the island with all the water it needed. A former government spy, experienced at weighing up intelligence, Phillip enjoyed the story enough to include it in his book, without believing a word of it. 'This wonder,' he noted wryly, 'though vouched by several voyagers, and by some as eye witnesses, vanished at the approach of sober enquiry, nor could a single native be found hardy enough to assert its existence.'

Phillip's main purpose in stopping at Tenerife was to replenish water and buy provisions, especially fresh meat and vegetables. Unfortunately, both were in short supply. Phillip had more success topping up the fleet's dwindling stock of wine, of which the marines were getting through 'a pint . . . *per* man, daily'. Tenerife was also good for spirits. Brandy, noted Tench, was a 'cheap article'.

As the fleet prepared to leave the island, a convict on the *Alexander*, John Powers, managed to jump ship and escape in a small boat tied alongside. Drifting in the dark, Powers made his way towards a Dutch East Indiaman that had just anchored in the harbour. He begged her crew to take him aboard, but they understood the diplomatic niceties and would have nothing to do with an escaped convict, even though they needed men. 'Having committed himself again to the waves,' wrote Surgeon White, 'he was driven by the wind and the current, in the course of the night, to a small island lying to leeward of the ships, where he was the next morning taken.' Clapped in irons and taken before the governor, Powers pulled out an 'artful petition' written for him by another convict and 'so wrought on the Governor's humanity as to procure a release from his confinement'.

Phillip's account of the escape said much about his worldly and compassionate approach towards the convicts. 'It is not probable,' he wrote, 'that [Powers] had formed any definite plan of escape; the means of absconding must have been accidentally offered, and suddenly embraced.'

As time went on, Phillip's calculated tolerance and his willingness to give convicts the benefit of the doubt would bring him into bitter conflict with the marines. For now, however, there were more pressing matters to worry about.

The fleet left Tenerife early on 11 June 1787, heading for Rio de Janeiro. The scarcity of fresh meat and vegetables at Tenerife forced everyone on to a diet of salt meat, increasing the risk of scurvy. When adverse winds brought the fleet almost to a standstill, Phillip had to cut the allowance of fresh water to officers, seamen, marines and convicts alike. Surgeon White on the *Charlotte* watched in horror as the dreaded scurvy took hold. Without plentiful fresh water to counteract the effects of the salt meat, the disease raged through the transports 'with such hasty and rapid strides, that all attempts to check it proved fruitless, until good fortune threw a ship in our way, who spared us sufficient quantity of water to serve the sick with as much as they could use'.

The renewed supply of fresh water, added to an abundant store of essence of malt, 'made in a few days so sudden a change for the better in the poor fellows, who had been covered with ulcers and livid blotches, that every person on board was surprised'.

Phillip's intention had been to stop at the Cape Verde Islands but, finding the wind and current against him, he decided to sail on, reaching Rio de Janeiro on 5 August.

Captain John Hunter, a future governor, considered the fleet 'remarkably healthy. The whole number buried since we left England was sixteen, six only of that number had died between Tenerife and this place ... Many of those whom we had lost since we left Portsmouth had been lingering under diseases which they were afflicted with when they embarked. Consequently little hope could be entertained of their recovery.'

For those still suffering from the effects of scurvy, Rio proved the ideal place to recuperate. Phillip ensured that the convicts were plied with oranges, 'this fruit being in such plenty that the expence attending the purchase of a few for each individual a day was too inconsiderable to be noticed. Indeed it was no uncommon thing to see the country boats, as they passed the ships, throw in a shower of oranges amongst the people.'

Unhappily for the marines, it proved to be the wrong season in which to buy wine. The only sellers were the Portuguese retail dealers, whose prices were considered by the British to be extortionate. With a relatively paltry £200 in Treasury bills to spend, the careful Phillip baulked at their demands, buying less wine than he needed. Some of the shortfall was made up for in rum, although again the cost caused Phillip some anguish. '[T]he rum on our coming in,' he informed Nepean, 'there being little in the place, rose more than five-and-twenty per cent.'

After nearly two months at sea, the female convicts' threadbare clothing was virtually falling off them. Lacking replacements, Phillip was forced to improvise. He bought 'one hundred sacks of casada [tapioca]', which he intended to issue to the convicts once the supply of bread was exhausted. The coarse burlap sacks containing the casada 'will be used hereafter in cloathing the convicts, many of whom are nearly naked'.

The ready supply of fresh meat and vegetables, oranges, limes, bananas, 'cocoa nuts' and guavas at Rio de Janeiro quickly removed 'every symptom of the scurvy'. Phillip reported with satisfaction that 'provisions were here so cheap that . . . the men were victualled completely . . . at threepence three-farthings a head'.

In recognition of his years of service as a captain in the Portuguese Navy, Phillip was treated by the Portuguese viceroy of Brazil as an honoured guest. His officers were allowed to walk the streets of Rio without the normal military escort. While they wandered around the town admiring the architecture and seeking out 'tender' attachments with the local beauties, the marines and convicts got down to their old tricks.

Despite the bulkheads designed to keep the female convicts apart from the seamen and marines, 'promiscuous intercourse' between them proved impossible to prevent. One Thomas Jones was sentenced to 300 lashes for trying to induce a guard to 'betray his trust in suffering him to go among the women' but was let off due to his previous 'good character'. Private Cornelius Connell was not so lucky, punished with 100 lashes 'for having improper intercourse with some of the female convicts, contrary to orders'.

On the *Friendship*, Lieutenant Ralph Clark could not conceal his horror of 'Sarah Mccormick . . . She is eat[en] up with the P[ox] . . . She is one of them that went throu the Bulk head to the Seamen – I hope She has given them some thing to remember her – never was ther a Set of greater rascals together than the[y] are – the[y] are ten thousand times wors than the convicts.'

Trouble of a different kind was brewing on board the *Alexander*, where Smyth noted that the crew and convicts were 'very mutinously inclined'. They 'threaten'd Capt. Sinclair & Mr. Long, the chief Mate, & Mr. Dunnivan 2d. mate . . . declaring they wd. do as they pleased for all Capt. Sinclair, who they sd. had no power over them, & who indeed appeared to have lost all Authority over his people'.

In the stifling heat below deck on the *Charlotte*, Thomas Barrett – a ringleader in the mutiny on the *Mercury* – and two accomplices had spent much of the Atlantic voyage coining quarter dollars 'out of old buckles, buttons belonging to the marines, and pewter spoons'. When they arrived at Rio, the temptation to try out their handiwork proved irresistible. Barrett and his mates were soon passing their coins to food sellers who swarmed around the convict ships to trade from their canoes.

Barrett's forgeries came to light almost immediately, when a boat manned by three Portuguese and six slaves came alongside the *Charlotte* with oranges, plantains and bread for sale. While haggling with the three Portuguese, the *Charlotte*'s officers discovered that one of the convicts, Barrett, had passed some fake quarter dollars. 'The impression, milling, character . . . was so inimitably executed that had their metal been a little better the fraud . . . would have passed undetected,' wrote Surgeon White. The forgery was all the more impressive since the convicts 'never were suffered to come near a fire' and 'hardly ten minutes ever elapsed, without an officer of some degree or other going down among them'. Marines searched diligently but in vain for the apparatus used to make the coins. The forgers' adroitness gave White 'a high opinion of their ingenuity, cunning, caution, and address; and I could not help wishing that these qualities had been employed to more laudable purposes'.

Barrett's punishment on this occasion must have been light, since White did not bother to record what it was. Three weeks later, however, James Baker, a private marine, received 200 lashes for trying to pass off one of Barrett's coins. It was not the last time a marine would be punished more severely than a convict for the same offence.

The fleet left Rio de Janeiro on 4 September, with Phillip able to declare the convicts 'much healthier than when we left England'. During their stay, 'every Man had 2lb of fresh meat allowed him every day wt. plenty of Vegitables,' wrote Smyth. If the food at Rio was excellent, the same could not be said of the water, which had a foul taste that suggested it would not keep long at sea.

Despite his complaints about the high price of liquor at Rio, Phillip laid in 'one hundred and fifteen pipes of rum [more than 12,000 gallons or 54,000 litres] . . . for the use of the garrison'.

The ships were now to head back across the Atlantic, stopping at the Cape of Good Hope to resupply for the last time before striking out across the Indian and Southern Oceans for New South Wales.

They made the trip through huge seas. '[T]he ship rouls very much,' wrote Ralph Clark. '[I]t blowd very hard all night . . . a great dele of water went between the decks and washt the marines out of ther beds.' Four days later, he complained, 'I never lived so poor in my life as we doe at this time – nothing every day except Salt Beef or Salt Pork – thank God we have got Some Rice in the mess otherwise I would Starve.'

On 5 October the fleet sailed through a thick fog that made it impossible for any of the ships' lookouts to see each other. It drizzled constantly. In the damp and dismal conditions, tempers frayed. Two female convicts on the *Friendship*, Elizabeth Pugh and Rachel Harley, were put in irons, 'the former for Qarling [quarrelling] and dirtiness and the latter for theft and dirtiness'. And it was not just the convicts who were quarrelling on that misnamed ship. 'Mr F. got very much in licour then came on board where he begane to abuse me in a very Publick manner to Capt. Meredith,' complained Clark.

The weather worsened. During a squall, one of the convicts on the *Charlotte* fell overboard '& was drown'd notwithstanding every means was employ'd to save him'. Despite 'gales' and 'mountenous' seas, the fleet managed to stay together, although the *Supply* was often far ahead of the rest.

Early on the morning of 13 October, the *Supply* hoisted her ensign to indicate that she had sighted land. By one o'clock in the afternoon, Ralph Clark had a clear sight of the high ground rising above the Cape. Anchored in the bay were one Dutch sloop of war, a Dutch East Indiaman and two French East Indiamen.

The spectacle that greeted them on shore would have made the convicts relieved to be the subject of British rather than Dutch justice. Numerous gallows and other 'impliments of punishment' stood along the shore in front of the town. They included wheels for breaking felons. The mangled bodies of the sufferers had been left to rot, their severed right hands nailed to the side of the wheel as a terrible warning to others.

For Phillip and his officers, Cape Town was a disappointment after Rio. By comparison with the hospitable Portuguese, the Dutch colonists at the Cape were skinflints, dour and suspicious of foreigners. Food, as always, was an overriding preoccupation, and the British had arrived in the wrong season to enjoy the Cape's famed tropical fruits. 'The oranges and bananas were not equal to those of Rio de Janeiro,' noted Collins. Even the currency was an annoyance, the flimsy paper notes often being 'torn from our hands by the violence of the south-east wind, when we were about to make a payment in the street, or even at the door of a shop'.

The meat, however, was 'excellent', and between official duties Collins found time to investigate the local wine, which 'formed a considerable article of traffic here'.

Resupplying at the Cape had been a key part of Phillip's plans. But the governor, Mynheer Van Graaffe, despite his 'extreme civility and politeness', was cagey about selling Phillip the provisions for which he asked. There was, in any case, not enough room aboard the ships to store all that he wanted and needed.

Phillip's priority was the livestock that would form the basis of a government herd after the fleet landed in New South Wales. Tench catalogued the purchase of 'two bulls, three cows, three horses, forty-four sheep, and thirty-two hogs, besides goats, and a very large quantity of poultry of every kind'. In addition, the officers bought animals for their own private use, although the high prices demanded by the Dutch for feed forced them to 'circumscrib[e] their original intentions . . . few of the military found it convenient to purchase sheep, when hay to feed them costs sixteen shillings a hundred weight'. (At home, the cost of hay was around 40 shillings a ton.) Even at that price, Smyth reported that 'a large quantity, when it came to be opened, was so rotten as to be totally unfit for use, and was thrown overboard'.

The convicts had to be moved around to make extra room. The women on the *Friendship* were taken off and reassigned among the other female transports. Lieutenant Ralph Clark, still lovesick for his wife and son, wasn't sorry to see them go. 'Women convicts away as order thank god,' he wrote. 'I am very Glad of it for the[y] wair a great Trouble much more So than the [men].'

Their replacements arrived a week later: '30 Sheep came on board this day and wair put in the Place where the women convicts Were – I think we will find [them] much more Agreable Ship mates.'

Room was found to cram more than 500 live animals aboard the 11 already overcrowded ships, creating an impression that, in Phillip's words, 'naturally enough excited the idea of Noah's ark'.

There is some conjecture that, amid the reshuffle of convicts, James Squires was moved from the *Friendship* to the larger *Charlotte*. If so, he would have crossed paths with three of the fleet's most prolific diarists – Clark on the *Friendship*, and Tench and White on the *Charlotte* – during his passage to Botany Bay. The fact that none of them mentioned him in their accounts of the voyage suggests that Squires kept his head down and did as he was told.

On 12 November 1787 the fleet left the Cape, but its progress was hampered by strong winds from the south-east. After nearly two weeks at sea Phillip was frustrated to find himself 'only 80 leagues [around 440 kilometres] eastward of the Cape'. It was then that Phillip, without consulting Major Ross, made the decision to divide the fleet, leaving Captain John Hunter in charge of the rump. The option had been flagged in Phillip's original instructions but he had not discussed it with his senior officers. The way he put his decision into effect would intensify criticism by Ross and others that Phillip was aloof, autocratic and secretive.

Switching from the *Sirius* to the smaller but more nimble *Supply*, Phillip sailed ahead with three of the faster ships, the *Alexander*,

Scarborough and *Friendship*, taking with him 'several sawyers, carpenters, blacksmiths, and other mechanics' whose job it would be to investigate the country around Botany Bay and put up buildings in time for the arrival of the main fleet.

Before long, the 'flying squadron', as those left behind called it, was out of sight. Bad weather and high seas dampened the mood of the following fleet. An outbreak of dysentery was beaten off by the surgeons with only a single death, but scurvy now began to appear among the female convicts.

The voyage from the Cape to Botany Bay was the longest leg of the journey and represented a symbolic departure from the known world into the unknown. For the convicts, however, and for the marines guarding them, life carried on as before. Their task from the beginning had been to stay alive, and to coexist with each other in the cramped and unwholesome conditions. In this floating marketplace private commerce thrived: articles were traded, debts were paid, favours returned, good behaviour rewarded. In the absence of money, goods and services had to be bartered. Sex was a desirable commodity, so was labour, and so was liquor, large quantities of which had been accumulated during stops at Tenerife, Rio and the Cape.

On 23 November Clark drew 'a Quart of Rum in part of that which is due me from my allowance'. The following afternoon he gave his quart of rum 'to the Boatswain and Carpenter of the Ship for things that the[y] have done for me'.

A week later Clark was again lamenting his diet of salt beef and salt pork: 'I must make the best of it I have nothing else in the Mess – I never lived So poor Since I was born – drew this afternoon three Quarts of Rum from the Stuart [steward] being part of my Allowance.' Of this, Clark gave half a pint to 'the Ships cook' and a bottle to 'the Seamen . . . for the[y] are very wett and cold and a Glas wont do them any harm'; later he gave one of the convicts a glass of rum as 'he appeard to be very cold'.

On 2 December Thomas Kelly, a convict sent on board the *Lady Penrhyn* from the *Alexander* 'to superintent the Governor's Horses', was discovered to have 'broach'd a puncheon of Rum between decks & drank & given to the Women a Considerable quantity. As it appear'd pretty clear that he was instigated by the Women to do it the Capt. did not get him punish'd but took care to secure the Rum in future.'

On the *Friendship*, alcohol fuelled tensions between Captain Meredith, Lieutenant Faddy and Lieutenant Clark. While Clark refused to drink anything stronger than lemonade, Meredith and Faddy, as well as Thomas Arndell, an assistant surgeon, were regularly 'tipsey'. Clark's journal records bouts of drunken bickering.

But the supply of wine for the officers could not last forever, and by mid-December the *Sirius* had run out. On 19 December Lieutenant William Bradley noted in his journal, 'The wine being out, our allowance was order'd a Quart of Grog and a Quart of Water per day.'

On the *Lady Penrhyn*, Smyth 'drank a cheerful Glass to the health of our Friends in England (as indeed we do every Saturday night)'. To celebrate Christmas Day, Smyth gave 'a quantity of Currants' to the three marines on board as well as to the boatswain and the second, third and fourth mates, while '[t]he Capt. allowed them a reasonable quantity of Grog to chear their hearts'. On the *Friendship*, 'Several of the Marines got much in Liquor.'

On 1 January 1788, after sitting down to a meal of 'hard Salt Beef and a few musty Pancakes', Lieutenant Clark 'gave to the men one Quart one pint and a half Pint of Rum it being New Years day'. A week later he 'drew a Quart of Rum to give the Tayler and the man that cut my hair a Glass of Grog each'.

Dreaming of 'My Beloved Betsy' and wishing he could have 'a pice of goose' for dinner rather than 'Pease Soup and Pork', Clark later 'drew one Gallen and a half of Rum from the Stewart . . . which I have Bottled up and will draw the remainder what is due to me to Morrow'.

Abetted by the informal commerce in rum, marines and sailors got drunk whenever they had the chance. On 8 January Surgeon White went on board the *Fishburn* to check on the boatswain, who, after climbing the rigging on New Year's Day while drunk, had fallen from the topsail yard, 'by which he bruised himself in a dreadful manner'. Already suffering from scurvy, the boatswain's condition worsened; 'the parts soon mortified, and he died about an hour after I got on board'.

The voyage from the Cape took a deadly toll on the livestock. On 10 January Smyth reported that 'almost all the Sheep on board the *Sirius*, 13 Goats out of 15, one Cow, big of a Cow Calf & almost the whole of the Poultry had died'.

A hurricane struck Hunter's squadron off the coast of Van Diemen's Land. 'I never before saw the Sea in such a rage, it was all over white as snow,' wrote Smyth. 'The *Prince of Wales* carried away her Main

Yard & Sail & Main topsail – The *Charlotte* carried away her Main Sail – The *Borrowdale* split her Foretopsail – The *Fishburn's* Jib sail was split all in pieces – The *Golden Grove* . . . split her foresail and Maintopsail all in pieces . . . During the Storm the Convict Women in our Ship were so terrified that most of them were down on their knees at prayers, & in less than an hour after it had abated, they were uttering the most horrid Oaths and imprecations that cd. proceed out of the mouths of such abandon'd Prostitutes as they are!'

At around seven o'clock on the morning of Saturday, 19 January 1788, 'abt 40 miles distant', the squadron under Captain Hunter sighted the outline of the coast south of Botany Bay. 'The joy everyone felt upon so long wish'd for an Event can be better conceiv'd than expressed,' wrote Smyth.

It took Hunter's ships all day to approach within seven or eight miles of the entrance to Botany Bay. By then, the fleet had sailed an extraordinary 15,000 miles, and Hunter, an expert navigator and a cautious commander, was in no mood to tempt fate by trying to enter the bay in darkness. Signalling to the convoy to pass in succession under the stern of the *Sirius*, Hunter decided to take advantage of the easterly wind to 'keep working off under an easy sail till daylight', when the ships would regroup and sail into Botany Bay.

Things did not quite go to plan. The next morning Hunter woke to discover that the convoy had been carried south by the current, but with a good breeze behind them the ships soon regained the distance they had lost during the night.

A joyful sight greeted the convoy as it entered the bay: the flying squadron, consisting of the *Supply* and the three transports, *Alexander,*

Scarborough and *Friendship*, lay at anchor near the shore. The *Supply* had arrived on the 18th, and the three others on the 19th. At eight o'clock on the morning of 20 January, Hunter's bedraggled convoy anchored in Botany Bay in eight fathoms of water.

The voyage that had begun on the Mother Bank and brought them around the globe had taken exactly 36 weeks, including 68 days spent in ports. 'To see all the ships safe in their destined port without ever having, by any accident, been one hour separated, and all the people in as good health as could be expected or hoped for, after so long a voyage, was a sight . . . at which every heart must rejoice,' wrote Surgeon White.

As the *Sirius* sailed into Botany Bay, Hunter noted that 'a number of the natives assembled on the south shore, and by their motions seemed to threaten'.

Whether the uninvited visitors would be met by anything more than 'threats', nobody could tell.

3

Doomed to everlasting barrenness

The words 'Botany Bay' would come to signify many things: penal settlement, outpost of empire, trading station, military base. But to each man and woman arriving on the First Fleet, those words held a private meaning: terror or bewilderment, professional advancement, or simply the opportunity to leave the past behind and start again. They had sailed not just 'to the extremity of the globe' but to the limits of their imagination. The little knowledge they brought with them was derived from the fragmentary reports and confused impressions of a handful of men who had spent a week there 18 years earlier, and who could not agree on what they had seen.

On 29 April 1770 Captain James Cook sailed the *Endeavour* into Botany Bay and found the country to be 'deversified with woods,

Lawns and Marshes; the woods are free from under wood of every kind and the trees are at such a distance from one another that the whole Country or at least great part of it might be cultivated without being oblig'd to cut down a single tree'.

Two days later, venturing further inland, Cook reported seeing 'a deep black Soil which we thought was capable of producing any kind of grain at present it produceth besides timber as fine meadow as ever was seen'.

Sydney Parkinson, a botanical artist who accompanied Cook on his great voyage of discovery, was equally taken by what he saw, enthusing about the level ground, the fertile soil and the mild climate. Although they had arrived on the cusp of winter, to Parkinson 'every thing seemed in perfection'.

Their feelings towards the human inhabitants were more ambivalent. An initial attempt to communicate directly with two 'Natives' came to nothing, since:

> neither us nor Tupia [a companion whom Captain Cook had
> brought with him from Tahiti] could understand one word
> they said. We then threw them some nails, beads, etc., a shore,
> which they took up, and seem'd not ill pleased with, in so
> much that I thought that they beckon'd to us to come ashore;
> but in this we were mistaken, for as soon as we put the boat
> in they again came to oppose us.

Cook was not normally trigger happy in his behaviour towards native peoples, but a series of hostile encounters with the Māori in

New Zealand had made him wary. He responded to the threatened resistance by firing three musket shots, wounding one of the pair. The Aboriginal men retaliated by throwing their spears before running off. It crossed Cook's mind to seize one:

> but Mr. Banks being of Opinion that the darts were poisoned, made me cautious how I advanced into the Woods. We found here a few small hutts made of the Bark of Trees, in one of which were 4 or 5 Small Children, with whom we left some strings of beads, etc. A quantity of Darts lay about the Hutts; these we took away with us.

Trespassing, shooting, stealing: Captain Cook's visit hardly made an auspicious start to Anglo–Aboriginal relations.

Nor was everyone on the *Endeavour* as impressed by what they had seen of the country as Cook and Parkinson. Joseph Banks, a wealthy naturalist who was reputed to have sunk ten thousand pounds of his own money into the expedition, compared the land south of Botany Bay to 'the back of a lean Cow', with 'scraggy hip bones' that stuck out 'further than they ought'. Where Cook and Parkinson saw broad tracts of fertile land, Banks saw only isolated patches of good soil surrounded by country 'doomed to everlasting barrenness' (although he conceded that the unexplored hinterland might, after all, be as fertile as England). Had Joseph Banks held to his initial opinion of the east coast of Australia, the plan to establish a penal settlement at Botany Bay might have been stillborn. But nine years later, when he was called before a House of Commons committee on transportation (the Bunbury Committee), he was singing a different tune.

The great naturalist was asked to suggest a place 'in any part of the Globe' that might be suitable for a 'colony of convicted felons'. Escape from the colony would need to be 'difficult' and the land would have to be sufficiently fertile for the felons to be 'able to maintain themselves, after the first year'. By now, Banks was busy establishing himself as England's authority on all things antipodean. Since returning from New South Wales, he seemed to have forgotten everything he had written in his journal about lean cows and scraggy hip bones. Reporting Banks's evidence to the committee, the *Parliamentary Journal* of 1779 noted that his favoured location for a convict colony was 'Botany Bay, on the Coast of New Holland'.

The climate now reminded Banks of 'Toulouse in the South of France . . . the Proportion of rich soil was small in proportion to the barren, but sufficient to support a very large Number of People'. In addition, he 'apprehended that there would be little Probability of any Opposition from the Natives, as during his stay there, in the year 1770, he saw very few, and did not think there would be above Fifty in all the Neighbourhood . . . and those he saw were . . . extremely cowardly'.

It took another six years and another House of Commons committee (the Beauchamp Committee) before Botany Bay was plucked from a list of more or less impractical sites around the globe to become the British Government's preferred location for a convict settlement. The formal decision to establish the colony was not made until August 1786, a mere 17 months before Governor Phillip dropped anchor in Botany Bay.

But the sight that greeted the men and women of the First Fleet bore little resemblance to the country Captain Cook had rhapsodised about in his journal, or the place Joseph Banks had spoken of so glowingly to the Bunbury Committee. From the decks of their reeking and overloaded ships, the passengers surveyed the alien shore. Fear of starvation must have been in the back of every mind. Much of the livestock intended to support the colony in its first year was already dead. Nobody could be certain that the plants and seeds they had brought with them would grow in the foreign soil.

Squinting through their telescopes at the shimmering Australian shoreline and the 'very large and lofty trees' that came down almost to the water's edge, the strangers in their ludicrous garb were being watched in return. 'We hauled in for the harbour at a quarter past 2 in ye Afternoon,' reported Lieutenant Philip Gidley King, who had sailed with Phillip on the *Supply*. 'When abreast of Point Solander, we saw several of ye Natives running along brandishing their Spears.'

An unnamed 'officer' whose account of the landing was published the following year described 'natives' running along the beach making confused noises in what seemed like 'great terror'. So frightened were these first witnesses to the white invasion that they 'took their canoes out of the water upon their backs, and ran off with them into the country, together with their fishing tackle and children'.

Arriving a day after the flying squadron, the officers in Captain Hunter's convoy encountered a reception that was more aggressive than fearful. The *Sirius* sailed close enough to the shore for the crew to hear the Aboriginal people speaking. 'They pointed their spears,' wrote Hunter, 'and often used the words *wara, wara, wara.*' The words and accompanying gestures left little doubt about their meaning: 'Get lost!'

We can only guess how many of the invaders had read Captain Cook's account of his visit in the *Endeavour.* To the Aboriginal people, however, Cook's short, violent visit must have been a frightening communal memory. Some of those watching the English ships sail into Botany Bay might even have witnessed the *Endeavour's* arrival 18 years earlier.

As the first to arrive, Governor Phillip had been anxious to make contact with the native inhabitants. After anchoring the *Supply* at a spot on the northern side of Botany Bay, Phillip, his protégé Lieutenant King and other officers went ashore, beaching their boats at a spot where two canoes had been left. King described the subsequent encounter in his journal. The small group of Aboriginal people nearby 'immediately got up & called to us in a Menacing tone . . . at the same time brandishing their spears or lances'.

Rather than shooting at them with muskets, as Cook had done, Phillip held up some coloured beads and ordered a sailor to fasten them to one of the canoes. Phillip's party then indicated with gestures that they wanted water. This simple request seemed to placate the Aboriginal men, who indicated a spot further around the point, where they 'directed us by pointing, to a very fine stream of fresh water'. Phillip, alone and unarmed, then advanced towards them with a gift of beads. One man approached, but not close enough to receive Phillip's offering. He:

seemed very desirous of having them & made signs for them to be lain on ye ground, which was done, he (ye Native) came on with fear & trembling & took them up, & by degrees came so near as to receive Looking Glasses &c, & seemed quite astonished at ye figure we cut in being cloathed & I think it is very easy to conceive ye ridiculous figure we must appear to those poor creatures who were perfectly naked.

The son of a Cornish draper, Lieutenant Philip Gidley King would later be appointed the colony's third governor, a position in which his humble origins were held against him by those who considered him their social inferior. But perhaps it was King's background that allowed him to see the absurdity of the scene in which he was participating.

Like King, who regularly compared his observations with those of Captain Cook, Phillip had a detailed knowledge of Cook's *Endeavour* journal. He was aware that Cook had struggled to find enough water for his single ship. With the arrival of the *Scarborough*, *Alexander* and *Friendship*, Phillip had four ships in urgent need of water.

At around 11 o'clock on the second morning, Phillip's party – now including the marines' commander, Major Ross – again went searching for water. At the north-western corner of the bay they found a river, which they followed 'for about 6 miles, finding the Country low & boggy, & no appearence of fresh water'. Returning to Botany Bay, they explored further along the shore before beaching the boats in the south-west corner, where they sat down to 'eat our salt beff & in a glass of Porter drank ye healths of our friends in England'.

The arrival of Hunter's convoy made it clear that the visitors were not preparing to leave but were consolidating their position. A confrontation seemed inevitable.

The next day Lieutenant King went out with Lieutenant Dawes and three marines to search again for water. Stopping at a hill on the southern shore, King encountered a party of 12 Aboriginal people. Following Phillip's example, he approached them unarmed, holding out gifts of beads and baize. None of the group dared take them from his hand, but, after King dropped them, the Aboriginal men snatched up the beads and material '& bound the baize about their head they then in a very vociferous manner desired us to begone'.

One, in a belligerent demonstration of his spear-throwing prowess, then hurled a spear wide of the visitors. It flew 'about 40 Yards' and required an exertion for the warrior to pull it out of the ground. King interpreted this gesture as a threat that 'more could be thrown at us if we did not retreat'. Realising his party was outnumbered and not wanting to shoot, King backed away, stopping at one point to offer more gifts, which were refused. As the visitors descended the hill, the Aboriginal men regrouped on top of it and were 'ten times more vociferous', hurling a spear into the midst of the retreating party, to which King responded by ordering one of the marines to fire with powder only, causing them to run off.

Some hours after the incident with the spear (which led to the place being named Lance Point), King was able to make peace by offering the Aboriginal party more trinkets, although what they wanted most was 'great coats and cloathing' and especially 'hatts . . . their admiration of which they expressed by very loud shouts, whenever one of us pulled our hatts off'. The tone of this meeting by the shore was far different from that of the earlier encounter on the hill. Finding the strangers 'so very friendly', several Aboriginal men ran up to the warrior who had thrown the spear '& made very significant signs of their displeasure at his conduct by pointing all their lances at him & looking at us, intimating that they only waited our orders to kill him'. King, however, had no wish to see the unfortunate man punished and instead 'made the culprit a present of some beads'. Attempting to seal their new-found friendship, King then 'gave two of them a glass of wine, which they had no sooner tasted than they spit it out'.

Governor Phillip's written instructions from the Home Office required him to 'endeavour by every means possible to open an inter-course with the natives, and to conciliate their affections, enjoining all our subjects to live in amity and kindness with them'. Anyone who harassed or killed an Aboriginal person was to be punished 'according to the degree of the offence'. In his own hand, Phillip added the following words: 'any man who takes the life of a native will be put on his trial the same as if he had killed one of the garrison'.

But merely enforcing the law would never be enough to cultivate 'amity and kindness' between the races. In his vision for the future of the colony, Phillip stated his hopes of establishing friendly relations with the 'natives', a few of whom 'I shall endeavour to persuade to settle near us, and who I mean to furnish with everything that can tend to civilize them, and to give them a high opinion of the new guests'. In order to do this, Phillip was determined to prevent the sailors from 'having any intercourse with the natives, if possible. The convicts must have none, for if they have, the arms of the natives will be very formidable in their hands, the women abused, and the natives disgusted.'

In lieu of words, the British brought beads, 'ribbands' and trinkets, in return for which they took spears, clubs, fishing nets and other articles. The lack of a common language made it difficult but not impossible for both sides to communicate. Humour and gestures took the place of speech. Soon after the wine was spat out, Lieutenant King noticed 'a great number of Women & Girls with infant children on their shoulders, make their appearance on the beach, All *in puris naturalibus pas meme la feuille de figeur*'. The men immediately 'made signs for us to go to them, & made us understand their persons were at our service'. King sensibly declined this mark of their 'hospitality'. Instead, he beckoned to one of the women, offering her a handkerchief if she would approach. The woman 'put her child down & came alongside ye boat & suffered me to Apply the handkerchief where Eve did ye Fig leaf'. The others roared with laughter as King watched his 'female visitor' wade ashore.

The Aboriginal people were prepared to allow the visitors to catch and eat their fish, provided they shared their haul. They would take their trinkets and show them where to find water (although Watkin Tench noted that 'our toys seemed not to be regarded as very valuable'). But at the first sign of the strangers putting down roots, the locals reacted with dismay. 'The natives were well pleased with our people until they began clearing the ground, at which they were displeased and wanted them to be gone,' wrote Lieutenant Bradley.

The irony was that the visit *was* only temporary. Governor Phillip quickly decided that Botany Bay was no place to build a permanent settlement. Although the bay itself was large, it offered little shelter from easterly winds. The land surrounding the bay was not nearly as good as Cook had led them to believe, and there was little fresh water. '[I]f we are oblige to Settle here,' Ralph Clark wrote gloomily, 'there will not a Soul be [alive] in the course of a Year.'

On 21 January Phillip set out with Hunter, David Collins, the masters of the *Sirius* and *Supply*, and a party of marines in three boats, 'intending, if we could, to reach what Captain Cook has called Broken Bay, with a hope of discovering a better harbour as well as a better country'. En route, they noticed a 'large opening or bay, about three leagues and a half to the Northward of Cape Banks'. Although unpromising at first, the bay proved to have good deep water, while the surrounding country was 'greatly superior in every respect to that round Botany Bay'.

After spending two days exploring Port Jackson, Phillip found what he considered to be an ideal site for the new colony. 'We got into Port Jackson early in the afternoon,' he told Lord Sydney in a dispatch dated 15 May, 'and had the satisfaction of finding the finest harbour in the world, in which a thousand sail of the line may ride in the most perfect security.'

After briskly exploring various coves, Phillip chose the one that had the best spring of water. It was about a quarter of a mile across at the entrance and half a mile in length. Phillip judged that its geography and deep water would allow ships to anchor so close to the shore that the quays necessary to unload them could be built very cheaply. He named it Sydney Cove.

The 11 ships of the First Fleet thus prepared to sail away from Botany Bay, having stayed for less than a week. They left behind some trinkets and looking glasses and a small patch of roughly cleared ground. The bay had been a bitter disappointment, its poor soil and lack of fresh water a stark warning to the colonists that their survival in the new country hung in the balance. Those familiar with Cook's expedition felt doubly let down. 'The fine meadows talked of in Captain Cook's voyage I could never see,' wrote Surgeon White, 'though I took some pains to find them out; nor have I ever heard of a person that has seen any parts resembling them.'

The British Government's rushed scheme to establish a convict settlement on the shores of Botany Bay was over before it had begun. Not a single convict had set foot on shore. Tentative contact had been made with the Aboriginal people; there had been no overt violence, but the potential for it had been made clear enough by both sides. 'I am well convinced,' White noted complacently, 'that they know and dread the superiority of our arms.'

A final shock awaited the fleet. 'I rose at the first dawn of the morning,' wrote Tench. 'But judge of my surprize on hearing from a serjeant, who ran down almost breathless to the cabin where I was dressing, that a ship was seen off the harbour's mouth. At first I only laughed, but knowing the man who spoke to me to be of great veracity, and hearing him repeat his information, I flew upon deck, on which I had barely set my foot, when the cry of "another sail" struck on my astonished ear.'

Initial fears that the visitors might be Dutch warships, sent to seize New South Wales for the Netherlands, were quickly followed by excitement at the possibility that the ships might be British, carrying fresh supplies for the colony. In fact, the 'strange ships' were French. Commanded by the distinguished navigator Jean-François La Perouse, *La Boussole* and *L'Astrolabe* were on a voyage of discovery, mapping coastlines and exploring uncharted parts of the Pacific Ocean.

La Perouse's unexpected arrival with two large ships represented a possible threat to Britain's plan to claim its new territory unopposed. Having decided on Sydney Cove as the site of the settlement, Phillip wasted no time returning to Port Jackson in the *Supply*, leaving the rest of the fleet to follow when the wind was more favourable.

The French ships struggled for two days to get into Botany Bay. Each side was as astonished as the other at the extraordinary coincidence of their having arrived at this remote spot on the far side of the world within a week of each other.

Captain Hunter, in charge of the fleet in Phillip's absence, 'sent a boat with an officer to assist them in'. The usual courtesies were paid. Perhaps the French, having recently seen the captain of the *Astrolabe* and a dozen men stoned and bludgeoned to death in Samoa, were in need of more material assistance. But Hunter was in a hurry to leave and, in any case, the colony needed everything it had brought for its own use.

The French ships remained in Botany Bay for six weeks and would cause plenty of trouble for the English colonists before they sailed away.

4

A vile pack of baggages

The south-east breeze that brought the big French ships into Botany Bay made it treacherous for the smaller British ships to get out. Ralph Clark watched in horror as the *Prince of Wales* ran into the *Friendship*, carrying away her jib boom, while her own mainsail was 'rent in pieces'. Next it was the *Charlotte*'s turn to batter the *Friendship*, losing part of her carved stern and forcing both ships against the rocks so that Clark feared 'the Ships must have all been lost and the greater part . . . on board drownd'. The *Lady Penrhyn* narrowly avoided being struck before the fleet managed to work its way out of the bay with what Smyth called 'ye. utmost difficulty & danger wt. many hairbredth escapes'.

At the sight of the First Fleet riding at anchor in Botany Bay, La Perouse had been moved to remark that 'all Europeans are countrymen at such a distance from home'. But it is hard not to imagine guffaws from the French sailors crowding the decks of *La Boussole* and *L'Astrolabe* at this exhibition of British seamanship.

It took until seven that evening for the fleet to sail the six miles to Sydney Cove, where several of the ships were able to come so close to shore that they tied up to trees rather than having to drop their anchors.

With the destination of the settlement decided and the ships secured, it was time to crack open a bottle. At sunset, 'the Governor & a number of the Officers assembled on Shore where they Displayed the British Flag and each Officer with a Heart glowing with Loyalty drank his Majesty's Health and Success to the Colony'. The marines 'fired several vollies', but on this festive occasion it was 'the governor and the officers' who did the drinking.

The troops and male convicts were disembarked the next day. 'The confusion that ensued will not be wondered at, when it is considered that every man stepped from the boat literally into a wood,' wrote Collins.

Mollie Gillen, in *The Founders of Australia: A Biographical Dictionary of the First Fleet*, gives a total of 1373 people landed at Port Jackson, of whom 754 were convicts and their children. Seventeen convicts and three children died before the fleet left England, most of them from typhus on board the *Alexander*. The mortality rate at sea of less than 3 per cent was far lower than the average for British convicts transported across the Atlantic to America – and far lower than in the Second Fleet that followed two years later.

'Business now sat on every brow,' wrote Tench. 'In one place, a party cutting down the woods; a second, setting up a blacksmith's forge; a third, dragging along a load of stones or provisions; here an officer pitching his marquee, with a detachment of troops parading on one side of him, and a cook's fire blazing up on the other.'

A fresh water stream – later called the Tank Stream – rose from the marshy land of what is now Hyde Park and flowed north to the head of Sydney Cove, bisecting the infant colony. Phillip had his canvas hut erected on the eastern side of the stream, alongside the majority of the convicts; the marines and the rest of the convicts pitched camp on the west.

Alert to the risk of convicts trying to find their way to the French ships at Botany Bay, Phillip sent the marines to patrol the surrounding country with orders to round up absconders. Convicts were warned that 'the severest punishment would be inflicted on transgressors'. In spite of the warnings, many were keen to try their luck. 'Several of the convicts have Run away,' Clark wrote a few days after landing. '[O]ne or two of them have Come back having been to Botany Bay to see if the French Ships which we left there would take them but the[y] would [not].'

Everyone except the governor was sleeping in tents. '[I]n all the course of my life I never Slept worse . . . than I did [last] night,' whinged Clark, 'what with the hard cold ground Spiders ants and every vermin that you can think of was crauling over me.'

Despite the best efforts of the surgeons, disease was soon raging through the camp, overwhelming the tents assigned to the sick and forcing Phillip to bring forward plans to establish a general hospital. 'The scurvy . . . broke out, which, aided by a dysentery, began to fill the hospital, and several died,' wrote Collins. Edible plants were used to supplement the antiscorbutics that had been brought from England. Collins noted the abundance of 'wild celery, spinach, and parsley' growing around the settlement.

The female convicts were not landed until 6 February, 11 sweltering summer days after the fleet's arrival at Sydney Cove. What happened next has been transformed into one of the great convict myths – a 'drunken spree', in the words of Manning Clark, brought on by 'extra rations of rum'; an orgy, according to Robert Hughes, in which 'the women floundered to and fro, draggled as muddy chickens under a pump, pursued by male convicts intent on raping them'.

The previous day, the commissary and his clerk, together with Mr Shortland, the naval agent for the transports, had come aboard the *Lady Penrhyn*, and all the female convicts and children had been given fresh clothes. As they were shuttled to shore in the long boats, even the censorious Smyth was able to admit that '[t]hey were dress'd in general very clean & some few amongst them might be sd. to be well dress'd'. By six o'clock that evening, Smyth 'had the long wish'd for pleasure of seeing the last of them leave the Ship'.

The female convicts had not been on shore for an hour when a violent thunderstorm broke over the settlement, a bolt of lightning splitting a tree in two and killing a lieutenant's pig and five sheep belonging to Major Ross.

After the women had been disembarked:

The Sailors in our Ship requested to have some Grog to make
merry wt. upon the Women quitting the Ship indeed the
Capt. himself had no small reason to rejoice upon their being

all safely landed & given into the Care of the Governor, as
he was under the penalty of 40£ for every Convict that was
missing – for wh. reason he comply'd wt. the Sailor's request.

Cooped up in his cabin on the *Lady Penrhyn* while the thunder
roared and the crew got plastered, Smyth could have had no idea
of what the women were getting up to on shore, but that did not
prevent him writing about it.

The Men Convicts got to them very soon after they landed,
& it is beyond my abilities to give a just description of the
Scene of Debauchery & Riot that ensued during the night
. . . The Scene wh. presented itself at this time & during the
greater part of the night, beggars every description; some
swearing, others quarrelling others singing, not in the least
regarding the Tempest, tho' so violent that the thunder shook
the Ship exceeded anything I ever before had a conception of.
I never before experienced so uncomfortable a night expectg.
every moment the Ship wd. be struck wt. the Lighteng. – The
Sailors almost all drunk & incapable of rendering much
assistance had an accident happen'd & the heat was almost
suffocating.

Ralph Clark, who never passed up an opportunity to rail against
the 'damed whores' on the *Friendship*, and who was ashore during
the night the female convicts were landed, wrote about the lightning
strike and Major Ross's dead sheep but did not mention an orgy.

Nor did George Worgan, the surgeon on the *Sirius*, who in a letter to his brother Richard described the female convicts as a 'vile pack of Baggages continually violating all Laws, and disobedient to all Orders', or Surgeon White, Captain Hunter or Collins. As for the 'drunken spree', the convicts at Sydney Cove were not issued rations – let alone 'extra rations' – of rum.

Something happened that night, but not the fabled drunken orgy. Tench, more humane and less judgemental than most of his companions, remarked that during the long voyage 'the two sexes had been kept most rigorously apart; but, when landed, their separation became impracticable, and would have been, perhaps, wrong. Licentiousness was the unavoidable consequence.'

The day after the female convicts came ashore, the whole colony assembled to hear Governor Phillip's commission. The convicts were mustered early in the morning, and nine were found to be missing. They were assumed to be among those who had gone stumbling into the bush in search of the French ships at Botany Bay. La Perouse, however, had 'given his honour' not to take any fugitives on board, informing Lieutenant King on 1 February that 'a number of ye Convicts had been to him & offered to enter but he had dismissed them with threats; & gave them a days provisions to carry them back to ye settlement'.

Some of the stragglers were never seen again. 'A woman, named Ann Smith, and a man have never since been heard of,' reported White. 'They are supposed to have missed their way as they returned, and to have perished for want.'

After receiving the governor with 'flying Colours & a Band of Music', the marines formed themselves into a circle; the male and female convicts were then herded into the middle and 'order'd to sit down on the ground'. All the 'gentlemen' present were then invited into the centre to join Governor Phillip and the lieutenant-governor, Major Ross; Collins, the deputy judge advocate; the Reverend Richard Johnson; and Surgeon White. Two red leather cases containing Phillip's commissions were 'open'd & unsealed in the Sight of All present' and the commissions outlining the governor's powers were read aloud by Collins.

His authority established, Phillip addressed the private marines, thanking them 'for their steady good conduct on every occasion'. Those hoping for more tangible rewards were disappointed. Not only did the King's instructions forbid Phillip to grant land to marines; they expressly authorised him to 'emancipate convicts for good behaviour and industry and . . . to grant land to them'.

While the marines smarted from yet another slight, Phillip 'harangu'd the Convicts', according to Smyth, 'telling them that he had try'd them hitherto to see how they were disposed; that he was now thoroughly convinced there were many amongst them incorrigible, & that he was persuaded nothing but severity wd. have any Effect upon them to induce them to behave properly in future. He also assured them that if they attempted to get into the women's Tents of a night there were positive orders for firing upon them.'

Unless the convicts could be forced to work, the colony could not survive. Phillip left his listeners in no doubt that slackers would not be tolerated. Not more than 200 out of 600 male convicts had done any work, he said, warning them that 'the industrious shd. not labour for the idle; if they did not work they shd. not eat'.

As always, the critical issue was food. The fleet had brought a limited quantity of food from England; the rest the colonists would need to produce for themselves. There would be draconian penalties for anyone caught stealing. 'In England thieving poultry was not punish'd wt. Death; but here, where a loss of that kind could not be supply'd . . . stealing the most trifling Article of Stock or Provisions wd. be punished wt. Death.'

Phillip was pleased with how the day had gone. 'A rising government could not easily be committed to better hands,' he observed in his journal. That evening he and his officers sat down to dine on one of the sheep killed by lightning during the previous night's thunderstorm. '[T]he Mutten was full of maggots nothing will keep 24 hours in this country,' Clark wrote miserably in his journal.

The purpose of Phillip's harangue was not just to chastise the work-shy and to spell out the harsh penalties for breaking the law; it was also to encourage active – and willing – participation in the social experiment that the new colony represented. The effects were immediate, if not necessarily long-lasting. Within a week, 14 marriages had taken place among the convicts. (Some quickly regretted the decision. 'The Misfortune,' George Worgan quipped to his brother, 'is one half of them have asked the Governor if the Chaplain cannot Unmarry.')

Demanding good behaviour and hard work was one thing; enforcing them was another. Convicts who could be spared from clearing the land were assigned to gangs and put to work as 'Carpenters,

Sawyers, Shingle Makers, Stone Cutters, Masons, Brick Makers, Blacksmiths, &c.' Overseers were chosen from among the convicts on the basis of their conduct during the voyage from England, but few showed much enthusiasm for the job. The appointment of a provost marshal and constable to oversee the overseers made little difference.

Men such as William Parr were torn between their loyalty to fellow convicts and their duty as overseers. Described in court records as a 'noted swindler', Parr achieved a certain celebrity on account of his marriage to Mary McCormack on 10 February 1788 – the first marriage recorded in the colony. In the course of investigating the alleged theft of some property belonging to a man named Daniel Gordon, Parr was abused and threatened by another convict, Joseph Levi. The court found Levi guilty of abusive conduct and sentenced him to a hundred lashes, but before the sentence could be carried out, Parr interceded with the governor on Levi's behalf. As a result, Levi was pardoned. Whether Parr genuinely regretted his own role in the prosecution or whether he was intimidated into trying to overturn the sentence hardly matters: the role of convict overseer was an invidious one and Parr probably feared for his own safety. Others simply turned a blind eye.

'Notwithstanding these Precautions to keep them at their tasks,' wrote Worgan, 'they found means to evade this Vigilance . . . Ten or 14 of Them would take their Provisions (which is served them once a Week) and instead of going to work skulk about the Woods, and return by the Time of serving Provisions again.'

Tools were pilfered and lost; convicts stole from each other and grog began to find its way ashore. 'The sailors from the transports,' wrote Collins, 'although repeatedly forbidden, and frequently punished . . . persisted in bringing spirits on shore by night, and drunkenness was often the consequence.'

All of these problems had been foreseen by Phillip, who had pleaded while the fleet was still in England for the appointment of 'proper persons to superintend the convicts'. It was implicit in the government's plans for the colony that this job would fall to the marine corps, but after the fleet landed the marines did everything they could to avoid contact with the convicts. In his first letter to Lord Sydney, Phillip complained that most of the officers 'have declined any interference with the convicts except when they are employed for their own particular service'. Even Phillip's simple request for the officers to 'encourage such as they observed diligent and point out for punishment such as they saw idle or straggling in the woods' was ignored.

Barely a fortnight had passed since the landing at Sydney Cove, yet Phillip's vision of a colony in which 'industry and good behaviour' would redeem the convicts was already in tatters.

'This day our Carpenter, one of our Sailors, & a Boy belong[ing] to the *Prince of Wales* were caught in the Womens Tents,' wrote Smyth. '[T]hey were drum'd out of the Camp wt. the Rogue's March playing before them & the Boy had petticoats put upon him, they had all of them their hands tyed behind 'em. The Anarchy & Confusion wh. prevails throughout the camp, & the Audacity of the Convicts both Men & Women, is arrived at such a pitch as it not to be equalled, I believe, by any set of Villains in any other Spot upon the globe.'

To check these 'enormities', the criminal court sat for the first time on 11 February 1788.

A convict, Samuel Barsby, who was working on 'the other side of the water', had been stopped by two sailors wanting to know the way to the women's camp. In exchange for directions, Barsby was given three parts of a bottle of rum, most of which he drank. Later that afternoon, he quarrelled with another convict. When Drum Major Cook told the two men to get back to work, Barsby struck him with an adze. As he was being hauled off to the guard house, the drunken Barsby attacked another marine, Drummer West, 'putting him in Fear of his Life'. That evening, Barsby was so violent that he had to be bound and gagged.

In court Barsby did not dispute the facts but asked for mercy, blaming his actions on the rum. The court found him guilty and sentenced him to 'Receive 150 lashes on his bare back with a cat of nine tails'. The case was an ominous sign of the trouble that grog would cause in the years ahead.

In two other cases heard that day, a convict named Hill was found guilty of stealing some biscuit and sentenced to a week in irons, on bread and water, on a rocky island in the harbour that would come to be known as Pinchgut (now Fort Denison); and William Cole, another convict, was sentenced to 50 lashes for stealing a plank of wood, but was pardoned, apparently for not realising he was committing a crime.

Phillip was determined to prevent grog from getting into the hands of convicts, but its scarcity and desirability made it a valuable commodity for barter. A fortnight after Samuel Barsby went on the rampage while drunk on rum, Captain Marshall, master of the *Scarborough*, was reprimanded by the governor for allowing his steward to 'purchase an Animal of the Squirrell kind from one of the Convict men, & giving him Liquor for it'. Told by the steward that 'the price of the animal was a gallon of rum', Marshall told him to pay it, despite Phillip's strict orders against any private transactions with convicts. The steward was sentenced to 100 lashes for giving a bottle of rum to a convict, later reduced by Phillip to 50.

'[I]t appears to many a stretch of the Governor's prerogative,' commented Smyth, 'to inflict so severe a corporal punishment upon a seaman . . . without any form of legal tryal . . . an evident discontent prevails among the different Officers throughout the Settlement; the Marines and Sailors are punish'd wt. the utmost severity for the most trivial offences, while the Convicts are pardon'd (or at most punish'd in a very slight manner) for Crimes of ye. Blackest die.'

Fifty lashes, however, was no deterrent to the smugglers. Another seaman, Charles Clay, was soon before the court on a charge of bringing a bottle of liquor ashore. The officer of the guard, Lieutenant Faddy, testified that he had inspected a bundle Clay had brought ashore and discovered a bottle of brandy concealed inside. On the governor's orders, Clay was put in irons. He did not deny smuggling the bottle, saying that he was keeping a promise to two convicts who had done some work for him. He swore not to do it again but was nevertheless found guilty of disobeying orders and sentenced to 50 lashes, later reduced to 25.

Despite Smyth's complaint about the 'severity' of the penalties given to marines and sailors, most of the punishments meted out since the fleet had left England had been pragmatic rather than exemplary. While there had been occasional floggings, male offenders were more often punished by being forced to wear heavy irons. In the case of female convicts, at first '1 or 2 were flog'd with a cat of 9 tails on the naked breech' but in the interests of 'decency' such punishment 'was totally laid aside'. Instead, '[u]pon any very extraordinary occasion such as thieving fighting with each other or making use of abusive language to the Officers, they have thumb Screws – or Iron fetters on their wrists . . . and sometimes their hair has been cut off and their head shaved'.

But the thieving and fighting was getting worse.

While Phillip had been supplied with a small amount of money to buy provisions (and bribe Dutch officials) at Java and 'the Molucca Islands', his instructions said nothing about the need for money once the settlement was established. Where the colony had to pay for labour or buy goods from outside, Phillip used bills of exchange, which were effectively IOUs against the Treasury in London; these often passed through many hands before they were eventually presented for payment. 'These small bills will give the Treasury some trouble,' Phillip conceded in a letter to Under-Secretary Nepean, 'but this country has no Treasury.'

Smuggled and stolen liquor was already rippling through the colony's cashless economy. In mid–February another convict, William Murphy, was picked up by the night patrol for being 'very drunk'. Zachariah Clark, the contractor's agent, counted 18 bottles of wine missing from his store tent. Three convicts – George Whitaker, Daniel Gordon and John Williams – were accused of stealing the wine. Days later four convicts – Thomas Barrett, Henry Lovell, Joseph Hall and John Ryan – were charged with 'feloniously and fraudulently' stealing 'Butter Pease and Pork' from the public store. (Thomas Barrett was the forger who made a name for himself during the voyage by passing off quarter dollars 'out of old buckles . . . and pewter spoons'.) Captain Tench described the four as 'desperate and hardened villains'.

Their trials before the criminal court in the last days of February 1788 marked a turning point. The theft of food from the public store was a felony, punishable by death, but also a real and existential threat to the survival of the colony.

During the early planning for the colony, there had been some ambiguity over how the law was to be applied in New South Wales. The administration was to be essentially military, with a criminal court made up of marine officers. Initially this raised concerns about its jurisdiction over convicts who had been sentenced to transportation under civil law. But once in New South Wales, Phillip's authority was clear. Any sentence, including the death penalty, could be imposed provided the accused was found guilty by a majority of the court. The deputy judge advocate, David Collins, wrote in his journal, 'If guilty, and the offence is capital, they are to pronounce judgment of death, in like manner as if the prisoner had been convicted by the verdict of a jury in England.' As long as five members of the court agreed with a guilty verdict, the death penalty could be carried out immediately, without approval from the British Crown.

The conspiracy to rob the stores went beyond the four principals, who had 'persuade[d] some others, less deeply versed in iniquity, to be the instruments for carrying it on'. Unfortunately for Lovell, Hall and Ryan, but above all for Thomas Barrett, one of these accomplices 'on being apprehended . . . impeached the rest, and disclosed the scheme'.

All four were found guilty. At one o'clock in the afternoon Barrett, Lovell and Hall were sentenced to death; Ryan to 300 lashes. The 'Arm of a large tree' between the men's and women's camps was chosen for a gallows, and a large party of well-armed marines stood guard to prevent an uprising or attempted rescue by their fellow convicts who had been 'summon'd to see the deserved end of their Companions'.

After the parson, Mr Johnson, had finished praying with the condemned men, a noose was put around Thomas Barrett's neck and he mounted the ladder. 'I don't think that he had the least thought that [he] was to Suffer but when the Provos Martial put a handkerchiff a bout his head he turned as white as a sheet,' wrote Clark. Moments later the ladder was pulled from under him and Barrett 'Lanched into the other world without a gron – from every Account he was a great Rascall . . . after Barret had hung the usuall time he was cut down and put into a Grave near the Tree by Some of the convicts.'

The executions of Lovell and Hall were postponed until the following day.

The hanging of Thomas Barrett did not go as smoothly as Clark's account implied. According to Smyth, the convict hangman baulked 'either from Timidity or Feeling' at doing his job, putting the provost marshal, Mr Brewer, 'under the disagreeable Necessity of mounting the Ladder Himself, in order to fix the Halter'. The hangman only 'complyd' with his instructions after Major Ross 'threaten'd to give orders to the Marines to shoot him'.

'Just before Barrett was turned off,' wrote Smyth, 'he confess'd the justice of his sentence & that he had lead a very wicked life, he requested leave to speak to one of the Convict men (a very bad kind of man) . . . wh. was granted him, & he also expressed a wish to speak to one of the women convicts, but was refused, he then exhorted all of them to take warng. by his unhappy fate & so lanched into Eternity . . . The Revd. Mr. Johnson prayed very fervently wt. the Culprit before he was turn'd off.'

The next day a torrential downpour turned the camp to mud; Ralph Clark, whose job it was to deliver the temporarily reprieved prisoners to the gallows, had never seen it rain harder. Barrett's execution had a sobering effect on the other convicts, who sent a petition to the governor begging that Barrett's two co-accused, Lovell and Hall, be forgiven and spared the gallows. In return, they 'promised that not one amongst them he [i.e. Governor Phillip] would have reason to find falt with'.

It continued to pour with rain as Lovell and Hall awaited their fate. 'Whilst they stood at the place of Execution expecting every minute to be order'd to mount the Ladder Major Ross informed that his Excellency the Governor (wishing still to try what influence Mercy wd. have upon them) authoriz'd him to acquaint them that he wd. pardon them.'

Lovell and Hall were ordered to be banished 'to some uninhabited place', while Ryan was forgiven his 300 lashes.

On 29 February three more convicts were sentenced to death: John Freeman, for stealing seven pounds of flour; and John Williams and Daniel Gordon, for 'feloniously and fraudulently taking and carrying away' 18 bottles of Tenerife wine from Zachariah Clark (George Whitaker was acquitted of the same charge).

Williams, described by Surgeon White as 'an ignorant black youth', was recommended for mercy and pardoned. Gordon, who was also black, was pardoned as well. Both were banished along with Lovell and Hall. That left Freeman, who 'while under the ladder, with the rope about his neck . . . was offered a free pardon on condition of performing the duty of the common executioner as long as he remained in this country; which, after some little pause, he reluctantly accepted'.

'[H]ere was an Opportunity,' quipped White's medical colleague George Worgan, 'of establishing a Jack Ketch, who should in all future Executions either *Hang* or *Be Hanged*.'

From the outset, Governor Phillip's promise of rough justice for thieves was hopelessly compromised. Of the first six convicts sentenced to death in New South Wales for stealing food and provisions, five were reprieved, ostensibly in return for a 'guarantee' of future good behaviour by their fellow convicts. Phillip's preference for leniency, demonstrated time and again since the fleet had left England, risked exposing both himself and his administration to ridicule, not just from the convicts but also from the marines charged with guarding them.

After the condemned men had been reprieved, Major Ross 'inform'd All the Convicts that the Governor declared upon his

Word & Honour that whoever after this was found guilty of Theft shd. most assuredly suffer & that no interest or application whatever shd. save them'. Lieutenant Clark, for one, was not convinced. 'I think after his goodness the[y] ought to behave now well, but I am almost certain that before I am a fortnight older Some of them will be brought to trial for Capital offences.'

He was not far wrong.

5

The natives stole an ax & a spade

At first the seedlings grew, the native timber looked useful and the Aboriginal people offered nothing more than theatrical displays of violence. But it was all an illusion.

'The seeds that were sown . . . on first appearing above ground, looked promising and well,' wrote Surgeon White, 'but soon after withered away.' It was high summer and the worst season for planting. 'All the culinary plants that have come up, degenerate exceedingly,' complained Worgan. 'Peas, beans, cabbage plants etc do not thrive, and many of them have withered.'

On 14 February, spurred by the appearance of the French ships in Botany Bay, Phillip sent a small party of marines and convicts under Lieutenant Philip Gidley King to settle Norfolk Island, which had flax and pines seen by the British Government as valuable strategic assets. King's written instructions commanded him to 'proceed to the cultivation of the Flax Plant, which you will find growing spontaneously on the island: as likewise to the cultivation of cotton, corn, and other plants'. The *Supply* sailed with six months' provisions and the promise of more, but Phillip had little to spare and urged his protégé to make the provisions he had been given last as long as possible.

With a thousand convicts and marines sleeping rough amid primitive sanitation at Sydney Cove, dysentery swept through both the camp and the ships anchored in the harbour. On 19 March Surgeon Smyth reported, 'The Dysentery prevails very much on Shore & many have dyed of it.' Susannah Blanchard, a convict, died and was buried on 24 March. The next day John Fisher, a seaman, died 'of a Dysentery'. On Saturday 5 April Mary Spencer, another convict, was buried; followed on Tuesday by Thomas Lewis, a sailor from the *Friendship*; on Thursday by William McDonald, a sailor from the *Supply*; and on Sunday by James Thomas, a marine's child.

Cook's observation that 'the whole Country or at least great part of it might be cultivated without being oblig'd to cut down a single tree' proved cruelly inaccurate. The labour needed to fell the huge gum trees and grub roots out of bone-hard summer ground meant that a mere eight acres could be sown with wheat and barley in the first year. Pests attacked the little that grew. Anticipating the desperate problems that lay ahead, Phillip warned Lord Sydney, 'The immense number of ants and field-mice will render our crops very uncertain.'

Nor was the tall, straight timber everything it seemed. Although 'well described' by Cook, the wood had 'one very bad quality, which puts us to great inconvenience; I mean the large gum-tree, which splits and warps in such a manner when used green . . . that a store-house boarded up with this wood is rendered useless.'

Phillip's hopes of amicable relations between the colonists and the native inhabitants soon faded, despite the initial courtesies before the convicts had come ashore. The French were partly to blame. To keep the Aboriginal men from 'annoying' his crew while they worked on shore, La Perouse built a palisade 'wt. 2 or 3 Guns' at Botany Bay. La Perouse (like Phillip) had been instructed 'to endeavour by every possible means to acquire and cultivate the friendship of the natives . . . and to avoid exercising any act of hostility upon them'. But, lacking Phillip's patience and his motivation of establishing friendly relations with his long-term neighbours, La Perouse 'was obliged to fire upon them'.

While convinced that the French had done all they could to avoid confrontation and had only fired their weapons as a last resort, David Collins understood at once that it was the British colonists who would pay the price of La Perouse's actions, 'as those who had rendered this violence necessary could not discriminate between us and them'.

Governor Phillip had done his best to cultivate and maintain friendly relations with the Aboriginal people by 'strictly prohibiting every person from depriving them of their spears, fizgigs, gum, or other articles, which we soon perceived they were accustomed to leave under the rocks, or loose and scattered about upon the beaches'. But the sailors on the transports, who would soon be returning home, were mad for souvenirs. When a boatload of sailors tried to land in one of the coves to look for tools and weapons, they were driven off with stones. A party of warriors retaliated by landing on what is now Garden Island, where the crew of the *Sirius* had been trying to grow vegetables. 'Mr. Hill a Midshipman wt. 2 Marines were there on guard,' wrote Smyth. '[T]he Natives stole an Ax & a Spade & wd. persist in going off with them, wh. obliged Mr. Hill to give orders to the Marines to fire at their Legs, which they did wt. small shot, & the fellow dropt the Ax but the Spade they got clear off with.'

Ralph Clark had no hesitation declaring the Aboriginal people to be 'the Greatest thefs that ever lived – I think that we are in a fine stat we brought nothing but thefs out with [us] to find nothing but thefs'.

As relations worsened, Collins blamed the souvenir hunters for the:

termination of that good understanding which had hitherto
subsisted between us and them . . . the convicts were
everywhere straggling about, collecting animals and gum
to sell to the people of the transports, who at the same time
were procuring spears, shields, swords, fishing-lines, and
other articles from the natives, to carry to Europe; the loss of
which must have been attended with many inconveniences to
the owners, as . . . they were the only means whereby they
obtained or could procure their daily subsistence.

For a while, Aboriginal resentment towards the intruders manifested itself in avoidance, but few expected this to last. 'There is some reason to suppose they will not long remain quiet,' the unnamed 'officer' commented darkly. Retribution against the most vulnerable settlers – unarmed and often isolated convicts – was inevitable.

While drinking tea with Major Ross, Smyth learnt that 'the Natives had kill'd several of the Convicts who had elop'd from Port Jackson & taken up their residence near Botany Bay'. In some cases there was doubt over whether the absconders had been killed or had simply died of thirst after becoming lost in the bush. The deaths of two convicts named Allen and Macdonald in March were confirmed when 'their cloaths were found hanging up in a tree in triumph'.

The violence continued. On 22 May two of the convalescent convicts were sent out to get greens for the hospital. About a mile from the camp, the two men ran into a party of Aboriginal warriors, who attacked them with stones and spears. 'One of the Convicts escaped with a barbed spear broke in him entering at the small of the back . . . he reported that the other Convict was killed and that the Natives had stript him & taken the body away with them.'

The wounded convict, William Ayres, struggled back to the settlement, where Surgeon White was able to remove the spear, 'which had penetrated the flesh nearly three inches'. Ayres claimed to have received his wound from 'three of the natives, who came behind him at a time when he suspected no person to be near him except Peter Burn, whom he had met a little before'. After wounding him, they had beaten Ayres 'in a cruel manner' before stripping him of his clothes and carrying them off, making signs to him to return to the camp while he still could. As he staggered back to the settlement, he saw Peter Burn 'in the possession of another party of the natives, who were dragging him along, with his head bleeding, and seemingly in great distress'. Too weak from loss of blood to help his companion, Ayres 'was happy to escape with his life'.

According to a seaman on the *Borrowdale*, the two men had been attacked by the warriors out of 'revenge for taking away one of their canoes'. Suspicions that Burn might have been a victim of cannibalism were fuelled by a report from another convict who absconded and later returned, claiming to have seen 'the head of one of the convicts lying near the place, where the body had been burnt in a large fire'.

When Governor Phillip refused to allow a punitive expedition against the aggressors, some of the convicts took the law into their own hands. The day after the attack on Ayres and Burn, some canoes landed at Major Ross's garden beside the harbour. The Aboriginal men 'stole a jacket & several other things which were afterwards found in one of the canoes by some of the convicts, who followed them along the shore to the next cove where they landed & we have reason to suppose that one of the natives was murdered by them but the proof could not be got'.

More attacks followed, usually against convicts who had absconded or been sent into the bush to work. On 30 May Captain James Campbell of the marines took some boats down the south-west arm of the harbour (comprising what are now Rozelle, and Blackwattle and Johnstons Bays) to a spot where two convicts had been left with tents to cut rushes for thatching Campbell's house. Landing at the camp site, they 'found the Tent but not the Men'. While searching for the missing convicts, the marines discovered blood on the ground near the tent. According to Lieutenant William Bradley, '[T]hey followed it to the Mangrove bushes, where they found both Men dead & laying at some distance from each other. One of them had 3 Spears in him & one side of his head beat in: The other Man had no apparent wound but a blow on the fore head.'

Phillip set out the next day with a search party to look for the culprits. After dropping the party at the spot where the convicts had been killed, the boat headed back to the settlement. The officer who was in the boat called at Major Ross's farm, where he was told that a convict had killed one of the Aboriginal men some days before by cutting him across the belly with his knife. Bradley had no doubt the dead convicts were the victims of a revenge attack. 'They have attacked our people when they have met them unarmed, but that did not happen until they had been very ill treated by us in the lower part of the Harbour & fired upon at Botany Bay by the French.'

As well as killing convicts, the Aboriginal people began to slaughter what remained of the colony's livestock, spearing a he-goat belonging to the governor, and killing and carrying away a kid grazing near the hospital, both within the space of a fortnight. 'Whenever an opportunity offered,' wrote White, 'they have seldom failed to destroy whatever stock they could seize upon unobserved.'

As the year went on, the attacks on the convicts became more brazen, sometimes taking place within earshot of the marines sent from the settlement to guard – and protect – them. A convict named Cooper Handley, who went out with an armed party of marines to collect wild vegetables and sweet tea, became separated from his companions and was 'murdered and mutilated . . . in a shocking manner' by a group of Aboriginal warriors. 'The natives,' wrote Bradley, 'were so near our men that they heard them very distinctly shouting and making a great noise, yet were unable to overtake them in the pursuit. In the evening, a party of soldiers and convicts were sent out to bury the deceased.'

While individual attacks could be traced back to a particular act of provocation, at a deeper level the cycle of violence was a predictable outcome of the colonists' inability to empathise with the Aboriginal people. Written descriptions often sounded more zoological than anthropological, as if Aboriginal men and women were not human beings but another species of exotic wildlife to be observed and catalogued (and, later, dissected and preserved) like the possums and kangaroos.

'[D]uring our stay there of 3 months,' wrote Smyth, 'the different Animals we saw, were Kangaroos . . . a very large Species of Lizard, Dogs, Rats, Raccoons, flying Squirrels . . . There are also . . . great quantities of Ants of 8 or 10 different species & many flies & Musquito's. The Women are also quite naked & go in miserable bad canoes to Catch fish . . . The natives do not besmear their Hair or Bodies with any kind of Oil or paint as many Indians do . . . their Language is excessively Loud & harsh & seems to consist of a very short Vocabulary . . . they seemed altogether a most stupid insensible set of beings.'

Surgeon White was another who simply lumped the Aboriginal people among other forms of exotic fauna:

The natives of this country, though their mode of subsisting seems to be so very scant and precarious, are, I am convinced, not cannibals. One of their graves, which I saw opened . . . contained a body which had evidently been burned, as small pieces of the bones lay in the bottom of it . . .

The Pennantian Parrot . . . was about this time first noticed. The general colour of the body, in the male, is crimson.

Since the British and the Aboriginal people lacked a common language, information could only be exchanged with difficulty. First impressions – often based upon the most superficial 'evidence' – could be hard to dislodge. Rumours flourished, and some of them found their way into the published accounts. 'It has been suggested by a Convict who absented himself & remained some days in the Woods,' wrote Lieutenant Bradley, 'that the natives were Cannibals, & that he had seen a party of them eat the flesh of one who they had killed, the authority is not good yet I think that circumstance of their taking one of the Convicts into the Woods with them after having killed & stripp'd him favour the man's report.'

Not all the colonists were as scornful as Smyth, as haphazard as White or as credulous as Bradley. Refuting Joseph Banks's estimate that there would not be 'above Fifty in all the Neighbourhood', Captain Hunter counted Aboriginal people 'in very Considerable numbers' and found them 'a lively & inquisitive Race . . . Straight, thin, but well made people rather small in their limbs but very active'.

Watkin Tench, at 30 already a veteran of the American wars,

was unique in the lengths he went to in order to understand the Aboriginal people as individuals. Intuitive, compassionate and, above all, curious, Tench combined sharp physical observation with deeper insights born out of simple human empathy.

Encouraged and even charmed by their 'easy reception of us in the beginning', Tench was at first prepared to disbelieve Cook's cooler account, speculating that '[t]hat celebrated navigator . . . had somehow by his conduct offended them, which prevented the intercourse that would otherwise have taken place'.

Where others were inclined to see only impulsive 'hostility' directed against themselves, Tench searched for reasons. 'The result . . . of our repeated endeavours to induce them to come among us,' he wrote, 'has been such as to confirm me in an opinion that they either fear or despise us too much to be anxious for a closer connection.'

By contemporary standards, Tench was enlightened and humane. He was also disposed to see the best in other people where many of his colleagues – especially the sour and hypocritical Ralph Clark – habitually saw the worst. But Tench was still a soldier and an Englishman, convinced of the right of the 'new lords of the soil' to take possession away from the 'old'.

Few of his countrymen could have imagined, as Tench evidently did, the possibility of being *despised* by 'savages' of whom he himself had written, 'It is hardly possible to see any thing in human shape more ugly.' To Governor Phillip, the reason for their standoffishness was more pragmatic: 'They think perhaps that we cannot teach them any thing of sufficient value to make them amends for our encroachments upon their fishing places.'

When it became clear that Phillip's attempts to win over the Aboriginal inhabitants were not working, Tench blamed the 'fickle, jealous, wavering disposition of the people we have to deal with, who, like all other savages, are either too indolent, too indifferent, or too fearful to form an attachment on easy terms, with those who differ in habits and manners so widely from themselves'.

This dogmatic conclusion sounds out of character for Tench and must have reflected the impatience, exasperation and disappointment he felt at the failure to establish friendly relations. It did not stop him, during the rest of his time in New South Wales, from trying to understand the Aboriginal people and learn whatever he could of their languages.

As the first year wore on, hunger and malnutrition preyed on the demoralised colonists. The democracy of want eroded the social hierarchy, mocking the distinction between marines and convicts. The food was the same for both. 'Our allowance is very scanty,' complained Captain Campbell. 'I know not why . . . the only difference between the allowance of provisions served to the officer & served to the convict, be only half a pint (per day) of vile Rio spirits, so offensive both in taste & smell that he must be fond of drinking indeed that can use it.'

The kitchen garden on Garden Island grew barely enough green vegetables to supply the hospital. In April Phillip returned from a five-day expedition through the country south of the harbour to find that five ewes and a lamb had been killed, apparently by native dogs. The surviving livestock was too precious to eat. In the absence of other animal nourishment, wrote Surgeon White, 'the Kangaroo is considered as a dainty; but in any other country I am sure that such food would be thrown to the dogs, for it has very little or no fat about it, and, when skinned, the flesh bears some likeness to that of a fox or lean dog.'

Fish provided a useful – if unreliable – source of fresh protein, but catching it was laborious and the Aboriginal observers insisted on having their cut. '[T]hey often watch the moment of our hauling the seine,' wrote Tench, 'and have more than once been known to plunder its contents, in spite of the opposition of those on the spot to guard it . . . The only resource at these times is to show a musket, and if the bare sight is not sufficient, to fire it over their heads.'

By early May, nearly 200 convicts were too sick from scurvy and other diseases to work. A few days of wet weather seemed to promise that 'the rainy season had set in', but that too was an illusion: Sydney has no rainy season.

'No very good fortune had hitherto attended the livestock belonging to the settlement,' Phillip noted stoically at the end of May. But worse was to come. Two bulls and four cows, belonging to the government and to Phillip himself, were left to wander by the convict whose job it was to look after them. The animals strayed into the woods, and although they were tracked for some distance, it proved impossible to coax them back. 'This,' wrote Phillip, 'was a loss which must be for some time irreparable.'

Somehow, amid all these setbacks, the colony roused itself to celebrate King George III's birthday on 4 June. Phillip gave a free pardon to all convicts facing trial or undergoing punishment for offences committed since their arrival in New South Wales. 'Each convict was allowed a Pint of Grog,' wrote Worgan, 'and all Work was suspended for the day. Every Private Soldier drank His Majesty's Health &c . . . in a Pint of Porter, and every Seaman, in an additional allowance of Grog, and all this, at the Governors own Expence.' For one day, the settlement was awash with alcohol and, as Worgan put it, 'every Heart beat with Loyalty & Joy'.

The next day the colony woke to a grim but all too predictable hangover: '[W]hile many of the Convicts were rejoicing at the Bonfire, there were others practising their old Custom of Thieving, and many of the Officer's Tents & Huts had been robbed . . . One Officer's Chest was broke open, and robbed of 12 pair of Stockings & other Articles.' Alcohol, far from being the leveller Worgan imagined, had instead reopened the rift between convict and free settler.

The surgeon-general's report on the last day of June 1788 listed 36 convicts dead since the landing at Botany Bay, 66 under medical treatment and 52 'unfit for labour, from old age, infirmities, etc'. Yet, for all that, the colony was starting to take shape. A structure was emerging from the chaos of canvas. The lines of the intended town of Sydney had been laid down and all permanent buildings would have to conform with the plan. The main streets of the future town were to be 'two hundred feet wide'. Good clay had been found near Sydney Cove and 'very good bricks' were being made from it, although a lack of limestone would delay construction.

The generally benign climate convinced Governor Phillip that:

the cultivation of the vine may doubtless be carried to
any degree of perfection; and should not other articles of

commerce divert the attention of the settlers from this point, the wines of New South Wales may, perhaps, hereafter be sought with avidity, and become an indispensable part of the luxury of European tables.

Food remained the overriding problem. The colonists kept watch for the arrival of a supply ship from England, but none came. In early October, the *Sirius* set sail for Cape Town with orders to buy provisions.

The Aboriginal people watched aghast as the visitors continued to plunder their precious fish stocks. One day:

> about twenty of them, armed with spears, came down to the spot where our men were fishing, and . . . violently seized the greatest part of the fish which was in the seine. While this detachment performed this act of depredation, a much greater number stood at a small distance with their spears poized, ready to have thrown them if any resistance had been made. But the cockswain who commanded the fishing party, very prudently suffered them to take away what they chose, and they parted on good terms.

Without an interpreter to explain misunderstandings, the colonists found it impossible to overcome what Tench described as the 'unabated animosity that prevailed between the natives and us'. The dream of harmonious coexistence seemed more unattainable than ever. '[T]he natives were becoming every day more troublesome and hostile, several people having been wounded, and others, who were necessarily employed in the woods, driven in and much alarmed by them,' wrote Collins.

As the year dragged to an end, Governor Phillip decided the time had come for drastic action. If the colonists could not ingratiate themselves peacefully with the Aboriginal people, they would have to do so by force.

6

He is very fond of wine, but cannot bear the smell of spirits

On 31 December 1788 Governor Phillip sent two boats, under the command of Lieutenant Ball of the *Supply* and Lieutenant Johnston of the marines, to snatch and carry off some Aboriginal hostages. At Manly Cove, near the north head of the harbour, they spotted a group standing on the beach. Enticing them 'by courteous behaviour and a few presents', they lured them towards the boats. When the chance came, the marines 'rushed in among them and seized two men: the rest fled; but the cries of the captives soon brought them back, with many others, to their rescue'. One of the men was secured but the second, after dragging his captor into the water out of his depth, wrestled free and 'got clear off'. The boats made their escape under a hail of 'spears, stones, firebrands, and whatever else presented itself'. It took a volley of musket shots fired over their heads to drive the others off.

Fastened by ropes to the crossbeams of the boat, the captive 'set up the most piercing and lamentable cries of distress. His grief, however, soon diminished: he accepted and ate of some broiled fish which was given to him, and sullenly submitted to his destiny.'

Watkin Tench was among the eager crowd that came to ogle the frightened prisoner when he was landed at Sydney Cove:

> [H]e appeared to be about thirty years old, not tall, but robustly made; and of a countenance which, under happier circumstances, I thought would display manliness and sensibility; his agitation was excessive, and the clamourous crowds who flocked around him did not contribute to lessen it . . . though broken and interrupted with dismay, his voice was soft and musical, when its natural tone could be heard . . . To our ladies he quickly became extraordinarily courteous, a sure sign that his terror was wearing off.

The prisoner rebuffed repeated attempts to discover his name before Phillip gave up and started calling him Manly, after the cove where they had kidnapped him. (Later he came to be known by the name Arabanoo.) At the same time, he was happy to play tricks on his captors, studying illustrations of 'birds and beasts' that were shown to him and pointing to elephants, rhinos 'and several others' that he implied could be found roaming the woods around Sydney Cove.

At mealtimes he 'ate heartily of fish and ducks, which he first cooled. Bread and salt meat he smelled at, but would not taste: all our liquors he treated in the same manner, and could drink nothing but water.'

Having made the desperate decision to seize a hostage by force, Phillip needed to hold on to him long enough to teach him some English and to learn a few words of his language – enough, it was hoped, 'to unveil the cause of their mysterious conduct, by putting us in possession of their reasons for harassing and destroying our people'.

The kidnapping was a heinous betrayal of trust. If the prisoner absconded before his captors had a chance to redeem themselves through the 'mildness and indulgence' of their treatment, Phillip's hopes of better relations would be shot. 'To prevent his escape,' wrote Tench, 'a handcuff with a rope attached to it, was fastened around his left wrist, which at first highly delighted him; he called it "bengadee" (or ornament), but his delight changed to rage and hatred when he discovered its use.'

A convict was chosen to be Arabanoo's 'keeper', sleeping next to him and following him wherever he went. When Arabanoo's shirt caught alight after he stood too close to the fire, it was his convict keeper who rushed to douse the flames.

Anxious for it to be known that Arabanoo was being well treated, Phillip took him in a boat down the harbour to the cove where he had been snatched. Although initially fearful, some of Arabanoo's friends came out to speak to him as the boat lay at a safe distance off the beach. 'At length they began to converse,' wrote Tench. 'Our ignorance of the language prevented us from knowing much of what passed; it was, however, easily understood that his friends asked him why he did not jump overboard, and rejoin them. He only sighed, and pointed to the fetter on his leg, by which he was bound.'

Not for the first time, Tench was astonished by how much Arabanoo could eat. For supper that night, he polished off 'two kangaroo rats, each of the size of a moderate rabbit' and 'not less than three pounds of fish'. Then and later, however, he refused every invitation to drink liquor, turning from it 'with disgust and abhorrence'.

While Arabanoo grew at least partly reconciled to his captivity, he did not become the instrument for the wider reconciliation that Phillip had hoped for. The attacks continued. Three months after Arabanoo's capture, 16 convicts downed tools at the brick kilns and set off for Botany Bay to attack and pillage the local tribe. Guessing their intentions, a party of warriors ambushed them before they reached the bay, killing one and wounding seven.

Phillip was incensed by the convicts' sabotage of his campaign to befriend the Aboriginal people. Refusing to believe they were 'quietly picking sweet-tea' when attacked, he had the survivors flogged and forced Arabanoo to witness the punishment. If he expected Arabanoo to be impressed or even gratified by what he saw, Phillip had badly misjudged his sensibilities. While the British officers looked on, applauding themselves for this even-handed application of justice, Arabanoo displayed only 'symptoms of disgust and terror'.

A far more brutal demonstration of British justice followed a few weeks later, when seven marines were caught robbing the public store. The seven men had hatched an elaborate conspiracy involving multiple break-ins and the manufacture of duplicate keys. When one of them was put on guard duty, two or three of the others were to let themselves in to plunder what they could while the guard kept watch outside. The conspiracy was only discovered when one of the marines attempted to break into the store by himself, panicked at the approach of the night patrol and left part of the duplicate key in the lock.

One of the conspirators, Joseph Hunt, saved himself by informing on the rest. The other six – Luke Haynes, James Baker, James Brown, Richard Asky, Richard Dukes and Thomas Jones – were hanged on 27 March 1789. 'There was hardly a marine Present but what Shed tears, offacers and men,' Private John Easty wrote in his diary.

The list of stolen goods included modest amounts of butter, bread and tobacco, and a large quantity of flour, but what stood out was the grog: the marines had made off with '100 gallons of liquor – old rum, Rio rum and wine'. It was an extraordinary heist – around 30 times the amount of grog stolen from Zachariah Clark the previous year, for which John Williams and Daniel Gordon had been sentenced to death and reprieved. The scale of the theft hinted both at the thirst for grog building up amid the deprivations that gripped the infant colony, and at the deadly risks some people were willing to take to satisfy – or profit from – that thirst.

In the hierarchy of the colony, Governor Phillip's policy of making no distinction in rations (except for grog) between marines and convicts eroded the superiority that the marines felt belonged naturally and properly to them. The law, far from being even-handed, seemed weighted unfairly against the military. The death penalties imposed on Haynes, Baker, Brown, Asky, Dukes and Jones confirmed a perception that had existed among the marines since the fleet left England: that they were more severely punished than convicts for committing the same crime.

Three weeks after the six marines were executed, Sergeant James Scott made an ominous entry in his diary: 'I went with a party to Cut Grass tree for Lt. Johnstone. Found three Nativs under a rock, vis, a man and two Boys (of which one boy was dead).'

According to Collins, it soon became a daily occurrence to encounter 'either in excavations of the rock, or lying upon the beaches and points of the different coves . . . the bodies of many of the wretched natives of this country'. The cause of the deaths was smallpox, to which British of all classes had some immunity, while the Aboriginal people had none.

Returning from the Cape in the *Sirius* with a desperately needed cargo of flour, Bradley found the harbour and its numerous coves eerily deserted:

We did not see a Canoe or a Native . . . and were told that
scarce any had been seen lately, except laying dead in and
about their miserable habitations, whence it appears that they
are deserted by their Companions as soon as the disorder
comes out on them, and those who are attacked with this
disorder left to shift for themselves.

The smallpox epidemic lasted several months, killing as much as half of the local population while scarcely touching the colonists.

A handful of victims were found and brought into the settlement to be treated by Surgeon White. Arabanoo was at first reluctant to go near them, 'but his shyness soon wore off, and he treated them with the kindest attention'. When the patients died, Arabanoo buried them with his own hands. A boy, Nanbaree, survived the disease and was adopted by Surgeon White (who named him Andrew Snape Hamond Douglas White). A girl, Abaroo, was taken in by Reverend Johnson.

Arabanoo's concern for the sick and his implicit trust in Surgeon White's efforts to save their lives so moved Governor Phillip that he ordered his fetter to be struck off.

In May Arabanoo himself caught smallpox. At first, it seemed as if the attack might be relatively mild, or even that it might not be smallpox at all. But after a short time 'the disease burst forth with irresistible fury'.

Arabanoo's 'gravity and steadiness' had endeared him to everyone who knew him. 'His countenance was thoughtful, but not animated,' wrote Tench. '[H]is fidelity and gratitude, particularly to his friend the governor, were constant and undeviating . . . Although of a gentle and placable temper, we early discovered that he was impatient of indignity, and allowed of no superiority on our part. He knew that he was in our power; but the independence of his mind never forsook him. If the slightest insult were offered to him, he would return it with interest. At retaliation of merriment he was often happy; and frequently turned the laugh against his antagonist.'

Surgeon White tried everything he could to save him, and Arabanoo submitted to it all without complaint, swallowing all the doctor's vile-tasting medicines and even allowing himself to be bled. But it was all in vain, and on 18 May 1789 Arabanoo died. He was buried in the governor's garden with the governor looking on.

During the last few weeks of his life Arabanoo had been able to wander almost at liberty. If he had wanted to go back to his own people, there would have been little to stop him. But, for some reason, Arabanoo stayed. He was, Tench thought, perhaps 'the only native who was ever attached to us from choice; and who did not prefer a precarious subsistence among wilds and precipices, to the comforts of a civilized system'.

Despite Arabanoo's failure to learn much English, he had been Phillip's great hope for diplomacy between the two groups. His premature death was a catastrophe, seeming to confirm to the Aboriginal people that all contact with the visitors would be fatal. With Arabanoo gone, wrote Tench, 'the same suspicious dread of our approach, and the same scenes of vengeance acted on unfortunate stragglers, continued to prevail'.

Captain John Hunter, who had been en route for Cape Town in the *Sirius* when Arabanoo was brought in, immediately grasped the significance of the loss. 'If poor Ara-ba-noo had lived,' wrote Hunter, 'he would have acquired enough of our language to have understood whatever we wished him to communicate to his countrymen; he could have made them perfectly understand, that we wished to live with them on the most friendly footing, and that we wished to promote, as much as might be in our power, their comfort and happiness.'

Before the year was over, Governor Phillip resolved to try again. He chose Lieutenant Bradley to lead the kidnap raid. Encountering a 'great number of Natives' in one of the harbour coves, Bradley's party used the offer of two large fish to lure two men away from the group. The pair 'came round the rocks where they left their spears & met us on the beach near the boat & at a distance from their Companions sufficient to promise success without losing any lives, they eagerly took the fish'. Four sailors remained in the boat, which was brought as close as possible to the shore, while the rest of Bradley's party distracted the victims. At a signal from Bradley, 'the two poor devils were seiz'd & handed into the boat in an instant'.

As soon as the larger group realised what was happening, they rushed at the kidnappers waving spears and clubs, but Bradley's men were too quick for them, pushing the boat off and escaping down the harbour without the need to use their muskets. 'The noise of the Men, Crying & screaming of the Women & Children together with the situation of the two miserable wretches in our possession was really a most distressing scene,' wrote Bradley. '[T]hey were much terrified, one of them particularly so, the other frequently called out to those on shore apparently very much enraged with them.'

The boat returned to Sydney Cove. Nanbaree, the boy who had recovered from smallpox and been adopted by Surgeon White, recognised the two captives at once and addressed them by name as Colbee and Baneelon (or Bennelong). The first name was well known to the British; Nanbaree had often spoken of Colbee as 'a great warrior & a leading Man among them'. Both men had apparently survived smallpox; Colbee's face 'was very thickly imprinted with the marks of it'.

At the Governor's House, they were met by the girl named Abaroo, who 'called them by name, the same as the boy had done & was quite frantic with Joy'. The two children assured the men that they would be well treated and would be allowed to return to their friends, but for several days the captives were inconsolable. They were:

> shaved, wash'd & Cloathed; an Iron shackle was put on one leg with a rope made fast to it & a Convict charged with each of them, they were very sullen & sulky . . . yet it did not by any means affect their appetite if we may judge from the quantity they now eat, which is beyond every thing incredible.

Bradley took little personal satisfaction from his success in abducting Colbee and Baneelon. 'It was,' he wrote, 'by far the most unpleasant service I ever was ordered to execute.' He was relieved, however, to learn that 'neither of them had Wife or Family, who would feel their loss, or . . . be distressed by their being taken away'.

Despite Phillip's efforts to 'treat them indulgently, and guard them strictly', Colbee waited barely a fortnight before making his escape. It happened on a dark evening when the convict keepers were inside the house eating their supper. Baneelon was keeping them company indoors while Colbee sat outside the open door, pretending to pick at his own meal. The rope attached to Colbee's shackle was in the hand of his convict keeper. While Baneelon kept both keepers entertained, Colbee 'drew the splice of his rope from the shackle, and in a moment was over the paling of the yard, and out of sight'.

It wasn't the first time that either of the prisoners had worked themselves loose, with Colbee escaping 'by the very same means which had before been detected'.

A search was undertaken but the fugitive was nowhere to be found. '[H]is friends would certainly be something surprized to see him so well cloathed,' wrote Hunter, 'for he carried off his whole wardrobe.'

Baneelon, meanwhile, 'was nearly loose when the other was missed and in a minute more would have been after him'. Instead, Baneelon was to remain a prisoner for another five months.

Younger than Colbee by several years, and more high-spirited, Baneelon appeared to find captivity a lot more agreeable once the older man was gone. 'The presence of *Co-al-by*,' wrote Hunter, 'seemed to be a check upon the chearful temper of *Ba-na-lang*, which inclined us to think that he paid a kind of deference to him; he was always very silent in his company.' This seemed to confirm the impression given by the two children that Colbee was a more distinguished warrior than Baneelon.

With Colbee gone, Baneelon became the focus of everybody's attention. 'He quickly threw off all reserve,' wrote Tench, 'and pretended, nay, at particular moments, perhaps felt satisfaction in his new state . . . he became at once fond of our viands, and would drink the strongest liquors, not simply without reluctance, but with eager marks of delight and enjoyment. He was the only native we ever knew who immediately shewed a fondness for spirits.'

A fast learner and eager raconteur, Baneelon picked up English words and manners more easily than the teetotal Arabanoo and 'willingly communicated information; sang, danced, and capered, told us all the customs of his country, and all the details of his family economy'. He befriended Phillip, bestowing the name 'Beenena' (father) on him while 'adopting to himself the name of governor'.

Baneelon's storytelling, as recounted by Watkin Tench, suggested not so much a hostage as a feted guest enjoying his celebrity among strangers:

'But the wound on the back of your hand, Baneelon! How did you get that?'
He laughed, and owned that it was received in carrying off a lady of another tribe by force. 'I was dragging her away. She cried aloud, and stuck her teeth in me.'
'And what did you do then?'
'I knocked her down, and beat her till she was insensible, and covered with blood. Then . . .'

Hunter's account of Baneelon's captivity was more pedestrian and more equivocal, implying that Baneelon was frequently the unwilling butt of practical jokes:

He may be called a polite man, as he performs every action of bowing, drinking healths, returning thanks, &c. with the most scrupulous attention. He is very fond of wine, but cannot bear the smell of spirits, although they have often tried to deceive him, by mixing very weak rum or brandy and water, instead of wine and water; but he would instantly find out the deception, and on these occasions he was angry.

Although 'fermented liquor was new to him', Baneelon appeared to have no trouble holding his drink. The effect of wine or brandy upon him was no more perceptible, Tench reported, 'than an equal quantity would have produced upon one of us'.

Both his taste for liquor and his capacity for it marked Baneelon out from the other captives. Despite his prodigious appetite, Arabanoo had refused all offers of grog, drinking nothing but water. Colbee 'would at first not touch' the spirits that were offered to him, although he later overcame his distaste. It was Baneelon who adapted most easily to the social customs of the invader. '[H]is relish of our society [was] so great,' wrote Tench, 'that hardly any one judged he would attempt to quit us, were the means of escape put within his reach.'

In this, as in so many other things, Tench and his fellow colonists were deluded. While consolidating the settlement at Sydney Cove, Phillip mounted regular expeditions to explore the surrounding country. 'Benallon,' wrote Bradley, 'being now well reconciled, generally accompanies the Governor in little excursions.'

In February 1790, Phillip wrote to Lord Sydney informing him that of '1,030 people who were landed, many of whom were worn out by old age, the scurvy, and various disorders, only seventy-two have died'. Surgeon White's records showed that of those 72, 26 had been suffering from diseases 'of long standing'. In addition, 59 children had been born.

Phillip remained optimistic that 'a finer or more healthy climate is not to be found in any part of the world', but the hard truth was that the settlement was still incapable of feeding itself. 'Famine,' wrote Tench, 'was approaching with gigantic strides, and gloom and dejection overspread every countenance.' The hungry colony's hopes rested on the arrival of a supply ship. 'If thunder broke at a distance, or a fowling-piece . . . resounded in the woods, "a gun from a ship" was echoed on every side, and nothing but hurry and agitation prevailed.'

For the first 18 months, a party of marines had left Sydney Cove each week to walk to Botany Bay in hopes of seeing a visiting ship. Captain Hunter now came up with a more orderly system, posting sailors at the south head of the harbour with instructions to hoist a flag whenever a ship was spotted. 'Here on the summit of the hill, every morning from daylight until the sun sunk, did we sweep the horizon, in hope of seeing a sail.'

The dwindling stock of food forced Phillip to cut the ration to every person in the settlement to 4 pounds of flour, 2½ pounds of salt pork and 1½ pounds of rice per week. 'We shall not starve,' Phillip assured Nepean, 'though seven-eighths of the colony deserves nothing better.' Few shared his implacable optimism.

'If a lucky man,' wrote Tench, 'who had knocked down a dinner with his gun, or caught a fish by angling from the rocks, invited a neighbour to dine with him, the invitation always ran, "bring your own bread". Even at the governor's table, this custom was constantly observed. Every man when he sat down pulled his bread out of his pocket, and laid it by his plate.'

Nobody felt the pangs of hunger more keenly than Baneelon, whose voracious appetite had startled his hosts in better times. Trapped between the roles of guest and prisoner, he continued to be 'as well taken care of as our desperate circumstances would allow'. There was a motive behind Phillip's forlorn hospitality: had Baneelon absconded with news of their 'diminished numbers and diminished strength', the local tribes might have been emboldened to attack the settlement.

Whatever the British could spare for their captive, it was not enough. 'We knew not how to keep him,' Tench admitted, 'and yet were unwilling to part with him . . . the ration of a week was insufficient to have kept him for a day.'

Phillip tried to make up for the deficiency with fish and some Indian corn that had been reserved for Baneelon's own use, but even this special treatment couldn't fend off the ravening hunger that made Baneelon 'furious and often melancholy'.

In the end, Baneelon could bear it no longer. 'About two o'clock in the morning, he pretended illness, and awaking the servant who lay in the room with him, begged to go down stairs. The other attended him without suspicion of his design; and Baneelon no sooner found himself in a backyard, than he nimbly leaped over a slight paling, and bade us adieu.'

The ease of his escape seemed to confirm Tench's belief that he could have absconded at any time if he had wished, but had chosen to stay.

Afterwards, nothing was heard of Baneelon for several months. During this time food became even scarcer. Phillip was forced to reduce working hours, since hard physical labour was impossible on the pitiful rations. No new laws were enacted against food theft, but existing ones were ruthlessly applied. Sixty pounds of flour – an amount 'more tempting than the ore of Peru or Potosi' – was offered for anyone who caught a food thief. A convict found guilty of stealing potatoes was given 300 lashes on the spot and chained for six months to two others who were already fettered for previous offences, as well as having his allowance of flour stopped. For six months, he had to survive on 'two pounds of pork, and two pounds of rice' per week.

Tench recalled seeing another convict, a man 'with a wild haggard countenance', drop dead of hunger moments after collecting his 'daily pittance'.

For men and women slowly starving to death, perhaps it didn't seem strange to risk execution for a night on the grog. In April 1790 John Bates and John Russell were charged with feloniously breaking and entering the house of Mr John Palmer, the purser on the *Sirius*, in order to steal 'One Gallon of the Wine called Cape Madeira of the Value of Five Shillings, and One Quart of Wine called Red Port, of the value of One Shilling'. The two men pleaded not guilty and were acquitted, but what happened to the stolen grog is not recorded.

On the same day that Bates and Russell were acquitted, William Chafe stood trial for burglary. Chafe had been thatching James Tennyhill's roof and had broken in through an unsewn section. When he was taken to the watch house, straw was found in his hat. He denied being the thief and called another convict to give evidence, but the evidence didn't help him, and Chafe was found guilty and hanged.

The next month Joseph Elliott, alias Trimby, was found of guilty of stealing one and a quarter pounds of potatoes worth twopence halfpenny and sentenced 'to receive Three hundred Lashes on his bare Back, with a Cat of nine Tails' and to have his ration of flour stopped for six months. (Phillip reinstated the flour ration – without which Elliott would soon have starved – but did not interfere with the flogging.) Three days later Thomas Paul was sentenced to receive 500 lashes for stealing six cabbages worth one shilling; a plea of clemency reduced the punishment to '100 only' on account of his good character. In mitigation, both men pleaded that they were driven by hunger to commit the crime. A marine was sentenced to and received 500 lashes for stealing from a garden he was supposed to be guarding.

Hunger was the great leveller. 'It might have been supposed,' wrote Collins, 'that the severity of the punishments which had been ordered by the criminal court on offenders convicted of robbing gardens would have deterred others from committing that offence; but while there was a vegetable to steal, there were those who would steal it.'

With famine creeping ever closer, alcohol provided at least a memory of hangovers past to the few who could lay their hands on it. A furtive trade in grog had been going on ever since the First Fleet left Portsmouth, with officers such as Ralph Clark using their daily allowance to pay off favours and settle debts. Inside the settlement, more gallons of wine and spirits were reported stolen than were ever recovered. The supply of illicit grog circulated around the colony until it had all been drunk.

While grog was officially forbidden to convicts, those who had something valuable to sell – their skills and labour, for instance – could insist on being paid in alcohol. William Frazer, a convict blacksmith, was one of these. Although acknowledged as an expert blacksmith, Frazer (or Fraser) had a record for insolence and insubordination. In January 1789 he was accused of insolence to Sergeant Connor, who had given him an order only to be told, 'You may kiss my arse.' Found guilty, he was sentenced to 100 lashes but was 'forgiven by the Governor all but 25, which he received'.

Despite his sharp tongue and evil temper, Frazer made a lasting impression on Watkin Tench, who singled him out as an exemplar of 'perverted genius' and 'mechanical ingenuity'.

A skilled locksmith in a community of thieves, Frazer found his skills much in demand. Having ordered a special set of locks to secure the public stores, Governor Phillip sent for Frazer and asked him to examine them, while assuring him that they could not be picked. According to Tench, 'Frazer laughed and asked for a crooked nail only, to open them all. A nail was brought, and in an instant he verified his assertion.'

Some days later, Frazer's 'ingenuity' was again put to the test. 'He was sent for in a hurry . . . to the hospital, where a lock of still superior intricacy and expense . . . had been provided. He was told that the key was lost and that the lock must be immediately picked.' Frazer inspected the lock closely, and then demanded ten minutes to make an instrument to 'speak with it'. Leaving the lock in place, the blacksmith went back to his shop. He returned ten minutes later with his 'instrument', and in front of several astonished spectators 'open flew the lock'.

It was not only the authorities that sought out Frazer's talents. 'Had not his villainy been still more notorious than his skill,' remarked Tench, 'he would have proved an invaluable possession to a new country . . . When too lazy to work at his trade he had turned thief in fifty different shapes, was a receiver of stolen goods, a soldier and a travelling conjurer. He once confessed to me that he had made a set of tools, for a gang of coiners, every man of whom was hanged.'

The demand for Frazer's blacksmithing skills was reflected in his ability to insist on – and receive – payment in grog. Frazer's story ended in July 1791 when he went on a bender that killed him. 'He was an excellent workman,' wrote Collins, the deputy judge advocate, 'and was supposed to have brought on an untimely end by hard drinking as he seldom chose to accept any article but spirits in payment for work done in his extra hours.'

Amid the extreme deprivations of life in the colony, where alcohol was banned and a man could be flayed alive for the theft of a few potatoes, it showed a certain swagger for a convict to drink himself to death. Perhaps William Frazer was envied as well as mourned.

7

One hundred and fifty now, and the remainder when able to bear it

On 15 February 1790, after a hiatus of nearly two years, Lieutenant Ralph Clark resumed the journal he had started writing as a marine officer on the First Fleet. The previous entry, for 'Munday' 10 March 1788, related another of his many dreams – this one about the barracks catching fire – and had Clark sitting on a court martial at which 'Tray Davey and [another] Marine' were sentenced to 100 lashes 'for bringing each a Convict woman in to ther tents'.

Between the two entries, Clark wrote a number of letters that have survived, but if he kept a journal during the intervening 23 months, it is now lost. The interval did not improve his atrocious spelling, but it broadened his experience and in some ways deepened his engagement with the country.

By the time he embarked on the new journal, Clark had acquired two convict servants: Richard Davis and James Squires (whom we last saw on board the *Charlotte*), a chicken thief doing his best to stay out of trouble. If Clark selected James Squires because he knew him to be capable, then it is possible the two men had met on the *Friendship* and that Squires was indeed transferred from the *Friendship* to the *Charlotte* during the reshuffle of convicts after the Cape.

Squires was undoubtedly capable, but his record since arriving in New South Wales had not been spotless. On 14 November 1789 he was charged with 'feloniously stealing a certain quantity of medicines, being Hospital stores, the property of the Crown, and one pound of pepper, the property of Mr White and others, while employed in the laboratory tent at Port Jackson'. Captain Collins and Captain Hunter sat as magistrates. John Frederick, a seaman from the *Supply*, gave evidence, along with Surgeon White and Squires himself. Squires was found guilty. His sentence read, 'To receive three hundred Lashes, one hundred and fifty now, and the Remainder when able to bear it.'

Exactly what kind of medicines Squires stole from the hospital is not recorded, but in that critical year when the seemingly abandoned colony faced starvation, perhaps any 'medicine' would do, especially if it contained alcohol. (Wine for medicinal use was among the provisions aboard the First Fleet.)

On the same day that Squires faced the magistrates, a convict named John Coffin was charged with 'feloniously stealing one quart of brandy, the property of Mr White, and one quart of red wine, the property of the Crown'. It wasn't the first time Coffin had stood before the court. In May he had been charged with stealing flour, only to be discharged owing to 'an Equivocation and Inconsistency' in the evidence of one of the witnesses. Six witnesses, including Surgeon White, were called to give evidence on the charges of stealing wine and brandy, but Coffin was acquitted of both.

The punishments for stealing were necessarily harsh, and the difficulty of proving the crime led to many of the accused being found not guilty. Misdemeanours involving drunkenness were much easier to prove and were evidence of the thriving illicit trade in grog. After John Coffin was acquitted, another convict, Francis Jones, was brought before the magistrates charged with drunkenness and insolence. John Bazley, a habitual witness against his fellow convicts, told the court that Jones had abused him after being ordered to go to work. Jones 'confessed to being in liquor and was sentenced to fifty lashes'.

The same day, Ann Davis, a female convict, 'was found drunk and in possession of some articles missing from Robert Sidaway's house' and taken into custody. A week later Davis, alias Judith Jones, was charged with feloniously breaking and entering Sidaway's house and stealing clothes and other goods including 'four Linin shirts of the Value of Twenty nine shillings and Six pence . . . one Silk Waistcoat of the value of Two shillings' and 'Two Linin Caps of the Value of Six pence'.

It was a capital charge, and 12 witnesses were called to give evidence. Ann Davis was said to have called at the house occasionally 'to light a pipe as she passed by'. On 14 November she had found the house deserted and a window shutter halfway down 'so that the fowls would fly in'. Overturning a tub of water beneath the window, she climbed in and stole the clothing. Perhaps she got drunk while she was inside. Found guilty, she was sentenced to hang.

'On receiving sentence to die,' wrote Collins, 'she pleaded being quick with child; but twelve of the discreetest women among the convicts, all of whom had been mothers of children, being impanelled as a jury of matrons, they pronounced that she was not pregnant; on which she was executed the Monday following . . . She died generally reviled and unpitied by the people of her own description.'

There is no record of James Squires receiving the balance of his 300 lashes. He was keeping poor company, however. In March 1789 Squires was caught up in a case involving the theft of some cabbages. Two women, Jamasin Allen and Mary Turner alias Wilkes, were charged with stealing 'six heads of cabbages' out of William Parr's garden. Squires knew enough about what happened to be called as a witness, along with Parr and the two accused. Collins found both women guilty and sentenced them to 50 lashes each: '25 now, and 25 on the next Provision Day – Saturday.'

On 14 February 1790 Lieutenant Clark rowed up the harbour to a place called Lane Cove and exchanged a hatchet for two spears with men he called Dourrawan and Tirriwan. The next morning Clark and another marine, Private William Ellis, went looking for the two Aboriginal men again, accompanied by Davis and Squires. Of his two servants, Clark evidently had a much higher opinion of Squires, who he trusted to carry a gun.

At Lane Cove the party noticed smoke curling from Aboriginal cooking fires. Guessing that they couldn't be far away, Clark called out to the men, who called back. 'I then got out of the Boat,' wrote Clark. '[Davis] my Convict Servant who was in the Boat with me begd of me not to goe on Shore – he is one of the greatest Cowards living – I cald to them again . . . the[y] could See me although I could See nothing of them.'

Recognising Clark as the person who had given them the hatchet, the Aboriginal men came down to speak. Clark had given orders to Private Ellis ('the most Stuppid Mortal that I ever Saw') and Squires to open fire immediately if the men attempted to throw their spears. But the meeting went off peacefully (although Davis 'trembled the whole time') and after a couple of hours the two groups parted on friendly terms, despite Clark's attempt to barter his 'hatt' for the two men's infant sons. Although it would have been easy for Clark to have kidnapped both men 'without running any danger', he 'could not think of doing it for if I had taken them both what would have become of there young children the[y] must have Starved'.

Accepting a gift of mussels that had been roasting on the fire (and afterwards 'made me very Sick'), Clark set off with Davis, Squires and Private Ellis and 'went up the cove about Six miles' before returning to the settlement after dark.

Although Clark never mentioned James Squires again by name in his journal, Squires certainly accompanied him the next day, when Clark embarked on another trading expedition up the harbour. On their way back to Sydney Cove, Clark caught sight of a 'Native on the Shore with two Spears and a throwing Stick in his hand'. After tying up the boat, Clark grabbed his gun and started in pursuit of the 'Native', ordering his convict servants to follow.

They lost him in the woods. Disappointed, Clark was heading back to the boat when he:

> found the Skeleton of a man or Woman – the Skin was
> Still entire on the back part of the Head and the Hair Still
> adhering to it which was in colour of light Brown from which
> I was certain that it could be non of the natives but must
> belong to Some Unfortunate person that was Kild by the
> Natives or what is much more dreadful than been Kild by the
> Natives that of lossing one self and perishing with hunger – it
> Struck me as it did every body in the Boat that it must be the
> Skeleton of Mr. Hill a midshipman belon[g]ing to the *Sirius*.

Hill had gone missing on 7 November 1789, having lost his way while walking along the north shore of the harbour. 'Parties were sent day after day in quest of him,' wrote Collins. 'Guns were fired from the *Sirius* every four hours, night and day, but all to no effect.' It was not the first time Hill had got lost, and he had predicted to his shipmates that he would probably get lost again 'for a day or two'. His fears were more than confirmed, Collins noted grimly: '[H]e lost himself for ever, and thus added one to the number of those unfortunate persons who had perished in the woods of this country.' In a curious footnote to the story, it was later suggested that the skull might not have belonged to Midshipman Hill at all, but rather to a missing convict, also called Hill, who had vanished a year earlier from the settlement at Rose Hill, now Parramatta.

While the Aboriginal people had quickly learnt to keep their distance from the marines, they showed little fear of the ragged convict labourers sent to cut reeds on the margins of the settlement, or of the disoriented absconders they found wandering the bush in search of China. '[T]he Natives . . . are ready to attack the Convicts in the woods when ever the[y] think the[y] can get the better of them,' Clark wrote to a friend in England, 'but the[y] never Meddle with a red Coat.'

James Squires knew better than to try to abscond. However bad the food situation was, as long as a convict stayed in the settlement, he could count on the 'red Coats' for protection. Squires, in any case, had his eye on a different future – a future that did not involve being ordered around by the likes of Ralph Clark.

Two days after the excursion to Lane Cove, Clark was visited by Major Ross, the commander of the marine corps. After the pair had chatted for a while about 'different subjects', Ross 'put the following Questions to me Viz how should I like to goe to Norfolk Island – I made him for answer not at all – he then Said I am going – I said it is impossible – he said it was very true.'

Clark eventually relented and agreed to be part of the marine detachment that Phillip had decided to send to Norfolk Island, along with more than 200 convicts. Among them was James Squires's common-law wife, Mary Spencer (or Spence), who was pregnant with his son. Convicted of stealing 'one cotton and one black silk handkerchief, a green quilted tammy [a fine worsted cloth] petticoat, and a black silk cloak', Mary had been sentenced to five years' transportation and sailed to Australia on the *Prince of Wales*, aged about 19.

The record of James Squires's life with Mary Spencer is sketchy, although it is interesting to note that Mary was listed as a witness when John Coffin was charged with stealing brandy from Surgeon White – a case that went to court on the same day that Squires was found guilty of stealing medicines from the hospital stores.

In the early years of the colony, relationships between convicts were often short-lived. Among the professional thieves, streetwalkers and pickpockets sent to New South Wales, the terms 'husband' and 'wife' did not have to signify any more than that a couple were in the habit of sleeping together. Long-term attachments were probably the exception. As one contemporary commented, 'upon the least Disgust they separate'. Not surprisingly, Squires's liaison with Mary Spencer ended with her removal to Norfolk Island.

There was a final blow for Clark before he embarked for his new posting. Having already been robbed of 'the Greatest part of a fine Bed of Onions' and, three days later, of 'all my potatoes', Clark visited his garden to gather his crop of Indian corn, only to find most of it gone. No more than a bushel remained of the six that Clark had been expecting: 'about fifteen hundred Cobbs of corn' had been plundered. '[I]t is impossible for any body to attempt to raise any Gardin Stuff,' he commented sourly, 'for before it comes to perfection the[y] will steal it.'

On 5 March the *Sirius* and the *Supply* sailed for Norfolk Island. Mary Spencer survived the voyage and the catastrophes that followed

– including the wrecking of the *Sirius* on 19 March, when it struck a reef – and returned to Sydney two years later, leaving her infant son behind.

James Squires, meanwhile, set about transforming himself into a man of property. His problems with the law, however, were not quite over. On 19 August 1791 Squires and another convict, John Cross, were charged with 'buying the Necessaries of Francis MacQween [or MacKewen or McEwin], Private Soldier in the New South Wales Corps'. MacQween gave evidence at the trial. 'The prisoners say they did not know they were doing any Thing wrong. The Soldier said he was starving, and assured them they could not be brought into Trouble.' Squires and Cross were both found guilty and ordered 'To pay each the Penalty of five Pounds – to appear this Day three Weeks.'

The meaning of the word 'necessaries' was looser than it appeared. According to the influential political economist Adam Smith, the term embraced not just commodities 'indispensably necessary for the support of life' but also:

> whatever the custom of the country renders it indecent for
> creditable people, even of the lowest order, to be without.
> A linen shirt, for example, is, strictly speaking, not a necessary
> of life . . . But in the present times, through the greater part of
> Europe, a creditable day-labourer would be ashamed to appear
> in public without a linen shirt.

Leather shoes, according to Smith, would also come under the heading of 'Necessaries'.

The fact that Squires and Cross were able to buy Private MacQween's 'Necessaries' demonstrated that the two men had money. The fine was as revealing as the crime. At a time when stealing goods worth more than a shilling was a capital offence, five pounds was a large sum. The imposition of such a penalty indicated that the magistrates believed Squires and Cross were capable of paying it.

James Squires was both prosperous and entrepreneurial – unusual characteristics in a transportee at a time when other convicts were stealing food to survive.

8

At length a bottle was held up

After Baneelon's escape from the settlement there was no friendly contact between the British and the Aboriginal people for four months. Fights over fishing catches continued, while convicts wandering unarmed into the bush ran the risk of being speared.

On 7 September 1790 Governor Phillip went by boat to South Head with Captain Collins and Lieutenant Waterhouse to supervise the building of a column visible to ships out at sea. The same day, another boat took Captain Nepean, Surgeon White and some others to Manly Cove, where they saw a large group of Aboriginal men feasting on the rotting carcass of a beached whale. Among them, White recognised Baneelon, who had become 'greatly emaciated' since he last saw him, and his fellow escapee, Colbee.

From Manly Cove, White's party set off on foot on a hunting expedition to Broken Bay, leaving the boat to return to Sydney Cove with 'three or four great junks of the whale' as a personal gift to Governor Phillip.

Seeing Phillip's boat returning from South Head, the coxswain of the second boat signalled that he had important news. '[T] he Coxswain,' wrote Waterhouse, 'inform'd the Governor that Mr White had had a long conference with Benalong & Colby, that they had inquir'd for everybody they knew particularly for the Governor, that he had sent him a piece of Whale & said he would come up if the Governor would go down for him.' Encouraged by the coxswain's report, if not by the chunks of rotting whale meat, Phillip quickly gathered up an assortment of gifts he thought 'would be acceptable', jumped in a boat and 'immediately went to Collins Cove [later renamed Manly Cove] where they had been seen'. As a precaution, he took four muskets.

Finding the group still at Manly Cove, Phillip landed. The Aboriginal men, wary of another attempted kidnapping, promptly withdrew. Leaving the four muskets in the boat, Phillip advanced – as he usually did – unarmed and alone except for a seaman carrying some food and gifts. Calling Banéelon 'by all his names', Phillip walked up the beach until one man stepped away from the rest and came forward to meet him. '[T]he few months Bennillong had been away had so altered his person,' wrote Collins, 'that the governor, until joined by Mr. Collins and Mr. Waterhouse, did not perfectly recollect his old acquaintance.'

There was a way, however, for the wasted and battle-scarred figure to prove to Phillip that he was Baneelon:

At length a bottle was held up, and on his being asked what it was, in his own language, he answered, 'the King'; for as he had always heard his Majesty's health drank in the first glass after dinner at the governor's table, and had been made to repeat the word before he drank his own glass of wine, he supposed the liquor was named 'the King'; and though he afterwards knew it was called wine, yet he would frequently call it King.

His identity confirmed, Baneelon chatted to Phillip for a while. Physically diminished as he was, he soon rediscovered his old gusto, the wine perhaps playing a part in an uninhibited performance that saw Baneelon:

expressing pleasure to see his old acquaintance, and inquiring by name for every person whom he could recollect at Sydney; and among others for a French cook, one of the governor's servants, whom he had constantly made the butt of his ridicule, by mimicking his voice, gait, and other peculiarities, all of which he again went through with his wonted exactness and drollery. He asked also particularly for a lady from whom he had once ventured to snatch a kiss; and on being told that she was well, by way of proving that the token was fresh in his remembrance, he kissed Lieutenant Waterhouse, and laughed aloud.

Curiously, he refused to explain his wounds, saying only that he had received them at Botany Bay.

To Baneelon's annoyance, the gifts Phillip had brought did not include hatchets. After promising to return with some in two days' time, Phillip expressed an interest in an unusual spear, 'barbed and pointed with hard wood', which he noticed lying on the grass. Baneelon wouldn't let him have the spear but threw it on the ground beside another man and gave Phillip a common short spear instead.

The second man seemed frightened of Phillip, who behaved as he always did in such a situation, dropping the dirk (or dagger) he wore at his side and approaching with his arms spread to show that he had no weapon. The same approach had always worked before. Confident that his peaceful intentions would be as obvious to others as they were to himself, Phillip kept walking. The Aboriginal warriors then began to close around them. Fearful of being surrounded, Phillip instructed his men to retreat. By now, Lieutenant Waterhouse counted '19 armed men near us & more in great numbers that we could not see'. Phillip again assured Baneelon that he would return in two days, and he would bring with him the clothes he used to wear, along with the hatchets, 'one for Colby & one for himself, with which he seemd much pleased & often repeated it that it should not be forgot'.

While the British were preparing to leave, Baneelon pointed out and named several of his companions who were standing nearby. Phillip, anxious as ever to improve relations, attempted to take advantage of the introduction by approaching one of the men and presenting his hand. But the warrior 'seem'd frighten'd & seis'd the spear Benalong had laid in the grass, fixed his throwing stick & immediately threw it with astonishing violen[ce]'. The others immediately ran off. The spear had entered Phillip's right shoulder 'just above the Colar bone & went through about 3 inches just behind the shoulder blade', narrowly missing the backbone.

As Collins shouted to the men in the boat to bring up the muskets, Phillip staggered towards the shore, 'holding the spear with both hands to keep the end off the ground'. But the spear was nearly 12 feet long, and Phillip couldn't stop the end from jamming into the sand. 'He then begged me for Gods sake to haul the spear out,' recalled Waterhouse, who realised that by pulling the spear he would drag the barb back into the wound and tried instead to snap the shaft in two, a feat he eventually managed as spears rained down around them. With the help of a seaman, Waterhouse 'lifted the Governor into the Boat as he was very faint Capt Collins immediately follow'd with the Boats crew & put off'.

The party reached Sydney Cove in two hours; the surgeons were summoned and Phillip demanded to be told 'how many hours he had to settle his affairs'. But the wound was less serious than they had imagined, striking Phillip high enough to avoid major organs. 'Mr Balmain made us all happy by confidently assuring the Governor he did not apprehend any fatal consequences from the wound. The spear was then extracted & in six weeks he was able to go about again.'

Captain Nepean and Surgeon White, having landed at Manly Cove before the spearing took place, started walking north towards Broken Bay. Fearing that White and his companions would be ambushed, Phillip gave orders for a detachment of marines under Lieutenant Long to bring them back. It was already dark by the time the rescue party reached Manly Cove. Stumbling blindly through the bush, Long and the marines caught up with White's group around two in the morning at the place where they had made camp, roughly halfway between Port Jackson and Broken Bay.

Phillip's fears of an ambush were well founded. The next morning, the soldiers were surprised to find fresh footprints in the sand leading 'almost the whole way from the place where they had slept to the Cove'. They concluded that the Aboriginal warriors 'had secretly followed them, probably with hostile intentions but, on discovering their strength, and that they were on their guard, had abandoned their design'.

Returning to Manly Cove, they found three Aboriginal men waiting for them. The trio 'informed them that the man who had wounded the governor belonged to a tribe residing at Broken Bay, and they seemed highly to condemn what he had done'. Baneelon and Colbee had loitered around the cove chatting amiably to the crew of the boat that brought Lieutenant Long's party. 'Like the others,' wrote Tench, they 'pretended highly to disapprove the conduct of the man who had thrown the spear, vowing to execute vengeance upon him.'

Had the spear been thrown out of panic, or could the whole episode, with its elaborate preamble and enigmatic postscript, be explained as a ritual spearing to enact payback for the numerous offences committed by the British against their hosts? 'It may naturally be supposed,' wrote Phillip, 'that many would be desirous of punishing what was generally deemed an act of treachery, but Governor Phillip did not see the transaction in that light, and as soon as he arrived at Sydney he gave the necessary directions to prevent any of the natives being fired on, unless they were the aggressors.'

Intent on establishing peaceful communications between black and white, Governor Phillip made up his mind 'as soon as he should be able to go out, to endeavour to find Bannelong, and, if possible, to have the man given up who wounded him, or some of his tribe; not with a view of inflicting any punishment, but of detaining one or more of these people till they understood each other's language'.

On the morning of 15 September, eight days after the spearing, a fire was spotted on the north side of the harbour. A party was sent out from the settlement to investigate. They found Baneelon and several others. No attempt was made to oppose their landing and the two groups chatted for a while before agreeing to meet again that afternoon at the same place.

The second encounter, as Tench described it, was equally friendly. Gifts were handed around and Baneelon was pleased to be given a hatchet and a fish. A group of children who had been standing nervously some distance away was persuaded to join the men. At this point:

> a bottle of wine was produced, and Baneelon immediately
> prepared for the charge. Bread and beef he called loudly for,
> which were given to him, and he began to eat, offering a part

of his fare to his countrymen, two of whom tasted the beef, but none of them would touch the bread. Having finished his repast, he made a motion to be shaved, and a barber being present, his request was complied with, to the great admiration of his countrymen, who laughed and exclaimed at the operation. They would not, however, consent to undergo it, but suffered their beards to be clipped with a pair of scissors.

Gregarious as always, and eager to lord it over his companions, Baneelon appeared to have forgotten all about the spearing. Drinking the governor's wine was a gesture of reconciliation, understood as such by both parties.

After revelling for a while in his celebrity, Baneelon persuaded a woman to join him. Her name was Barangaroo, and he described her as his wife. 'At the request of Baneelon,' wrote Tench, 'we combed and cut her hair, and she seemed pleased with the operation. Wine she would not taste, but turned from it with disgust, though heartily invited to drink by the example and persuasion of Baneelon.'

Arrangements were made for another meeting the next day, at which some stolen fishing gear would be returned and Baneelon would give back the governor's dirk. Both sides showed up as promised. 'Baneelon inquired, with solicitude, about the state of the governor's wound, but he made no offer of restoring the dirk; and when he was asked for it, he pretended to know nothing of it, changing the conversation with great art, and asking for wine, which was given to him.'

Before leaving, the British urged Baneelon to visit the governor in Sydney, 'assuring him, that he would be well received, and kindly treated'. Baneelon resisted the invitation, insisting that Phillip visit him first.

It was several weeks before Baneelon and three companions undertook the promised visit, and only after the chaplain, Mr Johnson, agreed to remain behind as a hostage. When Baneelon arrived at the settlement, 'such numbers flocked to view them that we were apprehensive the crowd of persons would alarm them, but they had left their fears behind, and marched on with boldness and unconcern'.

After receiving another hatchet, Baneelon seemed to consider himself 'quite at home, running from room to room with his companions, and introducing them to his old friends, the domestics, in the most familiar manner'. Among the latter, he was especially pleased to see the governor's orderly sergeant, kissing him 'with great affection', and a woman who worked in the kitchen.

The minute the visitors asked to leave, they were carried back across the harbour and exchanged for the chaplain. 'Thus ended a day,' wrote Tench, 'the events of which served to complete what an unhappy accident had begun. From this time our intercourse with the natives, though partially interrupted, was never broken off.'

In those early years of signalling across the water and meeting awkwardly on the beach, Baneelon alone made himself at home at the governor's table. While most of his people spurned British attempts to ply them with grog, Baneelon drank on his own terms, demanding wine when he wanted it and mimicking (or mocking) the toasts that went with it. Alcohol was part of his prestige, both a factor in the events that led to the governor's spearing and a symbol of reconciliation afterwards. While Baneelon drank exclusively at the officers' table, he was allowed his prestige. When he turned his back on the British, their amusement and admiration for his drinking would turn to derision.

9

The two convicts got drunk

Keeping alcohol away from 'undeserving' convicts remained one of Phillip's preoccupations as governor, but the most 'undeserving' were often the most enterprising. As long as there was grog in the colony, there would be convicts willing to risk life and limb to obtain it.

On 23 March 1790, four days after the *Sirius* struck a reef off Norfolk Island, Captain Hunter allowed two convicts to swim out to the wreck to see how many animals could be saved. Their instructions, according to Ralph Clark, were to throw the livestock into the sea. The two men scrambled on board the ship and set about throwing 'a great number of Hogs, Goats, fouls over board'. Most of the animals made it safely to shore, but the pigs were dead already. Clark lost all his fowls 'except my Cocks who Swam on Shore'.

Their job done, the two convicts turned the ship upside down for the grog that they must have known would be on board and spent the next few hours drinking. '[T]he two Convicts got drunk and Some how or other got a Light which been Seen from the Shore the[y] were desired to come on Shore Several times and the[y] answerd that the[y] could not – every one was afraid the[y] would Set the Ship on fire – if so we would loose all the provisions which we are now in great hopes of Saving.'

With the drunken convicts refusing to move, another convict volunteered to swim out to the *Sirius* 'and Stay there if he could not get them out of the Ship to prevent them doing any Mischief to the Ship – he got Save on board and finding them both Drunk and that the[y] had set fire to the Ship he made them assist him in putting the fire out'. The sober convict then ordered his drunken colleagues over the side and forced them to swim to shore, while he stayed on board with the grog, ostensibly for the purpose of making sure the fire did not break out again. After swimming ashore the next morning, he informed Major Ross and Captain Hunter that 'had he not got on board as he did there would not have been a pice of the Ship but what would have been burnt as She was on fire in two places'.

The two convicts who got drunk and set the ship alight, James Branigan and William Dring, were put in irons and sent to the guard house, where they were confined for the next eight weeks.

The wreck of the *Sirius* confirmed Ralph Clark's belief that he was 'a child of bad Luck'. Most of his personal belongings were washed away after the ship hit the reef, and Clark struggled ashore 'without five Shirts a waistcoat a pair of trousers a pair of old shoes a hat or a coat and Jacket and not a Single thing to dress me . . . nor a Single bit of Soap'.

David Collins told essentially the same story about the drunken convicts setting fire to the ship in his *Account of the English Colony in New South Wales*. However, Captain Hunter's version of the incident, published three years later in London, failed to mention grog, convicts or the torching of the stricken ship. In Hunter's version, it was sailors, not convicts, who braved the crashing surf to return to the *Sirius*:

> The second day after the landing of the crew, the weather
> being more moderate, and the surf less dangerous, a few of
> the seamen, who could depend, in case of accident, upon their
> good swimming, were got on board by the hawser, and the
> utmost exertion used to get some part of the provisions sent
> on shore.

On his return to England in 1792, Hunter, in accordance with navy regulations, faced a court martial for the loss of the *Sirius* at Norfolk Island. He was honourably acquitted of all blame. Twelve years later he would be court-martialled for the shipwreck of another vessel under his command, the 74-gun warship *Venerable*. Again he was honourably acquitted. In all, Hunter was shipwrecked three times.

Hunter's book, *An Historical Journal of the Transactions at Port Jackson and Norfolk Island*, was written to bolster his credentials as a future governor of New South Wales. The bacchanalian scene depicted by Ralph Clark, an eyewitness to the shipwreck and its aftermath, would not have impressed Hunter's patrons or been good for his reputation, so he simply omitted it. The strategy worked. At the age of 58, Hunter would return as the colony's second governor.

But Clark's version – in which convicts, rather than sailors, swam out to the ship – was the truth. In Phillip's report about the wreck of the *Sirius*, dated 11 April 1790, the governor told Lord Sydney that two convicts had 'set the ship on fire', but he notably failed to mention that the men were drunk. Hunter was not the only one covering up the colony's grog problem.

The three convicts in the story of the *Sirius* had contrasting fates. After two months sobering up in the guard house, Branigan and Dring were 'permitted to goe to there own Hutts but Still to Remain in Irons'. In December 1791 Branigan was among those marked as having absconded before his term was up. Dring, described by Ralph Clark as 'the greatest Rascall living', served out his sentence and in 1793 was listed as 'a well behaved free man'. The convict who put out the flames, John Ascott (or Arscott), was later given his freedom by Governor Phillip and sailed to Calcutta on the storeship *Atlantic*.

10

It will certainly be a great evil

At Sydney Cove, the food shortage was reaching a crisis point. 'The dread of perishing by famine stares us in the face,' wrote an anonymous officer. '[W]e have but eight weeks provisions in the public store, and all chance of a reinforcement under seven months is cut off, unless ships from England should yet . . . come in upon us. The hope of this is however very feeble.'

His fears were echoed by Surgeon White. '[A]ll the grain of every kind which we have been able to raise in two years and three months would not support us three weeks,' he wrote to a friend.

The malnourished colonists, worn down by a diet of salt rations, were barely capable of working. 'Was this a ration for a labouring man?' asked Collins. 'The two pounds of pork, when boiled, from the length of time it had been in store, shrunk away to nothing; and when divided among seven people for their day's sustenance, barely afforded three or four morsels to each.'

This was the desperate state of the colony when, on 3 June 1790, the *Lady Juliana* – with 222 healthy female convicts on board – sailed into Port Jackson after 11 months at sea. It brought shocking news: the *Guardian*, a fast-sailing ship loaded with stores for the colony, had struck an iceberg and been abandoned at Cape Town with the loss of everything. The *Guardian* had carried enough flour, pork and beef (not to mention 15 casks of wine) to supply the colony for two years. Besides a small quantity of flour, the *Lady Juliana* brought nothing but hungry mouths to feed.

In the last week of June, the remaining ships of the Second Fleet – the *Neptune*, *Surprize* and *Scarborough* – limped into Sydney Cove. They had set out with more than a thousand convicts, but a quarter had died at sea. Of those landed, nearly 500 were sick: in the coming days and weeks, more than 100 would die in the hospital at Sydney.

The contract for the Second Fleet had gone to Camden, Calvert & King, a firm of London slave traders, and many of the convicts (unlike those embarked on the First Fleet, whom Phillip had made sure were well fed and cared for) were in a dismal physical condition when they left England. Emptying the county gaols of the 'disordered and helpless' might have eased the load on the parishes, but only by shifting it onto the settlement. Phillip warned Lord Sydney that if the practice were continued, the colony, rather than being able to support itself, would 'remain for years a burthen to the mother-country'.

Conditions on board the Second Fleet were far harsher than they had been on the First. 'The irons used upon these unhappy wretches were barbarous,' wrote Captain William Hill. 'The contractors had been in the Guinea trade, and had put on board the same shackles used by them in that trade, which are made with a short bolt, instead of chains that drop between the legs and fasten with a bandage about the waist . . . so that they could not extend either leg from the other more than an inch or two at most; thus fettered, it was impossible for them to move but at the risk of both their legs being broken . . . The slave trade is merciful compared with what I have seen in this fleet.'

The Reverend Richard Johnson, chaplain of the settlement, insisted on going on board the *Surprize* to see the convicts for himself. His account corroborated Captain Hill's. After visiting the *Surprize*, Johnson boarded the *Scarborough*, but the state of the convicts was so disgusting that he was 'dissuaded' by the captain from going below. The *Neptune* was even worse; the conditions were so 'wretched and intolerable' that Johnson did not dare venture down.

After the survivors had been brought ashore, Johnson began collecting evidence about their mistreatment, finding that 'for a considerable time together they had been to the middle in water, chained together hand and leg, even the sick not excepted – nay, many died with their chains upon them'.

Many of the convicts were too sick to be moved; some died on deck and others as they were being rowed ashore. The living, rather than being helped off, were often 'slung over the ship's side in the same manner as they would sling a cask, a box, or anything of that nature'. The dead were simply tossed into the harbour, their bodies floating to shore, where they could be seen lying 'naked upon the rocks' – a practice that went on until Johnson protested to Governor Phillip, who ordered that the dead be carried to the north shore of the harbour and buried.

As the contractor was paid by the number of convicts embarked, rather than the number landed, deaths at sea made the voyage more profitable. Once the ships reached Sydney, their masters were able to make a fortune selling surplus provisions to the starving colonists. 'Several of the masters of the transports immediately opened stores,' wrote Watkin Tench, 'and exposed large quantities of goods to sale, which, though at most extortionate prices, were eagerly bought up.'

Of the scanty amount of food destined for the public stores, 20 casks of flour had to be condemned as unfit for use.

As well as convicts, the Second Fleet brought two companies of the newly formed New South Wales Corps to take over some of the duties resented by the marines. The officers would do jury duty while the enlisted men would take over the hated job of guarding the convicts. Unlike the marines, the New South Wales Corps had been raised exclusively for the purpose of serving in the colony. Within a few years, its officers would turn the government of the colony upside down. Initially nicknamed the Botany Bay Rangers, they would soon be known by another name: the Rum Corps.

Few good words have ever been written about the New South Wales Corps. 'As soldiers, the Botany Bay Rangers . . . were poor stuff even by the current low standards of the British Army,' Robert Hughes wrote in *The Fatal Shore*. 'Most of them were scum . . . Few of the officers were better than the men.'

Hunter, the colony's second governor, complained that the corps consisted of 'Soldiers from the Savoy [a military prison], and other characters who have been considered as disgraceful to every other regiment in his Majesty's service'.

It was true that the New South Wales Corps (like other regiments in the British Army) recruited men from the country's prisons, and that after landing in Australia the corps bolstered its numbers with ex-convicts. It wasn't the criminality of the common soldiers, however, but the rapacity of their officers that would make the New South Wales Corps notorious.

Major Francis Grose, a veteran of the American Revolutionary War, was the recruiting officer charged with raising a corps of infantry for service in New South Wales. If anything, Grose seems to have considered the New South Wales Corps a cut above the average. In a letter written on 30 July 1790 Grose assured the secretary at war, Sir George Yonge, that the men under his command had behaved with the greatest propriety and had given 'constant satisfaction' to everyone concerned.

But friction quickly arose between the marine officers and the new arrivals, a detachment of whom were sent to relieve the marines on Norfolk Island. 'I am Sorry to Acquaint you that we have not lived on Such good terms with the New South Wales Corps as . . . I flatterd myself we should,' Ralph Clark complained in a letter to Captain Campbell. '[T]hey are without Exception the most Selfish Set of men I ever cam a Cross . . . we are Constantly in hot water with them.'

To Captain Johnston, he wrote, '[W]e here have had nothing but Court Martials Since you have been gone and all of them in the N:S:W: Corps.'

The officers and men of the New South Wales Corps were dismayed by the condition of the colony, which was teetering on the brink of starvation. Attempts to cultivate the land around Port Jackson had been abandoned, 'the crop of last year being so miserable, as to deter from farther experiment', and agricultural hopes were focused on the outlying settlement at Rose Hill.

'Vegetables are scarce, although the summer is so far advanced, owing to want of rain,' Tench wrote in November 1790. 'I do not think that all the showers of the last four months put together, would make twenty-four hours rain. Our farms, what with this and a poor soil, are in wretched condition. My winter crop of potatoes, which I planted in days of despair (March and April last), turned out very badly when I dug them about two months back.' The previous wheat harvest had been so poor that almost nothing except Indian corn could be sown.

Hardly a day went by without a burial: on Monday, 21 November, Richard Penny, Thomas Spencer, James Sennett and Mary Price; on Tuesday, Thomas Howard and Alexander Keiff; on Wednesday, George Holdsworth, Stephen Hilliard, Christopher Stephens, John Lewis and James Kennedy; on Friday, a child named Elizabeth Williams.

Reserves of flour and rice were dwindling; a cargo of flour, bought at an extortionate price from the Dutch in Batavia, had turned out to contain 'full one-sixth bran'. 'There are neither pease nor butter in the colony,' Phillip informed Lord Grenville, Sydney's successor as home secretary, in March 1791.

As the colony's cellars ran dry, the soldiers lost their precious grog ration. An anonymous piece published in the Edinburgh journal *The Bee: Or Literary Weekly Intelligencer* painted a dismal picture. Under the title 'Authentic Advices from Sydney Cove, New South Wales', the article described the plight of the newly arrived garrison as 'pitiable':

'It is probable Government does not intend to continue the allowance of spirits any longer, for, except a three months' proportion, which has lately been served, there has not been any issued for eight months past. The soldiers feel the want of that article very much, as they live but poorly, and have been long accustomed to it.'

Access to liquor was one of the few privileges for a soldier in New South Wales, where the distinction between 'free' and 'captive' had largely become meaningless. Under Governor Phillip's policy of equal food rations for all, the grog allowance alone signified the difference in status between the two groups.

Deprived of their longstanding entitlement, some soldiers inevitably resorted to stealing. On 19 July 1791 two private marines, William Norris and William Roberts, were tried by the criminal court for having 'at sundry times, between the first of May and Seventeenth Day of July' broken into the wine cellar next to the home of Zachariah Clark and stolen 'nine Gallons of Rum of the

Value of twenty two Shillings and Six-Pence, and five Gallons of red Wine of the Value of One Pound fifteen Shillings'.

While on night patrol between midnight and one o'clock, Sergeant Thomas Smith had found the sentinel, William Godfrey, missing from his post outside the 'Rum Cellar'. Seeing the cellar door open, Smith 'ordered the two men who were with him, to load their Musquets, which being done, he gave them Orders to blow out the Brains of the first Person who attempted to come out'. A warning shot was fired as a signal to the guard and William Godfrey emerged sheepishly from the cellar, saying there was nobody else inside. After being taken away, Godfrey admitted that he 'got in by picking the Lock with a Nail'.

Questioned by the deputy judge advocate, Godfrey made a full confession, implicating Norris and Roberts. Both men pleaded not guilty, calling a number of fellow marines to give evidence on their behalf. Collins preferred the version given by Private Godfrey, but 'for want of evidence sufficiently strong to corroborate the testimony of the accomplice, they were necessarily acquitted'. Private John Easty made a note in his diary: 'Every Person thought them Gulty.'

Court-martialled for 'Disobedience of Orders and Neglect of Duty', Godfrey was 'Sentenced to Receive 800 Lashes and to be Drummed Out of the Core of Marines. Recd 300 the same day and Drummed Out; got his Discharge (but No pay list).' Norris and Roberts were sent to cool their heels at South Head, far from the temptations of the settlement.

Relations between the New South Wales Corps and the marine corps did not improve. By Admiralty rules, the marines, 'at the expiration of their Station of three years', were entitled to be discharged on their return to England or, if they preferred, to be discharged and allowed to settle in New South Wales. Most were sick of the place and couldn't wait to go home. They could not leave, however, until a ship was available to take them.

Further detachments of the New South Wales Corps came on the Third Fleet, reaching Port Jackson between August and October 1791. Their arrival coincided, ominously, with an influx of liquor. 'The town beginning to fill with strangers,' wrote Collins, 'and spirituous liquors finding their way among the convicts, it was ordered that none should be landed until a permit had been granted by the judge-advocate; and the provost-marshal, his assistant, and two principals of the watch, were deputed to seize all spirituous liquors which might be landed without.'

Like the captains on the Second Fleet, those on the Third Fleet had crammed their ships with goods to sell to the colonists at whatever inflated prices the market could bear.

'I hope we shall soon see the *Gorgon* here to carry us to England,' Lieutenant George Johnston wrote indignantly to Ralph Clark, 'otherwise they must allow us Field officers pay for at present they ask a Guinea a gallon for Rum, and the same for a Pound of Tobbacca and everything else in proportion.'

Writing to his father, Collins complained about the 'most exorbitant Prices' charged by the profiteering ships' masters, 'three, four thousand per Cent being charged on many Articles'.

Thus began the systematic exploitation of the colony by speculative traders bringing food, clothes, tools and (most profitably of all) alcohol to settlers who would pay almost anything to have them. The most avaricious exponents of this trade would turn out to be the officers of the New South Wales Corps themselves.

The marines were not alone in their eagerness to go home. Many convicts had come forward insisting that their sentences had expired, but there was no paperwork in the colony to prove or disprove their claims. 'The language they hold is, that the sentence of the law has been carried into execution, that they are free men, and wish to return,' Phillip told Lord Grenville. While the men claiming to have served out their sentences had so far been reasonably well behaved, Phillip predicted that 'they will become troublesome as their numbers increase'.

Worn down by hunger and isolation, Collins lamented that he was 'spending the Prime of my Life, at the farthest Part of the World, without Credit, without, or with but very little, Profit, secluded from my Family, my Connexions, from the World, under constant Apprehension of being starved, and constantly living on a reduced Ration of Provisions'.

The bulk of the marines finally sailed for England on 18 December 1791 on the troopship *Gorgon*. Even those, like Watkin Tench, who had once been eager to stay could see no future for themselves in the colony. 'If I be allowed to speak from my own feelings,' Tench wrote of their imminent departure, 'I will not say that we contemplated its approach with mingled sensations:- we hailed it with rapture and exultation.'

Anxious to share in the rapture, two convicts tried to escape as stowaways, but they were found and brought back. A female convict who was thought to have escaped was discovered 'disguised in men's apparel at the native's hut on the east point of the cove'.

While the majority of marines were only too happy to leave, some stayed on as settlers; some had died and six had been executed.

Major Ross had been a thorn in the governor's side from the outset, and Phillip could not have been sorry to see him go. The marine corps, however, had left a significant mark on the colony. Collins, a marine himself, considered it 'as valuable a corps as any in his Majesty's service. They had struggled here with greatly more than the common hardships of service, and were now quitting a country in which they had opened and smoothed the way for their successors.'

Within a year of the marines' departure, the colony was showing signs of the self-sufficiency that Phillip had dreamt of since the day he sailed into Botany Bay. Nothing much would ever grow in the feeble soil around Sydney Cove, but hardworking settlers were carving out productive land at Rose Hill. By October, Phillip had granted land to 66 people around Rose Hill and nearby Toongabbie, most of whom were time-expired convicts. In 12 months, the amount of land under cultivation had roughly doubled.

The prospect of a self-supporting British colony on the far side of the world was no longer fantastical. The idealists' vision of convicts making good and becoming productive citizens was starting to come true. For Governor Phillip, however, the transformation had come too late. The man whose shrewdness, pragmatism and humanity had dragged the colony through the years of starvation had worked and worried himself into the ground. His 'health now is very bad, he fatigues himself so much. He fairly knocks himself up & won't rest till he is not able to walk,' William Chapman, a family friend, wrote in September 1792.

While Phillip complained at times about lack of sleep, he also confided in Joseph Banks that he suffered from 'a violent pain in the left Kidney . . . [which] renders me at times unable either to ride or walk'. But the physical toll was only part of the story. Exhausted by the demands of intractable convicts and feuding officers, demoralised by the failure of his diplomacy with the Aboriginal people, and disillusioned by the government's refusal to acknowledge his achievements, Phillip had had enough.

After his request to return temporarily to England went unanswered by Grenville, Phillip was left with no choice but to make the decision himself.

As governor, Phillip had done his best to keep the colony sober. Until the trading ships began to arrive, the circulation of grog had been limited by the scarcity of supply. Wine and spirits could not be squeezed out of dry cellars and the shortage of grain meant that convicts lacked the wherewithal for illicit distilling. Phillip foresaw the dangers of a free flow of booze and intervened to stop it, informing Under-Secretary Nepean on 18 November 1791 that, 'The landing of spirits without having a permit has been prohibited in the Port Orders, in order to prevent the convicts procuring any.'

Advised by the new home secretary, Henry Dundas, that the colony might need to relax its import restrictions on 'certain commodities, such as spirits' in order to encourage international trade, Phillip replied grimly on 11 October 1792 that the 'permitting of spirits amongst the civil & military may be necessary, but it will certainly be a great evil'.

Within two months, Phillip would be gone. As a parting gift, he distributed the government sheep among the free settlers, hoping that the new owners would breed from the animals to enlarge the colony's flock. The settlers, however, had other ideas about what to do with their windfall.

On 10 December 1792 the governor boarded the storeship *Atlantic*, accompanied by Baneelon and another Aboriginal man named Yemmerawannie. 'His excellency,' wrote Collins, 'was received near the wharf on the east-side . . . by Major Grose, at the head of the New South Wales Corps, who paid him, as he passed, the honors due to his rank and situation.'

As commandant of the New South Wales Corps and lieutenant-governor of the colony, Grose was now in charge. It was supposed to be a temporary arrangement, necessitated by Phillip's having sailed for England before a new governor could be appointed, but Grose would run the settlement for more than two years. During that time, Phillip's prophecy about the evils of spirits would prove more far-sighted than even he could have imagined.

11

Ardent diabolical spirit

No sooner had the *Atlantic* sailed than notices went up throughout the colony advertising sheep for sale. It was clear that their owners had no intention of breeding from the animals, as Phillip had hoped, and would eat them if they could not find buyers. While some 'exchanged their sheep for goats, deeming them a more profitable stock', they were in the minority. Most wanted to trade their sheep for grog. This meant doing business with the officers of the New South Wales Corps, who had secured most of the newly arrived spirits and who were now encouraged by Lieutenant-Governor Grose to buy up the sheep before they could be eaten. '[S]pirits were the price required by the more ignorant and imprudent part of them,' Collins wrote disapprovingly, 'and several of their farms, which had been, and ought to have always been, the peaceful retreats of industry, were for a time the seats of inebriety and consequent disorder.'

The commercial ambitions of the New South Wales Corps under Grose had become apparent even before he assumed command of the colony. In July 1792, five months before Phillip's departure, the *Britannia* storeship had sailed into Port Jackson bringing much-needed supplies. She was discharged from government service on 17 August. By the start of October, the *Britannia* was ready to sail to New Zealand. At this point, Major Grose and his officers put forward a proposal to hire the ship and send her to the Cape of Good Hope to buy 'a freight of cattle, and such articles as would tend to the comfort of themselves and the soldiers of the corps, and which were not to be found in the public stores'. The officers paid £2000 to hire the ship and a further £2200 as trading capital to buy livestock and other goods.

'The situation of the soldiers under my command,' Grose informed Governor Phillip, 'who at this time have scarcely shoes to their feet, and who have no other comforts than the reduced and unwholesome rations served out from the stores, has induced me to assemble the captains of my corps for the purpose of consulting what could be done for their relief and accommodation.' Having agreed terms with the *Britannia*'s master on what he called 'money matters', Grose pleaded with Phillip to 'protect this ship from interruption as much as you can' in order to help his soldiers 'escape the miseries' of their 'precarious existence'.

The tone of Grose's letter is unlikely to have impressed Phillip, who had endured nearly five years of the 'precarious existence' that some of Grose's men had experienced for just a few months. 'I cannot acquiesce with you in thinking that the ration served from the public stores is unwholesome,' Phillip wrote in reply. 'I see it daily at my own table.'

The *Britannia* plan also presented Phillip with a diplomatic problem, since Grose's proposed business venture represented a flagrant breach of the charter that granted the East India Company a monopoly on private trade to and from the colony. While aware of the dangerous precedent being set, Phillip acknowledged that he 'could not prevent it'. After initially informing Grose that he could not 'with propriety, take any official step in this business', he later gave the venture a tepid endorsement, reassuring Dundas that 'I do not think his Majesty's service will suffer'.

While Phillip continued to prohibit the 'free use' of spirits in the colony, knowing they would inevitably reach the convicts, he was prepared to tolerate the limited sale of 'porter', a strong brown beer, a cargo of which had just arrived on the *Royal Admiral*. As the *Britannia* set sail for the Cape of Good Hope, Phillip gave permission for goods brought for private trade by the *Royal Admiral* to be sold in shops at Sydney and Parramatta. 'A licence was given for the sale of porter,' wrote Collins, 'but, under the cover of this, spirits found their way among the people, and much intoxication was the consequence. Several of the settlers, breaking out from the restraint to which they had been subject, conducted themselves with the greatest impropriety, beating their wives, destroying their stock, trampling on and injuring their crops in the ground, and destroying each other's property.'

The punishments imposed by the magistrates were relatively light: one settler bound over for two years' good behaviour on a surety of 20 pounds and another put in the stocks for an hour. But the deputy judge advocate's private verdict was damning:

> The indulgence which was intended by the governor for their
> benefit was most shamefully abused; and what he suffered
> them to purchase with a view to their future comfort, was
> retailed among themselves at a scandalous profit; several of
> the settlers houses being at this time literally nothing else but
> porter-houses, where rioting and drunkenness prevailed as
> long as the means remained.

In an artificial society that lacked the usual regulating structures of family, community and employment, the line between order and lawlessness was always thin. Widespread public drunkenness warned of more dangerous transgressions: violence, disobedience, the destruction of property and even insurrection.

A month after the *Britannia* set sail for the Cape, an American ship, the *Philadelphia*, arrived in Port Jackson carrying what an unnamed correspondent described as 'a cargo of assorted notions much needed in the settlement'. According to the writer, 'the speculative skipper sold the lot at a high figure, in addition to which he found employment for his ship between Sydney and Norfolk island in the transport of stores'.

The 'assorted notions' consisted of 'American beef, wine, rum, gin, some tobacco, pitch, and tar'. The beef, pitch and tar were bought by the colonial government at a cost of £2829. The rest was snapped up, for an unknown sum, by the officers of the New South Wales Corps for resale to the public.

So began a trading partnership between American shippers and the New South Wales Corps that would significantly enrich both parties (but especially the latter) while undermining some of the founding principles of the colony. In the decades to come, the cargoes brought by American (and British) masters to New South Wales would consist increasingly of grog, for which there was seemingly limitless demand. The amount of grog relative to other provisions climbed steadily year by year. Profits from foodstuffs, iron pots, shoes, clothes and other useful goods might have paled beside those from wine and spirits, but the arrival of these much-needed articles offered a reliable way of pressuring the colonial administration to allow grog to be landed.

With Grose in charge, life rapidly improved for the officers and men of the New South Wales Corps, and became worse for the convicts. On the day after Governor Phillip sailed out of Port Jackson, Grose issued a direction to the commissary, John Palmer. Formerly the purser on the *Sirius*, Palmer was the man responsible for receiving and issuing government stores and keeping the public accounts. From now on, Palmer was directed by Grose to issue to 'the Civil, Military, Superintendents, Settlers from the Free People, Overseers, Watchmen, and People employed in the Storehouses' three pounds of flour weekly in lieu of three pounds of rice.

Flour was – and always had been – the mainstay of the ration. No decent substitute had been found for it, and its lack was felt acutely during periods of reduced rations. Before leaving, Phillip had set the weekly allowance of flour at three pounds, supplemented by five pounds of rice, for free and convict alike. Writing to Dundas, Grose declared that he 'considered it expedient . . . to make some little distinctions between the convicts and the civil and military people'. These 'little distinctions' meant that, while the colony was on reduced rations, the military would receive twice as much flour as the convicts.

On the same day that Lieutenant-Governor Grose issued his edict about the flour ration, Richard Atkins, a free settler who had sailed with Grose on the *Pitt*, noted in his journal:

Commencement of a New Government . . . the
Superintendents receiv'd orders to report every thing to
Capt F[oveaux] and the convicts to work from 5 to 9 in the
morn – and from 4 to sunset in the afternoon . . . The Settlers
have begun selling their Stock. 3 Eyes [ewes] that were given
them by Government to breed from were yesterday disposed
of to C.F. [Captain Foveaux]. No Soldier is to be interrupted:
Times are Changed.

The son of a baronet, Atkins charmed his way into the colonial administration by flaunting his family connections. John Macarthur, who would later play a leading role in the removal of Governor Bligh, accused him of being 'deeply plunged in infamy . . . a public cheater, living in the most boundless dissipation, without any visible means of maintaining it than by imposture on unwary strangers . . . drunkenness and indecency are almost inseparable from him'.

Soon after Atkins's arrival in the colony, Phillip had appointed him a magistrate at Parramatta. Under Governor Hunter, he became acting deputy judge advocate after the departure of David Collins, a position he held (with one interruption) until the end of 1809. Bligh himself described Atkins as 'a disgrace to human jurisprudence' who 'has been the ridicule of the community: sentences of death have been pronounced in moments of intoxication; his determination is weak, his opinion floating and infirm; his knowledge of the law is insignificant and subservient to private inclination; and confidential cases of the Crown he is not to be entrusted with'.

Infamous or not, Atkins saw clearly enough how the colony was changing under the new administration. 'Waited on Lieut Govr who received me very kindly,' he wrote three days after Grose had altered the rations. '[H]e ordered a convict 50 Lashes for striking a Soldier, who it seems is never to be interrupted however wrong he may be . . . for the first time since it has been a colony a distinction on the ration. The Civil and Military, Constables and Overseers have 3 [lb] of Flour more than the Convicts.'

Under Phillip, the colony's routine magisterial duties had been carried out by three men: the chaplain, Mr Johnson; the surveyor-general, Augustus Alt; and Atkins. Grose wanted judicial authority firmly under the control of the military. While not formally stripping the three men of their appointments, he emasculated the magistrates by handing their powers to the officers of the New South Wales Corps.

Whether he knew it or not, Grose was contravening not just the spirit but also the letter of the law that, as lieutenant-governor, he was bound to uphold. The Courts of Criminal and Civil Jurisdiction took their authority from Letters Patent under an Act of Parliament; Phillip's Commission explicitly called for the establishment of a Magistrates' Court. The British Government had never meant to hand over to the military the functions that belonged to the civil tribunals. By usurping the power of the magistrates, Grose was (presumably unintentionally) laying the foundations of an outlaw regime, the ramifications of which would bedevil more than one of Phillip's successors as governor.

The changes instigated by Grose in the first few days of his rule were profound (if temporary), but a more seismic transformation of the social and economic conditions of the colony was looming. Grose had a low opinion of the ordinary settlers, who he considered to be indolent and shiftless, and became convinced that the only way the government could keep its granaries full was by encouraging the officers of the New South Wales Corps to cultivate land.

While Governor Phillip had been given no authority from London to grant land (except for small garden plots) to his officers, Grose did have that authority. The dispatch giving the necessary power, addressed to Phillip, was dated 14 July 1792 and arrived in the colony five weeks after Phillip's departure. Following the advice it contained, Grose quickly began making grants of land to civil and military officers. Most officers received 100 acres or less, although one – Lieutenant John Macarthur, whom Grose had appointed inspector of public works at Parramatta – received significantly more.

In a letter to Dundas on 16 February 1793, Grose reported that the officers were making 'astonishing' progress improving their farms and that within six months he was confident of seeing newly cultivated land 'more than equal to a third of all that has ever been cleared in the colony'.

Having decided that the officers were 'the only description of settlers on whom reliance can be placed', Grose vowed to 'encourage their pursuit as much as in my power'.

The example of James Thorpe, who had been brought out from England to be the colony's millwright at a salary of £100 per annum, strongly confirmed Grose's prejudice against ordinary settlers. 'I am sorry to observe I do not expect much benefit from this man,' he told Dundas. '[H]e is by no means as expert as he pretends to be, and he has unluckily been on board the hulks as a convict. He is recollected by a number of his old associates, and, from some dirty tricks he has already attempted, I fear he has not forgotten all he learned when in that situation.'

Grose's promise to do 'as much as in my power' to help the officers understated his generosity, which went much further than the government in Britain had intended. While the lieutenant-governor had told Dundas that the officers were improving their land 'at their own expense', the truth was that Grose had allowed each officer the services of ten convicts, fed and clothed from the commissary at public expense. (Ordinary settlers had to make do with just one or two.) Officers willing to pay for extra labour could engage gangs of convicts, who, when not employed on government work, were permitted to hire themselves out in return for grog.

Under this one-sided arrangement, the government would effect-ively pay twice for everything it took into the public stores: once by supplying free convict labour (which could have been employed on its own farms) and again by buying the product of that labour.

On 24 December 1792 an American trading ship, the *Hope*, from Rhode Island, anchored at Sydney Cove. The master, Benjamin Page, had brought with him what Collins described as 'a small cargo of provisions and spirits'. According to Page, the reason for his putting into Port Jackson was to procure 'wood and water', of which his ship was 'much in want'; the sale of his cargo 'appear[ed] to be but a secondary object with him'.

It soon became apparent that selling his cargo was far from being Captain Page's 'secondary object', and that his cargo of grog was anything but small. In addition to 200 barrels of American cured beef, at four pounds per barrel; 80 barrels of pork, at four pounds ten shillings per barrel; and 44 barrels of flour, at two pounds per barrel, the *Hope* carried 'seven thousand five hundred and ninety-seven gallons of (new American) spirits', priced at four shillings and sixpence per gallon.

Grose inspected the inventory of the commissary and found supplies running dangerously low. This, along with his fear of drought, persuaded him to make Page an offer for the provisions carried on the *Hope*. But Page had no intention of selling the pork and beef without also selling the spirits; he knew he had Grose over a barrel. 'I lamented on this occasion being obliged to purchase the spirits, without which he would not agree to the disposal of his provisions,' Grose told London.

A portion of the *Hope*'s liquor was issued to the troops of the New South Wales Corps, some of whom disobeyed orders by bartering their allowance with convicts in return for rations and clothing. Grose gave instructions for the remaining spirits to be disposed of to the 'military and civil officers of the colony, in which were included the superintendents, and some others in that line'. It soon became clear that many of those buying the grog were doing so not for their own consumption but 'with the particular view of retailing it among the convicts'.

There was no shortage of customers among a convict population that had barely touched a drop of alcohol in more than five years. 'The fondness expressed by these people for even this pernicious American spirit was incredible,' wrote Collins. '[T]hey hesitated not to go any lengths to procure it, and preferred receiving liquor for labour, to every other article of provisions or clothing that could be offered them.' The consequences were predictable enough. '[A] discreet use of it being wholly out of the question with those people, intoxication was become common among them.'

It wasn't just the 'intoxication' of the convicts that worried Collins, but the prospect of this leading to wider insubordination. In an isolated colony in which convicts significantly outnumbered marines, keeping the convict population sober had been a way of keeping it under control:

It might therefore have been expected, that when that restraint was in ever so small a degree removed, they would break out into acts of disorder and contempt of former prohibitions. It was therefore indispensable to the preservation of peace and good order in the settlement, to prevent, if possible, the existence of so great an evil as drunkenness; which, if suffered, would have been the parent of every irregularity.

Aware of the danger and sensing, perhaps, an implicit challenge to his authority, Grose moved to snuff out the grog trade, declaring in public orders that:

it was his intention to make frequent inquiries on the subject; and it might be relied upon, that if it ever appeared that a convict was possessed of any of the liquor so supplied by the commissary, the conduct of those who had thought proper to abuse what was designed as an accommodation to the officers of the garrison, would not be passed over unnoticed.

Grose was still dealing with the problems caused by the *Hope* when a signal went up at South Head announcing the arrival of another ship. At about ten o'clock on the morning of 16 January 1793, the *Bellona*, from England, anchored in the cove. She brought 17 female convicts, five settlers and their families, together with a cargo of provisions including 'five pipes of port wine and a quantity of rum'.

Armed with fresh instructions from London aimed at thwarting the visiting profiteers and their 'shameful impositions', Grose gave orders for the *Bellona*'s grog to be 'consigned to the governor for the

purpose of being sold to the officers of the civil and military estab-
lishments at prime cost'. The wine, Collins noted, 'was immediately
distributed; coming to the officer, after every expence of wharfage,
&c. at 19l. 10s. per hogshead, and the rum at five shillings per gallon'.

The *Bellona*'s master had more trouble offloading his tobacco,
which 'was likely to remain for some time undisposed of, as a quantity
had been lately brought into the settlement, and was selling at a
lower price than could be taken for that imported by this ship'.
Unfortunately for him, the New South Wales Corps was speculating
in tobacco as well as grog, and several of the officers who had invested
in the *Britannia* were awaiting large consignments of tobacco. Spoilage
caused by improper storage had also led to the loss of 'seventy-nine
gallons of rum, and one hundred and ninety-eight gallons of wine'.

In order to avoid demurrage (a penalty imposed for taking too
long to unload a ship), convicts were brought in to help take off the
Bellona's cargo, with the promise that they would be given time off
in lieu. Some of these convicts had been employed in building the
new barracks, where the laying of bricks came abruptly to a halt.
Impatient to see work on the barracks restarted, Grose ordered the
convicts back to their old jobs as soon as the *Bellona* was unloaded.

Having worked up what they claimed to be 16 days' worth
of overtime, the convicts at the barracks insisted on having their
promised time off. 'As it would have proved very inconvenient to
have allowed them to remain unemployed for that number of days,'
wrote Collins, 'the lieutenant-governor directed the commissary to
issue to each person so employed half a pint of spirits *per diem* for
sixteen days.'

They were not the first convicts to be rewarded for their labour with grog, but until now this system of recompense had largely been informal. It was Grose's innovation to formalise the arrangement and to make the colonial government an official party to it.

Collins (rather surprisingly, given his censorious remarks elsewhere) was initially unconcerned by the transaction. 'Liquor given to them in this way operated as a benefit and a comfort to them,' he commented blandly. But it set a precedent that would have profound consequences in the years to come, and it helped cement and legitimise the role (previously illicit) of grog as a commodity ripe for barter.

A pattern was now established whereby provisions and other goods brought to the colony on American ships were taken by the commissary, leaving the grog to be purchased by the New South Wales Corps. Sometimes the officers bought the entire cargo. The quality of liquor was overwhelmingly poor, but the public demand for alcohol was such that even the reviled 'American spirits' could be resold for as much as 20 times the landed price.

In June 1793 the *Britannia* returned from the Cape. Of the 30 cows taken on board, 27 had died during the voyage, leaving the officers to pick over a cargo of 'flour, sugar, tobacco, and spirits'. Robert Murray, who kept the ship's log on the *Britannia*, calculated that after the spirits had been mixed with water ('with which every measure of liquor sold at pt. J. [Port Jackson] is adulterated') the officers stood to make a profit of nearly 900 per cent on every gallon sold.

The floodgates had opened. Grog was starting to pour into the colony and the bulk of it would end up in private hands – mainly those of the officers of the New South Wales Corps.

As the amount of grog in the colony increased, so did the number of crimes in which grog was involved. Accounts written by Collins and others reported settlers neglecting their farms, and convicts selling their rations and their clothes for drink, then robbing the settlers' gardens to feed themselves.

Convicts desperate for a drink had always found ways to barter food and other articles for grog, but Phillip's determination to suppress the practice had stopped it from becoming widespread. While Grose lacked Phillip's zeal, he did try to prevent liquor reaching the convicts, but the forces against him were too strong. Thanks to the American ships and the New South Wales Corps, there was simply too much alcohol coming into the settlement for the regulations against the distribution of spirits to be effective.

The reward for uncovering illicit booze was to share in the confiscated product. Collins reported that 'fourteen or fifteen gallons were found in one night; and, being seized by the watchmen and the guard, were divided among them as a stimulus to future vigilance'. Evidence of heavy drinking was seen in the number of prisoners found every morning in the watch house – 'for, when intoxicated, it could not be expected that people of this description would be very careful to avoid breaking the peace'.

The 'vigilance' of the watchmen was not enough to curb the traffic in grog, or to prevent the growing number of crimes and accidents associated with it. On 18 January, after a drinking binge in Sydney, a settler named Charles Williams (also known as Magee), his pregnant wife and their infant child, together with a woman named Mary Green, who was carrying a bag of rice, set out in a small boat for Parramatta. When the boat listed near Breakfast Point, Green reached out to try to stop the rice from getting wet, tipping both women and the child into the river. The two women drowned. The child, wrote Collins, 'was forced from the wretched mother's grasp just before she finally sunk, and brought on shore by the father; but for want of medical aid it expired'.

Williams, a former convict, had 'recommended himself to [the governor's] notice by extraordinary propriety of conduct as an overseer'. His reward, in July 1791, had been the grant of a farm 'on the Creek leading to Parramatta'. During the years that followed, Williams and his wife, Eleanor, had become notorious for their drinking. '[T]hey had been rioting and fighting with each other the moment before they got into the boat; and it was said, that the woman had imprecated every evil to befal her and the infant she carried about her (for she was six months gone with child) if she accompanied her husband to Parramatta.'

It was several days before the women's bodies were pulled from the river. The 'wretched and rascally' Williams buried his wife and child within a few feet of his door. Soon after laying his wife to rest, he was observed 'sitting at his door, with a bottle of rum in his hand . . . drinking one glass and pouring another on her grave until it was emptied, prefacing every libation by declaring how well she had loved it during her life'.

Alcohol was also the downfall of Thomas Daveney, a former superintendent of convicts at the government farm at Toongabbie. Although well regarded by Governor Phillip, Daveney had been dismissed (for reasons unknown) from his post by Grose and retired to his private farm at Toongabbie. According to Collins:

> He had been always addicted to the use of spirituous liquors; but he now applied himself more closely to them, to drown the recollection of his disgrace. In this vice he continued until . . . he came to Sydney in a state of insanity. He went to the house of a friend in the town, determined . . . to destroy himself; for he there drank, unknown to the people of the house, as fast as he could swallow, nearly half a gallon of Cape brandy.

Finding him unconscious on the floor, Daveney's hosts left him 'for ten or twelve hours' to sober up, 'in consequence he was seized with a violent inflammation . . . a mortification succeeded, and at last carried him off'.

Shortly before his death, Daveney asked to see the deputy judge advocate, assuring him that 'nothing lay on his conscience which could make his last moments in this life painful'. Unlike many others, Daveney had made a success of his farm and left his widow, Catharine, 86 goats, which were 'sold by public auction for three hundred and fifty seven pounds fifteen shillings'.

In April 1793, Richard Sutton, a convict, 'was stabbed with a knife in the belly by one Abraham Gordon, at the house of a female convict, on some quarrel respecting the woman, and at a time when both were inflamed with liquor'.

Punishment imposed by the military under Grose was proving no more of a deterrent than punishment handed down by the civil courts under Phillip. Collins decided it was time to make an example of somebody: 'The frequency of enormous offences had rendered it necessary to inflict a punishment that should be more likely to check the commission of crimes than mere flagellation at the back of the guardhouse, or being sent to Toongabbe.'

A convict named John Crow, who twice escaped from custody after being arrested for breaking into two houses in Parramatta, was convicted in the criminal court and hanged eight days later. Crow's execution disabused those who mistakenly believed that Grose, as lieutenant-governor, did not have the legal authority to carry out a sentence of death, but it did not have the deterrent effect predicted by the deputy judge advocate.

Grog was widely seen as a factor in the growing lawlessness. 'The passion for liquor was so predominant among the people, that it operated like a mania,' wrote Collins, 'there being nothing which they would not risk to obtain it: and while spirits were to be had, those who did any extra labour refused to be paid in money, or any other article than spirits, which were now, from their scarcity, sold at six shillings per bottle. Webb, the settler near Parramatta, having procured a small still from England, found it more advantageous to draw an ardent diabolical spirit from his wheat, than to send it to the store and receive ten shillings per bushel from the commissary. From one bushel of wheat he obtained nearly five quarts of spirit, which he sold or paid in exchange for labour at five and six shillings per quart.'

At the end of December 1792, in his annual survey of stock, grain and other articles for sale in Sydney and Parramatta, Collins had noted just two types of grog: 'spirits in exchange were estimated at from twelve to twenty shillings per gallon', while 'porter was sold from nine to ten pounds per hogshead, or from one shilling to one shilling and three pence per quart'.

By the end of 1793, in a column headed 'Wine, – Spirits, – Porter', Collins supplied the following table of prices at Sydney:

Jamaica rum per gallon from 1£. to 1£. 8s.

Rum (American) from 16s. per gall. to 1£.

Coniac brandy per gallon from 1£. to 1£. 4s.

Cape brandy per gallon from 16s. to 1£.

Cherry brandy per dozen 3£. 12s.

Wine (Cape Madeira) per gallon 12s.

Porter per gallon from 4s. to 6s.

At Parramatta, prices were significantly higher for poorer quality stuff: 'Neat spirits' were available for between one pound ten shillings and two pounds a gallon; and 'wine of the most inferior quality' could be had for 16 shillings a gallon.

The high prices of wine, spirits and porter in the colony were largely attributable, Collins believed, to the 'great avidity' with which they were snapped up by the settlers, who in their eagerness to obtain what they wanted often made extravagant offers rather than wait for the seller to set a price.

12

We brew for our lives

By the time Grose took over as lieutenant-governor, James Squires was a free man. His seven-year sentence had expired in April 1792 (although it is possible he was pardoned before then). Squires's prospects had improved dramatically since his days as convict servant to Ralph Clark and he was now making a name for himself as a brewer. Among his clients was Grose himself, who seems to have drunk Australian beer in preference to the 'pernicious' American spirits he was importing for the public stores.

After two years on Norfolk Island, Squires's de facto wife, Mary Spencer, had returned to Sydney, but her relationship with Squires was over. Squires was now living with Elizabeth Mason, who had been sentenced to death in Gloucester at the age of 22 before being reprieved and transported for 14 years. The couple had a daughter, Martha, who was baptised on 3 April 1793, and they would go on to have six more daughters and a son.

In December 1820 Squires gave oral evidence to John Thomas Bigge's Commission of Inquiry into the State of the Colony of New South Wales. He told Bigge:

> I have been in the Colony from its earliest establishment and
> for 30 years I have been a brewer. At first I lived in Sydney,
> and brewed beer in small quantities. I sold it then for 4d
> per quart and made it from some hops that I got from the
> *Daedalus*. I also brewed for General Grose & Col. Paterson
> for their own consumption from English Malt. I have been
> established at Kissing Point as a Brewer for 28 years, and have
> brewed beer from Indian corn and Colonial Barley.

If Squires was already brewing beer by 1791, as he told Commissioner Bigge, it is virtually certain that he was the colony's first brewer (although it is interesting that he does not make the claim himself). But others, inspired by his success, were soon following his example. Local beer became a plausible – and affordable – alternative to imported spirits. By the end of 1796, Collins's annual inventory of articles for sale in Sydney included 'Beer made at Sydney', which he described as 'brewed from Indian corn, properly malted, and bittered with the leaves and stalks of the love-apple . . . or, as it was more commonly called in the settlement, the Cape gooseberry'. (They were actually different fruits, but Collins did not pretend to be a botanist.) The recipe succeeded so well that the manufacturer, Mr Boston, 'erected at some expence a building proper for the business, and was . . . engaged in brewing beer from the abovementioned materials, and in making soap'.

John Boston arrived from England on 25 October 1794 as a free settler on the *Surprize*. His fellow passengers included four political prisoners belonging to a group known as the 'Scottish martyrs'. Grose was warned by letter to 'keep a watchful eye over their conduct and . . . give them clearly to understand what must be the consequence' of any future seditious behaviour. Although 'brought up a surgeon and apothecary', Boston was more interested in business and claimed to have a working knowledge of 'brewing, distilling, sugar-making, vinegar-making, soap-making, etc.'

The hope in government circles was that Boston would 'prove particularly useful to the settlement by curing fish and making salt'. Instead, he went into business with one of the Scottish martyrs, the wealthy clergyman Thomas Fyshe Palmer, and a Glasgow cotton-spinner named James Ellis who, like Boston, had come out as a free settler on the *Surprize*.

Boston and Palmer had become friends during the voyage. It seems likely that they arrived with high hopes of making a killing in the developing colony and were dismayed to find a virtual monopoly in place. In a letter to a friend, Palmer lamented the 'destructive and oppressive monopoly of the military officers', which prevented the other settlers from buying goods from visiting ships.

Grose's decision to transfer the powers of the magistrates onto the military had given the officers a powerful tool with which to defend their monopoly. 'The officers . . . suffer no one but themselves to board any ship that may arrive,' Palmer complained in June 1795. 'They alone buy the cargo, and sell it at 1, 2, 3, 400, and even 1000 per cent profit. Mr. Ellis and Boston were ordered into confinement for entering a ship and endeavouring to purchase things, not prohibited, for their use. With great respect, but firmness, they remonstrated against this invasion of the common rights of British subjects. This was construed into an audacious attack upon the privileges and interests of these military monopolists. And from that time . . . they have set their faces against them and me. They have had no grants and no servants. Mr. Boston . . . has been the whole time unemployed.'

Much as Boston protested against the officers' monopoly, their shameless profiteering on imported goods opened up opportunities for home-grown competition. By the middle of September 1795, Palmer was telling his clergymen friend Mr Lyndesay that Boston and Ellis 'manufacture beer, vinegar, salt, soap, etc, for sale. I have a farm.' A month later, he told another correspondent that 'Ellis lives with me to brew and farm'. On 16 September 1796, Palmer informed Lyndesay, 'We brew for our lives, sell our beer to considerable profit, which is in high estimation.'

No amount of beer, however, could curb the colony's thirst for imported spirits. Three years earlier, the home secretary had warned Grose, 'Great attention seems necessary to prevent spirits from being secretly sold and conveyed to the convicts' and instructed him to 'strictly enforce such orders and directions as appear most likely to prevent the secret and clandestine sale'.

Grose applied these instructions literally, taking measures to clamp down on the 'secret and clandestine' sale of spirits to convicts – for instance, by threatening to pull down the house of anyone caught selling spirits without a licence. He did little, however, to interfere with the officers' monopoly.

'Little other conversation is heard but buying, selling, bartering &c,' the chaplain, Richard Johnson, wrote to a friend in London. '[M]any of our officers have turned Merchants – Shopkeepers &c – wholesale and retail dealers in spirituous Liquors – a Convict can go & purchase a Bottle, a Pint of Rum from an officer & a gentleman. Some, not quite so open, employ their wash woman or others in this way – & in this way many are making their fortunes – spirits . . . adulterated with water, little better than the sailors grog, sold for 40 shillings a gallon.'

The reverend Mr Johnson was not alone in worrying that, under Grose, New South Wales was turning into a colony of bootleggers.

13

Grog purchases what money will not

In May 1794, after 18 months in charge of the colony, Grose wrote to the secretary of state of his intention 'to return by the first opportunity'. Plagued by wounds he had received as a soldier in the American Revolutionary War, Grose suffered in the Australian climate and had already indicated his desire to return to England. 'I am so very much teased in the hot weather with the breaking out of my wounds,' he wrote, 'that I feel I cannot in safety hazard the event of another summer.'

Pleased with his achievements as lieutenant-governor, Grose trusted himself to be 'able to give a satisfactory account' of his early departure. Although expensive to maintain, Grose's policy of entrusting the colony's future agricultural development to the civil and military officers rather than to free settlers and time-expired convicts had been a notable success. Domestic production had shored up the settlement's previously unreliable food supplies: land under cultivation was expanding at an ever-increasing rate and livestock was flourishing.

'The permission given to officers to hold lands had operated powerfully in favour of the colony,' Collins wrote in May 1794. 'They were liberal in their employment of people to cultivate those lands; and such had been their exertions that it appeared by a survey taken . . . by Mr. Alt that nine hundred and eighty-two acres had been cleared by them since that permission had been received . . . in the short period of fifteen months, the officers, civil and military, had cleared more than half the whole quantity of ground that had been cleared by government and the settlers, from the establishment of the colony to the date of the governor's departure. The works of government, however vigilantly attended to, always proceeded slowly, and never with that spirit and energy that are created by interest.'

Like Grose, Collins appeared to have forgotten that while private interest might have been the chief motivation behind the officers' energetic land-clearing, the work itself was being done by convicts fed and clothed at public expense. This fact had not gone unnoticed by the British Government, which strongly disapproved of Grose's generosity.

Before leaving New South Wales, Grose received instructions from London that, in future, civil and military officers were to be allowed two convicts each (rather than ten) 'to be maintained out of the public stores for two years longer, but after that period they should themselves maintain such as they are desirous of keeping'. Where grants of lands were made to officers who continued to receive their pay, the government expected them to feed and clothe any additional convicts out of their own pockets.

These orders put Grose in an awkward position. Under his administration, the officers of the New South Wales Corps had become a privileged class. Any attempt to wind back those privileges was certain to be met with hostility and resistance. Grose's response to Dundas's dispatch was to point out that any fewer than ten convicts per officer would not be enough to cultivate the land. He resolved to take no action until he had received further instructions from England. Long before those instructions arrived, Grose had sailed for home, leaving the problem to his successor.

Meanwhile, profiteering by the officers continued to provoke resentment from established settlers and newcomers alike. The Reverend Samuel Marsden, recently arrived from England, complained in his first letter home, 'I [could] have laid in Liquor at Rio for 6d. per Bottle, [which would] have been worth 5 [shillings] to me here.'

In June 1794 the *Britannia* returned with more goods for sale. The captain, Mr Raven, had diverted to Batavia after being warned of French privateers 'infesting' the Bay of Bengal. Collins's description of the cargo listed large quantities of beef, pork, sugar and rice but omitted to mention spirits. Richard Atkins, however, noted in his diary that the 'Private trade' included 'Arrack 164 Gall'.

American ships loaded with grog continued to come. A fortnight after the *Britannia* arrived from Batavia, the *Halcyon* from Rhode

Island showed up 'with a cargo of provisions and spirits on specula-tion'. Her master was Benjamin Page, who in December 1792 had brought 7597 gallons of American spirits in the *Hope*. His cargo this time was more modest: 'five thousand gallons of spirits', according to Collins, as well as 'eight hundred barrels of beef and pork' and 'a small quantity of tobacco, tea, nankeens etc'.

The colony had prospered in the 18 months since Page's last visit, and the day had come when the colonists were able to inform speculative traders that 'we were not in want of any casual supplies'. Page's salvation lay, as always, in the cargo of grog he was carrying. 'The whole of the spirits were purchased by the officers of the settlement and of the garrison at the rate of six shillings per gallon,' wrote Collins, 'and afforded, together with what had been received from Batavia by the *Britannia*, a large and comfortable supply of that article for a considerable time.'

For visiting ships, timing was everything. Just three weeks after Benjamin Page succeeded in offloading his spirits at six shillings per gallon, the *Hope* returned to Sydney under a different master, who was 'greatly disappointed' to be able to get a mere 'three shillings and sixpence per gallon' for his cargo of spirits, while 'his salted provisions no one would purchase'.

The regular arrival of trading ships and the fact that their provi-sions were no longer desperately needed – and could even be turned away – were further evidence of the colony's transformation under Grose. 'It might be safely pronounced,' Collins wrote in May 1794, 'that the colony never wore so favourable an appearance as at this period; our public stores filled with wholesome provisions; five ships on the seas with additional supplies; wheat enough in the ground to promise the realising of many a golden dream; a rapidly-increasing stock; a country gradually opening, and improving everywhere upon us as it opened; with a spirit universally prevalent of cultivating it.'

But wheat 'in the ground' did not automatically end up in the government stores. Collins regretted the tendency of some settlers to dispose of their grain by other means, 'some by brewing and distilling it; some by baking it into bread, and indulging their own propensities in eating; others by paying debts contracted by gaming'.

The increase in gambling seemed inextricably linked to the traffic in spirits. '[O]nly yesterday,' the chaplain reported in June 1794, 'sixteen were detected gaming near the Church, & during the Time of Service'.

In terms of productivity, nobody demonstrated the success of Grose's agricultural policies more than John Macarthur, who had arrived in New South Wales as a lieutenant on 28 June 1790 with his wife, Elizabeth, and their first child. Unpopular with Governor Phillip, who reprimanded him for his frequent quarrels, Macarthur was able to redeem himself under Grose, whose generous grants of land and stock quickly established Macarthur as the most powerful private landowner in the colony. His success in being the first to clear and cultivate 50 acres of land (albeit with the help of free convict labour) won him a grant of another 100 acres.

By August 1794, Macarthur was able to boast of having a farm 'containing nearly 250 Acres, of which upwards of 100 are under cultivation . . . Of this years produce I have sold £400 worth & I have now remaining in my Granaries upwards of 1800 Bushels of Corn.'

Macarthur's celebration of his own (and, by extension, Grose's) achievements was coloured by his antipathy towards Phillip:

The changes that we have undergone since the departure of Governor Phillip are so great and extraordinary that to recite them all might create some suspicion of their Truth. From a state of desponding Poverty, and threatening Famine, that this settlement should be raised to its present aspect, in so short a Time, is scarcely credible.

The slight against Phillip was unfair as Phillip had experienced problems rarely faced by Grose. While the convicts Phillip had at his disposal were often sick, weak with hunger and incapable of serious labour, the convicts Grose supplied to the officers were well fed and highly motivated, not by the distant promise of emancipation but by the immediate promise of grog. 'Not being restrained from paying for labour with spirits,' wrote Collins, 'they [the officers] got a great deal of work done at their several farms (on those days when the convicts did not work for the public) by hiring the different gangs.'

The result was a colony in which the possession of alcohol was a gauge of both prosperity and ruin. The monopolistic terms of trade, if allowed to continue, all but guaranteed that the officers would make their fortunes at the cost of making all the other settlers bankrupt.

'In a country like this, where money is really of no value, and rum everything, you must perceive the necessity of my having a constant supply by every vessel,' Thomas Muir, one of the Scottish martyrs, wrote to a friend in London. 'When any money is transmitted, cause a considerable part of it to be laid out at the Cape or at Rio Janeiro, in rum, tobacco, sugar, &c, &c, which are invaluable, and the only medium of exchange. We bought some rum at Oris for 18d the gallon, and can sell it for 30 shillings [a mark-up of 2000 per cent]. . . For a goat I should pay in money £10 sterling; now, for less than eight gallons of spirits, at 18d the gallon, I can make the same purchase.'

A member of the New South Wales Corps commented after two years in the colony, 'Liquor, or more properly grog, purchases what money will not.'

Regular importations ensured that cellars remained full. In September 1794 the *Britannia* sailed for the Cape of Good Hope on another voyage of speculation for some of the civil and military officers. In March she returned after what Atkins described in his diary as a 'remarkable quick passage of 6 Months'. She brought '33 horses, 9 Ewes & a Ram', together with 'a great quantity of Spirits, Sugar &c. the most of which was private trade on acc.t of the Officers'.

In an uncharacteristically wry paragraph, Collins noted, 'On the 17th St. Patrick found many votaries in the settlement. Some Cape brandy lately imported in the *Britannia* appeared to have arrived very seasonably; and libations to the saints were so plentifully poured, that at night the cells were full of prisoners.'

The combination of payment in spirits and a policy that diverted convicts away from public works onto private farms had led to a labour shortage on government land. 'Public field-labour was entirely at a stand[still],' Collins wrote in January. A muster found

50 convicts who should have been working for the public 'without any employment', while others were 'at large in the woods, runaways, and vagabonds'. Most were rounded up and 'sent to hard labour' in the government grounds at Parramatta and Toongabbie, along with 'a large gang, formed of bricklayers, brickmakers, timber-carriage men &c.' who were put to work preparing the ground for wheat.

According to Collins, they didn't work very hard. 'In several districts native boys between the ages of eight and fourteen were living among the settlers and in some cases were rationed from the public store. Some of the older boys were found to work twice as well as an assigned convict.'

Since Grose's departure in December, the colony had been under the command of Captain William Paterson, the senior officer in the settlement. There was still no sign of John Hunter, the man appointed by the British Government to be the next governor. (He was still in England.) Before leaving Sydney, Grose had given Paterson a letter to deliver to Hunter on his arrival. 'The colony is at this time in so flourishing a state,' he wrote, 'and the officer I leave to command every way so capable of the duty of it, that no evil consequences can possibly attend my going away.'

Certainly there would be no evil consequences for the New South Wales Corps. Under Grose, the officers had become a law unto themselves, and Paterson, as temporary administrator, made no attempt to check their often arbitrary use of authority or to rein in their trading and farming activities.

Under Governor Phillip, the granting of land had been strictly tied to an undertaking by the recipient to occupy and improve the land. The rum economy had put an end to that. In early 1795 Atkins reported land grants changing hands between soldiers and settlers for 'a few Gallons of Spirit . . . 2, 3, or 4 Gall. of Spirit will get a grant of 25 Acres . . . every Soldier indiscriminately has a grant, and of the whole amount[ing] to 400, not 30 have kept them.'

Many of the new grants were for land on the banks of the Hawkesbury River. The rich black soil was the best in the colony, so fertile that 'one man had in three months planted and dug a crop of potatoes'. But violence quickly erupted between the Aboriginal people and the settlers. The truce that Phillip had struggled so hard to achieve was now in ruins.

On 28 March 1795 a settler named Thomas Webb, who had moved from his farm at Liberty Plains to another on the banks of the Hawkesbury, was attacked while working on his land. At about the same time, an Aboriginal party threw a spear at some soldiers who were travelling up the river in a small boat. 'All these unpleasant circumstances,' wrote Collins, 'were to be attributed to the ill treatment the natives had received from the settlers.'

In one case, a group of settlers 'seized a native boy, and, after tying him hand and foot . . . dragged him several times through a fire, or over a place covered with hot ashes, until his back was dreadfully scorched, and in that state threw him into the river, where they shot at and killed him'. While grudgingly accepting the settlers' claims that the boy had been sent among them as a spy and 'was returning . . . with an account of their weakness, there being only one musket to be found among several farms', Collins commented, 'many still considered it as a tale invented to cover the true circumstance, that a boy had been cruelly and wantonly murdered by them'.

The situation rapidly worsened. By May, an 'open war' seemed to have broken out between the Aboriginal people and the settlers; news raced through the settlement that two Europeans had been killed, one a settler named Wilson and the other a freeman, William Thorp. Large groups of men, women and children ransacked the settlers' corn, carrying off the cobs in blankets and nets. 'In their attacks they conducted themselves with much art,' wrote Collins, 'but where that failed they had recourse to force, and on the least appearance of resistance made use of their spears or clubs.'

In just a few weeks, five people were killed and several wounded. Without drastic action, Paterson 'very much feared they [the settlers] would have abandoned the settlement entirely and given up the most fertile spot which had been discovered in the colony'.

The military response was swift and ruthless. Paterson sent a party of the New South Wales Corps from Parramatta with instructions to 'destroy as many as they could meet with of the wood tribe . . . in the hope of striking terror, to erect gibbets in different places, whereon the bodies of all they might kill were to be hung'.

Several Aboriginal people were reported to have been killed as a result of the punitive action, but as none of the bodies were found it was impossible to say how many. Several prisoners – a man, five women and some children – were also taken and sent to Sydney; one of the women, a nursing mother, had been shot through the shoulder and the same shot had wounded the baby. Both were 'placed in a hut near our hospital, and every care taken of them that humanity suggested'. The man, who was said to have played a role in several of the Hawkesbury murders, soon escaped from the settlement in Sydney and swam to safety across the harbour.

Like Phillip, Paterson hoped that, by treating his captives well, 'some good effect might result'. But, after reaching the conclusion that 'coercion, not attention, was more likely to answer his ends', he sent the women back.

As a deterrent to further violence, Paterson's punitive action was a failure. As soon as the soldiers were withdrawn from the Hawkesbury, Aboriginal warriors attacked a farm near Richmond Hill, killing the owner, William Rowe, and 'a very fine child'. Rowe's wife, 'after receiving several wounds, crawled down the bank, and concealed herself among some reeds half immersed in the river, where she remained a considerable time'. Eventually, she was rescued and taken to the hospital at Parramatta.

Another party of the corps was immediately dispatched to the Hawkesbury to stop the violence. The posting of garrison troops now became permanent. Soldiers were distributed among the settlers for their protection – a protection that Collins considered 'many of them did not merit'.

It was not only the settlers at the Hawkesbury who came under attack. Atkins described 'an unfortunate *rencontre* . . . between the Natives and the Constables who guard the corn at Toongabee'. In the morning, an Aboriginal party of about a dozen had been driven out of the corn, laden with bags full of cobs. That evening, an even larger group returned and again 'began filling their baggs'. When the constables attempted to drive them away, the Aboriginal men turned on them, hurling their spears without hitting anyone. In the struggle that followed, 'one was shott and one cut down with a sword, the head of one is brought in and the Lt. Govr. has preserved it, as a present for Dr. Hunter'.

By the winter of 1795 there were more than 400 settlers on the Hawkesbury. Land granted by the government extended for nearly 30 miles along the banks on both sides of the river. 'The new Settlement at the Hawkesbury is one continued scene of drunkeness,' wrote Atkins, 'the Settlers selling their crops for Liquor.'

Feckless settlers with no aptitude for farming flocked to the Hawkesbury, lured by the fertile soil. 'The farmers now every where began putting their wheat into the ground,' Collins wrote in April, 'except at the [Hawkesbury] river, where they had scarcely made any preparations, consuming their time and substance in drinking and rioting; and trusting to the extreme fertility of the soil, which they declared would produce an ample crop at any time without much labour.'

In May, Atkins reported that within the space of six days:

one man fell into the River and was drownded. A Woman drownded herself, A Man Kill'd his Wife; and a poor inoffensive Settler because he would not join in the debaucheries of his neighbours, had his stack of Corn and house set on fire and burnt. These are the effects of Liquor. It would be impossible to discribe the scenes of villany and infamy that passes at the Hawkesbury. If we have not soon a change of Government no mans life will be safe.

In a private letter to Edward Laing, assistant surgeon to the New South Wales Corps, Collins commented, 'the Natives at the Hawkesbury are murdering the Settlers – [Lieutenant] Abbott & [Ensign] Mackellar with Co Soldiers are, in return, murdering the Natives (but it cannot be avoided)'.

Such was the state of the colony when John Hunter made his long-awaited return, accompanied by the homesick Baneelon. Hunter was supposed to have sailed to Australia with the *Reliance* and the *Supply* in March 1794, but the ships did not leave England until February 1795. They anchored at Sydney Cove on 7 September 1795.

Besides a few barrels of salted provisions picked up at Rio de Janeiro, the ships brought a town clock and the components of a large windmill.

Four days after his arrival, Hunter was sworn in as governor of New South Wales. The following year, Paterson would return to England on sick leave.

Hunter's reappearance after an absence of four and a half years coincided with the return of some cattle that had strayed from the settlement seven years earlier and been given up as lost. During the colony's early months, livestock had been irreplaceable, and the loss of the cattle caused anguish. The herd now numbered 39, including 'three large bulls', and their recovery augured well for the new governor.

Fifty-eight years old when he took office, Hunter was widely respected for his naval skills but had little experience of government. His career had been steady rather than spectacular, characterised by competence, courage and loyalty but lacking the personal charisma and intellectual agility that would have strengthened his hand as governor.

For all his technical expertise as a seaman, it had taken him until the age of 43 to obtain his first commission as a lieutenant. (By contrast, his successor, Philip Gidley King, was commissioned at the age of 20.) As a naval officer, Hunter was able to exert his authority over subordinates who respected rank and discipline. The majority of the people whom he came to New South Wales to govern had scant respect for either. The officers on whom he would rely had no personal loyalty or allegiance to him; they had little to gain by supporting Hunter and much to lose. Hoping for cooperation, he would be met instead with obstructiveness and the threat of disobedience.

The population of New South Wales when Hunter took over from Paterson was approximately 3200, of which 59 per cent were convicts. Nearly all the rest were civil and military officers and convicts whose sentences had expired. Materially, the colony had never been healthier, but this did not stop the chaplain, Mr Johnson, from denouncing the Grose and Paterson administrations for 'their extortion, their despotism, their debauchery and ruin of the colony, driving it almost to famine by the sale of liquors at 1,200 per cent'.

In October, Hunter began to reverse the changes made by Grose by taking the 'police and civil duties of the town and district of Sydney' away from the military and returning them to the civil magistrates. Macarthur, whose powers as inspector of public works were 'practically absolute in the district of Parramatta', found himself replaced by Richard Atkins. On the contentious issue of how many convicts the officers should be allowed to keep, Hunter decided to ignore the government's instructions and leave things as they were.

Violence continued at the Hawkesbury, where Hunter's hopes of using Baneelon as a peacemaker foundered due to Baneelon's influence 'not extending to the natives at the river'. In December an Aboriginal group attacked some isolated settlers' huts, 'stripping them of every article they could find . . . An armed party was directly sent out, who, coming up with them, killed four men and one woman, badly wounded a child, and took four men prisoners.'

While Collins hoped that such ferocious punishment would teach the Aboriginal people a lesson, he suspected — correctly — that the soldiers' actions would not deter them from 'prosecuting the revenge they had vowed against the settlers for the injuries they had received at their hands'.

The new year brought two more ships, the *Experiment* from Bengal and the *Otter* from Boston. Arriving with a large consignment of Indian goods, the master of the *Experiment* confidently expected to make 'ten or twelve thousand pounds' from his cargo. The master of the *Otter*, however, 'declared he had nothing for sale; but that he could, as a favour, spare two hogsheads of Jamaica rum, three pipes of Madeira, sixty-eight quarter casks of Lisbon wine, four chests and a half of Bohea tea, and two hogsheads of melasses'.

In January 1796 'some of the more decent class of prisoners, male and female' were given permission to perform a play. The play they chose was Edward Young's *The Revenge*. 'They had fitted up the house with more theatrical propriety than could have been expected,' wrote Collins, 'and their performance was far above contempt. A seat in the gallery could be bought for one shilling or in lieu of a shilling, as much flour, or as much meat or spirits, as the manager would take for that sum.'

Towards the end of January, a number of settlers applied to the governor for licences to operate stills. Collins considered the request 'strange', since it represented 'a direct disobedience of his Majesty's commands'. Inquiries soon confirmed that the settlers were merely seeking official approval for a business that had been operating furtively for some time, turning out spirits 'of so destructive a nature, that the health of the settlement in general was much endangered'.

Hunter not only refused the application but also 'forbade all persons on any pretence whatsoever to distil spirituous liquors of any kind or quality'. Constables and other officials were ordered to be 'extremely vigilant' in discovering the whereabouts and ownership of 'any article or machine for the purpose of distilling spirits' and to give this information to the magistrates, who would pass it to the deputy judge advocate. In the course of this government-ordered sweep:

> several stills were found and destroyed, to the great regret of
> the owners, who from a bushel of wheat (worth at the public
> store ten shillings) distilled a gallon of a new and poisonous
> spirit, which they retailed directly from the still at five
> shillings per quart bottle, and sometimes more. This was not
> merely paid away for labour, as was pretended, but sold for
> the purposes of intoxication to whoever would bring ready
> money.

William Hogarth's 1751 depiction of a gin-sodden London was echoed half a century later by Jeremy Bentham's diatribe against a rum-drenched Sydney. (*Tate Images*)

Marine Lieutenant Ralph Clark complained about the officers on the *Friendship* regularly being 'tipsy'. The wine on the *Sirius* was finished five weeks before the fleet reached Sydney. On 19 December 1787 Lieutenant William Bradley noted grimly in his journal: 'The wine being out, our allowance was order'd a Quart of Grog and a Quart of Water per day.' *(National Maritime Museum)*

Admiral Edward Vernon, nicknamed 'Old Grog', earned the wrath of sailors by ordering their rum to be mixed with water. *(National Portrait Gallery, London)*

Sydney Cove. Port Jackson. 1788.

After an abortive landing at Botany Bay, Governor Arthur
Phillip chose Sydney Cove (TOP, in a watercolour by Lieutenant
William Bradley) as the site for the new settlement. The following
year, a kidnap party led by Lieutenant Bradley captured two Aboriginal men,
Colbee and Baneelon (BOTTOM). Bradley considered the kidnapping 'by far the
most unpleasant service I ever was ordered to execute'. With fewer than 250
marines to protect the colony, security was a constant worry. In this 1786
portrait by Francis Wheatley (INSET), Phillip is shown holding plans for a fort to
be built in New South Wales. *(Images courtesy State Library NSW)*

TOP: Under Governor King, Sydney rapidly expanded to the south and east. In 1803 alone the number of houses doubled. BOTTOM: If you look closely at 'Sydney Cove', painted by John Lewin in 1808, you can just make out the casks being rolled ashore. Born in England, Lewin became Australia's first professional artist. *(Images courtesy State Library NSW)*

Like his predecessors, William Bligh (LEFT) had firm orders from the Home Secretary to control the grog trade. He made a better job of it than most of them until his arrest in 1808. This painting of Bligh being pulled from under a bed at Government House (TOP) was put on display, no doubt with the aim of snuffing out support for the ousted Governor by depicting him as a coward. *(Images courtesy State Library NSW)*

PROCLAMATION.

GEORGE JOHNSTON.

THE PUBLIC PEACE being happily, and, I trust in ALMIGHTY GOD, permanently established, I hereby PROCLAIM the CESSATION of MARTIAL LAW.

I HAVE This Day appointed MAGISTRATES and other PUBLIC FUNCTIONARIES, from amongst the most respectable OFFICERS and INHABITANTS; which will, I hope, secure the impartial Administration of Justice, according to the LAWS of ENGLAND, as secured to US by the PATENT of OUR MOST GRACIOUS SOVEREIGN.

WORDS cannot too strongly convey my Approbation of the Behaviour of the whole Body of PEOPLE, on the late memorable Event.—By their manly, firm, and orderly Conduct, they have shewn themselves deserving of that Protection which I have felt it was my Duty to give them, and which, I doubt not, they will continue to merit.

IN future, no Man shall have just Cause to Complain of Violence, Injustice, or Oppression:—No FREE MAN shall be taken, imprisoned, or deprived of his House, Land, or Liberty, but by the LAW.—Justice shall be impartially administered, without Regard to, or Respect of Persons; and every Man shall enjoy the Fruits of his Industry in Security.

Soldiers!

YOUR Conduct has endeared YOU to every well-disposed INHABITANT in this Settlement!—Persevere in the same honourable Path, and you will establish the Credit of the NEW SOUTH WALES CORPS on a Basis not to be shaken.

GOD SAVE THE KING.

By Command of His Honor, the LIEUTENANT GOVERNOR.
NICHOLAS BAYLY, Secretary.

Head Quarters, Sydney,
Jan. 27, 1808.

RIGHT: Although not an active rum trader himself, Major George Johnston was on familiar terms with others who were. Johnston announced the end of martial law on 27 January 1808 with the above proclamation. He assured Viscount Castlereagh that Bligh's removal had aroused 'general joy that . . . displayed itself in rejoicings, bonfires, and illuminations'. The euphoria did not last. *(Images courtesy State Library NSW)*

TOP: John Eyre's 'First Government House, Sydney'. William Bligh remained there for a year after the coup, refusing to leave the colony until relieved by lawful authority. King George III's instructions to Governor Hunter (LEFT) cited the 'unrestrained importation of spirituous liquors' as the chief cause of the 'great evils' besetting the colony. After Hunter's removal from office, Governor Philip Gidley King (CENTRE) continued to fight a losing battle against the grog traders. Unable to 'prohibit the use of spirituous liquors', Governor Lachlan Macquarie (RIGHT) taxed them instead to fund an ambitious building program. This included ornate Gothic stables to complement a new government house that was never built. The stables are now home to the Sydney Conservatorium of Music. *(Images courtesy State Library NSW)*

TOP: Governor Macquarie took a keen interest in improving the colony's public houses and granted land to Richard Fitzgerald for 'a handsome commodious inn of brick or stone'. The Macquarie Arms, Windsor, was opened by Macquarie on 26 July 1815 (*sketch by Gary Bell*). ABOVE: James Squire's 900-acre estate at Kissing Point was emblematic of Governor Macquarie's policy of convict rehabilitation. (*State Library NSW*) RIGHT: 'Queen Gooseberry' and her husband 'King Bungaree' were well known in Macquarie's Sydney. Her Aboriginal name was variously recorded as Kaaroo, Carra, Caroo, Car-roo or Ba-ran-gan. It is possible she used this mug to collect her allowance of rum. (*State Library NSW*)

The spread of private stills was both an inevitable consequence of the popular thirst for grog and a manifestation of the entrepreneurialism that had spread through the colony as a result of the New South Wales Corps' trading practices. As much as Collins and others bemoaned its 'destructive' effect on the moral and physical welfare of the settlement, liquor had become an indispensable cog in the colonial economy, and played a key role in the machinery of law and order.

On 29 January 1796 the government posted a reward for the capture of the African-born convict Black Caesar, an absconder who was at large with six or eight vagabonds, all said to be armed. Reputed to have been 'the hardest working man in the country', with an appetite 'so ravenous that he could devour the full ration of three days in one', Caesar survived by stealing food from settlers and vowed never to come in 'nor suffer himself to be taken alive'.

A man named John Wimbow (or Winbow) and his companion spent several days searching for Caesar. 'Finding his haunt,' wrote Collins, 'they concealed themselves all night at the edge of a brush which they perceived him enter at dusk. In the morning he came out, when, looking round him and seeing his danger, he presented his musket; but before he could pull the trigger Wimbow fired and shot him.' Caesar was taken to the hut of Thomas Rose, a free settler at Liberty Plains, where he died a few hours later.

'Thus was the colony at length rescued from the depredations of a ruffian, whom no indulgence could reclaim, nor severity intimidate,' wrote the pickpocket-turned-chief constable, George Barrington,

In recognition of the 'vigilance' he showed in ending the life of Black Caesar, Wimbow was rewarded with five gallons of spirits.

14

Nothing but drunkenness

etween December 1792, when Governor Phillip left New
South Wales, and September 1795, when Governor Hunter
arrived, private enterprise had become the driving force of
the economy. Phillip had left a settlement in which most people were
employed either on public construction or on government farms.
By the time Hunter landed, agriculture was largely in the hands
of officers and small farmers, who produced most of the grain and
owned most of the livestock. So many convicts were employed on
private land that the government struggled to find labour for public
works.

At war with France once again, Britain was spending more than
it could afford propping up its European allies and wanted to limit

the drain on the Treasury caused by Grose's transfer of convict labour from the government to the officers. Hunter faced a dilemma: taking back the convicts and making the government the principal supplier of wheat to the commissary would ruin the livelihoods of the private farmers, who would no longer have a market for their produce. It would also make enemies of the most powerful individuals in the colony, the officers of the New South Wales Corps. Not doing so would mean disobeying direct instructions from the new home secretary, the Duke of Portland.

In a letter to Sir Samuel Bentham, Hunter bitterly regretted having accepted the job, admitting, 'had I been gifted with the power of looking into future events, happy as I shall ever be to obey the commands of His Majesty ... I never should have coveted that which now occupys my endeavours'.

Convinced that the government could never match the efficiency of private farming, Hunter allowed the officers to keep their convicts. '[I]f it is the wish or intention of Government to have this colony increase to a state of respectability,' he advised Portland in April 1796, 'some encouragement must be held out to respectable settlers and industrious people of all descriptions. This can never be the case if it be the intention of Government to cultivate land enough for the maintenance of all the convicts sent here. The farmer will be labouring for a mere subsistence; he can never cloath himself and family if he has no market for his surplus corn, and if Government does not become his purchaser he can have no market. What then, my Lord, must be the consequence? A general indolence, a total inattention to farming, dissatisfaction with their situation, and a desire to quit the country by every opportunity which offers.'

The illicit traffic and reckless consumption of spirits remained the colony's overriding moral concerns. Johnson, Atkins and Collins continued to rail against what they saw as an epidemic of drunkenness and immorality. Yet grog had its uses, as Hunter was forced to concede. 'I have already observed,' he told Portland, 'that much labour is often obtained by a small gratification in the article of spirits.'

Preventing the importation of spirits entirely, he told Portland, was 'next to an impossibility'. However, he could and did attempt to 'put a stop to the great inconvenience of having every little hut a settling-house for the retailing spirits'. The penalty for being caught included the threatened destruction of the offender's house. While some houses were demolished, Hunter admitted that even this draconian punishment 'did not effectually prevent it' and he moved instead to a system of tightly regulated licences for retailing spirits, 'which appear to answer the purpose well, prevent much intoxication, and seem to give general satisfaction'.

The introduction of licences for the sale of liquor brought a facade of legitimacy to an illicit traffic. But tinkering with the mechanics of supply did nothing to address the underlying problem of demand, which had begun to destabilise the settler economy.

The huge mark-ups on imported spirits, and the willingness of many farmers to pay for their grog with wheat, had burdened the settler population with crippling debts. Many of the smallholders were time-expired convicts with no way to pay their debts except by pledging future crops – sometimes for two or more seasons to come. The problem was especially widespread on the Hawkesbury. 'As this was an evil of great magnitude,' wrote Collins, 'the governor set on foot . . . an inquiry.'

The inquiry found a total debt of more than £5000 incurred by settlers at Prospect Hill, The Ponds, the Field of Mars, the Eastern Farms and on the banks of the Hawkesbury. An investigation into the 'appearance of the farms, and the general character of the settlers' found that many were industrious, 'but a great number were stated to be idle, vicious, given to drinking, gaming, and other such disorders as lead to poverty and ruin'.

Hunter's response was to issue a government order forbidding liquor sellers from accepting grain as payment. The penalty for any farmer breaching the order was to be stripped of his convict labour, while the liquor seller would lose his licence.

Granted 'for the purpose of accommodating the public with liquor in moderation', the licences had done little to curb consumption. On the contrary (and despite his assurance to Portland that they had 'prevent[ed] much intoxication'), Hunter lamented in one of his public orders that 'instead of their answering that salutary end, he finds nothing but drunkenness and idleness throughout every part of the settlement amongst that description of people, and he is sorry to add that robberies appear more frequent now than formerly'.

Atkins wrote a succinct entry in his diary: 'I really think that any thing short of a prohibition will fail of stopping this pernicious practice.'

Prohibition in a settlement already awash with spirits could never succeed, but Hunter attempted to reduce their availability by not allowing more to be landed. In August 1796 an American ship, the *Grand Turk*, arrived from Boston with a cargo of 'spirits, tobacco, wine, soap, iron, linseed-oil, broadcloth &c.'. Eighteen hogsheads of tobacco were quickly snapped up and the government bought 'some' spirits at seven shillings per gallon. But the master's hopes of a profitable visit were dashed when Hunter forced him to take away the bulk of his liquor. It would be the first of several attempts by Hunter to clamp down on the officers' import monopoly.

Towards the end of the year, a spate of serious crimes resulted in eight men being sentenced to death at a single sitting of the criminal court. Martin McEwan, a soldier, and three convicts, John Lawler, Thomas Doyle and Michael Doland, were all found guilty of robbing the stores over a period of ten months; a convict, Francis Morgan, was found guilty of the murder of a man named Simon Raven at Cotton's Farm, north of the harbour; and another soldier, John M'Douall, was convicted with two convicts, Matthew M'Nally and Thomas Inville, of robbing the stores.

Morgan was the first to be executed, and his body was 'hung in chains at Pinchgut Island', within sight of Sydney Cove. (According to a much later account of the murder, 'His gain by committing the crime was a half pint of rum.') A week later, McEwan and Lawler were hanged at Sydney; M'Nally and Doyle were hanged the next day at Parramatta. The other three were given conditional pardons.

Collins had no hesitation in finding grog to blame for the crimes. The offences, he remarked, 'did not proceed from an insufficiency either of food or clothing; but from an inordinate desire of possessing, by any means whatsoever, those articles with which they might be able to procure spirits.'

Hunter reacted by issuing a proclamation against the 'danger of attending too great an indulgence in the use of spirituous liquors'.

In spite of the order forbidding the exchange of grain for spirits, the problem of settler debts continued to grow. At a sitting of the civil court in February 1797, writs were issued against a number of settlers for debts totalling thousands of pounds. 'It appeared that to obtain spirituous liquors, these people, the settlers, had incurred debts to so great an amount, as to preclude the most distant hope of liquidating them, except by selling their farms,' wrote Collins. 'Thus all their former industry must be sacrificed to discharge debts which were contracted for the temporary gratification of being steeped in beastly intoxication for a certain length of time.'

Collins was no longer a witness to the events he was reporting, having left the colony in August 1796, and was forced to rely on information (presumably from Hunter) to complete the second volume of his *Account of the English Colony in New South Wales*. In a letter to the Duke of Portland, Hunter expressed his own dismay at the 'vast variety of debts' incurred by settlers to buy spirits, and at the resulting lawsuits that had caused 'the complete ruin of many of them'.

On 6 July the governor informed Portland that newly arrived ships had 'brought spirits enough to deluge again this colony, and to throw it into such state of fermentation and disobedience as wou'd undo all I have been attempting to bring about for the public good'.

By now the full extent of the colony's mania for private trade –
'that rage for speculation and traffic' – had dawned on Hunter. It
wasn't just the military officers who were preoccupied with making
money, he realised, but also 'the majority of those holding situations
under the Crown . . . superintendents, storekeepers, and various other
descriptions of people'. The result, he advised Portland, was that
'public duty was intirely neglected . . . Their private concerns occupy
all their time, and £50 per annum seems to be no object where
£300, £400, or £500 is to be gained by trade.' The situation was so
serious, Hunter concluded, that 'many of these people, if they cannot
be prevail'd on to make their public duty their first consideration,
shou'd be remov'd'.

In an attempt to control the importation of spirits, the governor
had guards placed on board visiting ships, but this failed to stop
smuggling. Hunter now antagonised the officers by refusing to allow
any liquor to be landed beyond what each officer 'wanted for his
private accommodation'. This action, he told Portland, had 'given
much offence' and deepened the growing rift between the almost
60-year-old Royal Navy officer and the recalcitrant, prosperous and
much younger Captain John Macarthur.

Within a year of Hunter's appointment as governor, his enemies
were plotting to get rid of him. In June an 'infamous, scandalous
and anonimous' letter was found lying on a Sydney street. The writer
alleged that Hunter's servants were secretly trading in spirits 'under
the sanction of their master' and that they had 'imposed upon' those
with whom they did business.

Hunter's response to this grave attack on his integrity was to call for anyone who had been involved in trafficking spirits with his servants and had been 'wrong'd by them' to give evidence to the Court of Civil Judicature. He personally guaranteed that anyone coming forward to seek redress would receive his 'support and protection'. At the same time, Hunter promised a large reward of 20 guineas to anyone prepared to give evidence to prosecute and convict the 'authors or advisers' of the 'false, infamous, and scandalous' letter. If the informant was a convict, he or she would also receive 'full and absolute emancipation'.

Nobody claimed the reward, which Hunter believed must have been 'irresistible to a convict', and the governor was forced to conclude that whoever had penned the 'scurrilous' paper had done so with the connivance of 'their superiors'. While on this occasion he did not name names, his dispatches to the home secretary left no doubt that he blamed the officers of the New South Wales Corps. 'No character,' he protested, 'however sacred, however immaculate, is safe here in the present state of this colony if he attempts to oppose that disgraceful traffic [in spirits] which has done so much mischief.'

While the allegations in the anonymous letter might have been nothing more than smears, Hunter was a notoriously poor judge of character. The man he engaged as his 'principal servant', Nathaniel Franklin, was later alleged to have 'got himself link'd into a society of infamous characters of both sexes' and to have committed 'robberys of a very serious nature' against Hunter when he was away from Sydney. When he realised he was about to be exposed, Franklin shot himself in the head. 'I then, too late, discover'd, to my very great loss and expence, that those suspicions were but too well founded,' wrote Hunter.

It wasn't just the settlers who were victims of the officers' greed; the soldiers, too, were forced to surrender their pay for overpriced and unwanted goods pushed on them by their superiors. Joseph Holt, who was transported to Australia for his role in the Irish Rebellion of 1798, published a vivid account of the way the officers of the New South Wales Corps extorted from their men:

Captain Anthony Fenn Kemp, when a soldier came to him for his month's pay, would usually accost him with, 'Well, what do you want?'

'I want to be paid, Sir,' the soldier would say.

'What will you have?' was always Captain Kemp's answer. 'I have very good tobacco, ten shillings the pound, and good tea at twenty shillings the pound, prints at eight shillings a yard,' and so on.

If the poor soldier answered, 'Sir, I do not want any of your goods,' the Captain's comment was, 'You don't? You are a damned saucy rascal . . . Begone, you damned mutinous scoundrel, or I'll send you to the guardhouse, and have you flogged for your impertinence to your officer.'

The soldier, having no redress, would take his monthly pay in property, which he did not want, and then he would endeavor to dispose of what he had received to some person who had money; generally selling it for less than half the price he was charged by his Captain. This system of monopoly and extortion compelled the soldier to serve his Majesty for half his nominal pay; I can prove what I assert, as I have often bought goods from the soldiers myself, upon these terms. It was . . . very provoking to see the officers draw the goods from the public store, to traffic in them for their own private gain, which goods were sent out for the advantage of the settlers, who were compelled to deal with those huxter officers, for such articles as they may require, giving them from 50 to 500 per cent, profit, and paying in grain. It thus would happen, that one of these monopolizers, who never grew a grain, would sometimes have a thousand bushels of wheat to put in the store; and this was the manner in which all those old tailors, and shoemakers, staymakers, man-milliners, tobacconists, and pedlars, that were called captains and lieutenants, made their fortunes; by the extortion and the oppression of the soldier, the settler, and the poor.

Other witnesses confirmed Joseph Holt's account of the officers' rapacity. Robert Murray, who was aboard the *Britannia* when it arrived in June 1793, wrote in his journal, '[T]he meanness practised by the Officers of the N. S. W. Corps exceeds all I could possibly suppose Usurers capable of'. Returning a year later, Murray was even more scathing: 'Of the State of the Colony at this time I need only repeat what I have before said, with the addition that I now thought . . . that Tyranny Opression and Fraud had arrived at their Meridn [meridian] in port Jackson under the Auspiceies [auspices] of the Officers of the New South Wales Corps.'

If the officers' monopoly had been confined to spirits and tobacco, it would have been bad enough, but it extended, according to Maurice Margarot, to 'all the necessaries of life which are brought to the Colony'.

Another of the so-called Scottish martyrs, Margarot was sentenced to 14 years for sedition and arrived on the *Surprize* with the future brewer, John Boston. While in New South Wales, Margarot was linked to several would-be rebellions and became a thorn in the side of the officers, criticising them in letters to the Colonial Office and probably informing on their activities to Governor Hunter and his successor, Governor King. In his evidence to the 1812 Transportation Committee, Margarot explained how the officers cornered the market in 'luxuries; tea, sugar, rum, wine, little matters for clothing, silk handkerchiefs, etc' which they bought from visiting ships and retailed at a huge mark-up.

As well as luxuries, they controlled the trade in 'sieves, hats, clothes, linen, coarse cloth and a thousand other articles' shipped out by the government for the use of settlers and convicts. '[W]hen a ship of that kind has arrived,' Margarot told the parliamentary committee, 'and the goods have been landed in the King's stores, after a few days the stores are opened to the officers, who go in, lay their hands upon every thing of value, and have their names affixed to it as purchasers, and they leave nothing but the refuse for the Colony.' Having taken everything they wanted, the officers would then on-sell these goods 'at 500 per cent profit'. A sieve, Margarot told the committee, 'which cost them 5s 9d has been sold for three guineas, and rum I have known sold at £8 a gallon, which cost 7s 6d'.

Asked whether 'civil officers, or military, or both' were engaged in the trade, Margarot answered, 'All of them to a man.' He went further, alleging that in 1797 the officers had colluded in a 'bond' that committed them 'neither to underbuy nor undersell the one from the other', and attributing his later 'persecution' by the officers to his refusal to sign the bond.

Forced to pay exorbitant prices for essential goods, the small farmers also found themselves cut out of supplying food to the public stores. 'There may come a time when the settler shall reap what he has sown,' Thomas Palmer wrote to a friend in Scotland, 'at present, from necessity, he is obliged to sell to an avaricious huckster his wheat at 3s per bushel, who turns it into the stores at 10s, the price which government gives for it . . . If he raises Indian corn, or wheat, it is of little use to him. He must sell it for what he can get to these hucksters. He cannot, like them, turn it into the stores . . . By these means the colony is ruined . . . Every farmer and settler is only a tenant at rack rent to the officers.'

A stronger and more decisive governor, with the unequivocal backing of the home secretary, would have been better equipped to take on the entrenched interests of the officers, but Hunter's instinct was to look for a compromise, and he never felt he had the Duke of Portland's confidence, or even his attention. He was probably correct in both assumptions. Whatever confidence the duke might once have had in Hunter was steadily worn down by subversive letters from Australia criticising his administration.

In May 1798, worried that Portland 'may not have time at present' to read his account of the colony's problems, Hunter wrote in desperation to Lord Sydney. 'Many of our oldest & formerly our best Settlers, have of late been brought to Ruin, their familys beggard, & oblig'd to fall back on the Public store to prevent Starving, intirely thro' the effects of that dangerous & disgraseful traffic . . . which I have been struggling in vain to get the better of.' Since some of the people buying these distressed properties did not have the labour they needed to work them, paddocks were being left idle. As a result, Hunter warned, 'we shall I fear grow less Grain every year'.

It seems unlikely that Lord Sydney would have shared this fear, given the steady flow of letters celebrating the colony's agricultural achievements. The settler debt crisis was real enough, but so was the dramatic expansion of cultivated land under Grose's policy of giving free land and labour to the officers. Hunter's dire prediction reflected both his frustration and his deeply held belief that, 'since the year 1792 . . . the Public Intrest & that of private individuals has been . . . in direct opposition to each other'.

Determined to strike 'at the Root of this very Ruinous trade', Hunter told Sydney of his plans to set up a 'Public Store on Govt. account for the purpose of supplying the labouring People with every European Article they may want, at a moderate Expence, & to be paid in the produce of their Farms or Live Stock'. He also suggested that the government actively participate in the grog trade 'by way of preventing this article from being smuggled into the Colony by Speculators'. By forcing down the price, he was confident of being able to make spirits 'a very precarious article' for foreign traders, who would be 'afraid to venture it'.

These were fighting words. If Hunter followed through on his proposals, the officers' trading position would be under attack from all sides: at a stroke, they would lose their import monopoly, their control of agricultural produce and their retail market for imported goods. Hunter and the officers were now locked in a desperate power struggle.

Nearly two years earlier, the Duke of Portland had received an anonymous letter (perhaps from Macarthur, perhaps not) criticising the new administration and asserting that under Hunter 'the interest of Government is utterly disregarded, its money idly and wantonly squandered, whilst vice and profligacy are openly countenanced'. On 26 February 1799 Portland sent a copy of the letter back to Hunter, asking him to respond to the allegations it contained in order to satisfy the government that they were false. Portland's letter did not reach Hunter until November 1799, by which time another letter ordering him home had already been written.

It must have mortified Hunter to know that the scurrilous accusations against him had been circulating in London for two years, and would continue to circulate for another six months or more before his reply reached Portland. By then, the damage to his reputation would have been done. He brooded on the home secretary's letter for nearly a fortnight before sitting down to answer the allegations against him, dismissing the anonymous writer's 'scandalous insinuations' and railing against the 'horrid depravity and wickedness' of his heart. '[T]he sacred character of our Saviour, were he to appear in this colony in its present state, wou'd not be secure from the dark attack of those whose private views he might oppose in favour of the public interest.'

Hunter's long, petulant and self-righteous letter could only have convinced Portland that its author was not the man to tackle the rum traders. In little over a year, Hunter would be recalled. Until then, his battle against the grog continued.

Like the rabbits that had come out with the First Fleet, illegal stills were spreading through the colony. Hunter issued numerous General Orders aimed at finding the illegal distillers and destroying their stills. Typical was the order of 28 February 1799, which called on 'the aid and exertion of the whole body of officers, whether civil, military, or naval' to 'use every means in their power to detect the guilty person, and to seize or destroy the utensils they may have provided for a purpose so certainly calculated to ruin the present healthy state of the inhabitants of this territory'.

The penalty for free settlers was severe: 'every indulgence they may have hitherto received from Government shall be immediately withdrawn, and they shall be ordered to quit this colony by the earliest opportunity'. Convicts were to be punished in any way the court thought fit.

As usual where grog was concerned, the profits outweighed the deterrents. In March 1799 Hugh Murphy, Patrick Conway, William Flynn and Jacob Hamilton were all found guilty of operating a still. Another man, Owen McNanamy, confessed to having operated an 'unlawful still' for ten months with the help of a constable, Henry Kable. As well as warning him 'to put the still out of the way' when an inspection was likely, Kable had 'given a fair price for the liquor'.

Accepting Kable's improbable claim that he thought the law against stills had been suspended, the magistrates let both men off with a reprimand. 'A Bottle of Liquor [was] produced,' the court records noted drily, 'the Quality of which was declared to be good.'

Behind some of the small-time bootleggers stood more powerful interests. Writing to Portland, Hunter accused unnamed officers of having sought permission ('after I had given directions for the destruction of stills') to erect a still, which he had refused. Soon afterwards, Hunter received information that 'this party had hir'd some Irishman who had a knowledge of making what they call's whisky, and that they labour'd in the night-time in this forbidden trade, and that they sold this pernicious article at forty shillings p'r gallon'.

In March 1799 the recently promoted Lieutenant Colonel Paterson was ordered by the Duke of Portland to return to the colony to investigate reports of 'abuses which are practiced and countenanced by the officers of the New South Wales Corps, who, among other instances of impropriety, are stated to be in the habit of purchasing spirits and other articles in New South Wales and retailing them at the most exorbitant prices to the lowest orders of the settlers and to convicts'.

A trained horticulturist, Paterson had kept himself busy while on sick leave advising Sir Joseph Banks on plants and trees suitable for growing in the colony. He sailed for Australia on the supply ship *Walker*, charged with the task of putting an end to the 'abuses' of the New South Wales Corps and mending the 'sullied' reputation of His Majesty's officers.

Paterson would never see England again.

15

The children are abandoned to misery

lthough he did not know it, Hunter's time as governor was
already running out when Paterson arrived on 3 November
1799 to resume command of the New South Wales
Corps. While the order to recall Hunter had not yet been sent,
arrangements had already been made by Portland for Philip Gidley
King to take over the governorship.

Paterson's instructions were to investigate the rum traders. In
effect, he was investigating Hunter's tolerance of the rum trade, which
had continued in the face of repeated instructions from London to
stop all traffic by officers.

Aware of the scathing personal attacks against him, Hunter initially
suggested to Paterson that it was inappropriate for the investigation

to begin while he remained governor. Hunter knew that King was returning to the colony in the role of lieutenant-governor, and his solution was for Paterson to defer his investigation until King arrived. His procrastination only convinced Paterson that he was not up to the job. 'I cannot help declaring,' Paterson wrote to Sir Joseph Banks on 28 November, 'that a more active & a more determined person is wanted in this Colony for their Governor.'

Hunter's fecklessness in dealing with the rum traders was shown up by two incidents on either side of the new year. On 2 December a captured Spanish merchant ship was brought into Port Jackson. 'Her cargo,' Hunter told Portland, 'consists chiefly of a quantity of spirit, and a larger proportion of wine.' To nobody's surprise, 'officers of every description' applied for a share of the grog.

Although dismayed by the arrival of another cargo so 'dangerous to our general concerns', Hunter allowed the rest to be bought by settlers who would otherwise be 'oblig'd to pay some of the monopolists not less than £4 4s a gallon for an adulterated spirit, for the purpose of paying part of the labor employ'd upon their farms'. This, he assured Portland:

> will in some degree check the monopoly for a time, and ease
> the immense expences attending the cultivation of land . . .
> I am in hope [the cargo] will be found far less injurious than
> it otherwise would have been, for to prevent its being landed
> is not possible . . . of various evils, therefore, I am of opinion
> what I have proposed will be found among the least.

A month later the *Thynne*, a 150-ton square-rigger, arrived in Port Jackson laden with provisions from Bengal. The Danish-flagged ship had been secretly chartered by the officers of the New South Wales Corps. Among the 'many useful & much wanted articles' it brought to the settlement were '40 bales cloth, 542 mounds sugar, 100 chests tea, 35 mounds soap, 25 mounds black pepper, 7 mounds coffee . . . 500 pairs shoes' and '1 box indigo'. The cargo also included 9106 gallons of rum.

As usual, Hunter's instinct was to refuse permission for the spirits to be landed. He relented, however, after Macarthur convinced him that by allowing the officers to buy the *Thynne*'s cargo of grog 'at a moderate price', he would save them from having to make 'large purchases from adventurers', thereby leaving 'the lower description of inhabitants without any competitors in the purchase of any cargoes that may be brought for sale'. According to Macarthur, this magnanimous behaviour on the part of the officers would put a stop to 'unfounded' accusations of monopolising.

'Although this vessel's cargo consists of many things much wanted here,' Hunter told Portland, 'yet she has brought fifty legars of spirits, which the gentlemen say is for the benefit of their respective farms, and that when divided amongst their number will not appear so large a proportion as to be attended with inconvenience.'

Nobody, of course, was more adept at dealing with the 'inconvenience' of shifting large quantities of imported spirits than the officers of the New South Wales Corps. Hunter conceded that by allowing the importation he was confirming the allegations made against him in the anonymous letter, but he felt he had no choice.

'To oppose its being landed, my Lord, will be vain on my part, for the want of proper officers to execute such Orders as I might see occasion to give.'

At the same time as Hunter allowed the officers to land spirits from the *Thynne*, 18 settlers signed a petition asking the governor's permission to buy a cargo of spirits ('13 pipes of rum, at 7s. per gallon' and 'a cask of port wine, at 7s. 6d. per gallon') from the *Minerva*, which had recently arrived from Ireland with 162 male and 26 female convicts. 'They are desirous of procuring spirit at a moderate rate,' Hunter told Portland, 'which they say is intended to be applied to the advantage of their farms in hiring labour . . . If the officers receive permission to land what they want, and the others are refus'd, then we shall be accus'd of encouraging monopoly in the hands of the officers, and refus[ing] the comforts which are wanted by others.'

Hunter had been outfoxed. Unwilling to allow either importation, he grudgingly gave permission for both. 'I am sufficiently experienc'd here,' he told Portland, 'to know that whilst the article sought after is in this harbour, or indeed any other on this coast, it is impossible to counteract the designs of those who wish to have it.'

Paterson was horrified. 'I have not yet been four months in the colony,' he told Sir Joseph Banks, 'and in that time there has been upwards of Fifty Thousand gallons of Spirits brought into it. From all these circumstances you will easily conceive what a confused state we are in.'

The *Speedy* sailed into Port Jackson on 15 April 1800 with Captain Philip Gidley King on board. He brought a dispatch for the governor from the Duke of Portland. Its contents were devastating.

Portland chastised Hunter for the high costs of running the colony; the excessive consumption of spirits; the officers' trading activities; and the over-generous allocation of convict servants to the settlers. He berated him for ignoring or misunderstanding instructions from London. Hardly an aspect of Hunter's administration escaped criticism.

After stating his 'disapprobation of the manner in which the government of the settlement has been administered by you in so many respects', Portland delivered the final humiliation: 'I am commanded to signify to you the King's pleasure to return to this kingdom by the first safe conveyance which offers itself after the arrival of Lieutenant-Governor King, who is authorised by his Majesty to take upon him the government of that settlement immediately on your departure from it.'

Hunter was too much the dutiful naval officer to question his orders. While promising to give King everything he needed and to leave the colony 'at the first safe opportunity', he could not conceal the 'pain' Portland's letter had caused him. 'Had I, My Lord,' he wrote, 'been less an enemy to the wretched and disgracefull traffic carried on here, so much to the injury of this colony . . . your Grace, I am well persuaded, wou'd not have been troubled with so many of these despicable attempts and insinuations to my prejudice which appear to have been so very industriously press'd upon your mind.'

Portland's savage criticism finally roused Hunter to action. In April, reports reached him that many of the settlers on the Hawkesbury River had grown so addicted to spirits that they were no longer capable of sowing their land. 'Immediately on hearing their situation,' wrote Collins, 'he forbade the sending any more spirits to that profligate corner of the colony, as well as the retailing what had been already sent thither, under pain of the offenders being prosecuted.'

The home secretary's order to return on the first 'safe' ship gave Hunter a reason for delaying his departure, much to King's chagrin. The *Friendship* was safe and ready to leave by the first week of May, but Hunter felt he could not 'arrange his business' in time and proposed instead to sail on the *Buffalo* in August. In the interim, he refused to relinquish any part of his command.

Frustrated by the delay, and determined to justify Hunter's removal, King made his own damning assessment of the state of the colony. 'Vice, dissipation, and a strange relaxation seems to pervade every class and order of people,' he wrote to Under-Secretary John King in London. 'The children are abandoned to misery, prostitution, and every vice of their parents, and, in short, nothing less than a total change in the system of administration must take place immediately I am left to myself.'

The colony was already so steeped in grog that '[o]ne shipload of spirits is not more than half sold. Cellars, from the better sort of people in the colony to the blackest characters among the convicts, are full of that fiery poison.'

Unfortunately for Hunter, one of the pedlars of the 'fiery poison' was his own aide-de-camp, who was caught selling spirits to a sergeant of the corps at 24 shillings a gallon, having paid only ten shillings a gallon. The 140 per cent mark-up was modest compared with those imposed on the settlers, but it was enough for Paterson to demand that the captain be court-martialled.

Lacking a residence of his own, King had to spend several weeks lodging with Lieutenant Colonel Paterson. No doubt, they found an opportunity to discuss Paterson's investigation into the officers' monopoly.

Aware that he would have a fight on his hands with every shipment of grog that came into the colony, King attempted to choke off the traffic at its source. In May – almost five months before he took over the governorship – he wrote to Lord Mornington, the governor-general of India, asking him to use his influence to prevent grog being shipped from India to New South Wales. 'The quantities of this poison [rum] thrown into this colony,' he told Mornington, 'would be truly distressing to Your Lordship's feelings could you be informed of the evils attendant thereon.'

Whether Mornington had the kind of influence King required, or would be willing to use it, was far from certain. A return dated 31 May 1800 showed that in the previous six months nine ships had arrived at Port Jackson and that 36,590 gallons of spirits and 22,224 gallons of wine had been imported, much of it from India.

While speculative traders continued to visit, the colony had now reached a size that made it attractive to larger contractors. The Calcutta merchants Campbell, Clark & Co. had been trying for several years to establish a trading connection with the settlement. In 1798 one of the partners, Robert Campbell, bought a parcel of land at Dawes Point, on the Sydney Harbour foreshore, where he was given permission to build warehouses and a private wharf. Two years later, in a letter to King, Campbell outlined the company's hopes of obtaining a contract for supplying New South Wales and

Norfolk Island with 'necessaries', either on government account or for sale to the public from the company's warehouses on the harbour.

Campbell had already been negotiating for the same trading rights with Governor Hunter, who, characteristically, had told him to seek approval from the government in London.

As well as establishing a 'house of agency' in Sydney, Campbell wanted to have one of the partners based in the settlement to coordinate the importation of goods from India and London. If permission were granted, he told King, 'your Excellency may depend on the business being conducted on the most liberal footing circumstances will admit'.

The scheme, if it went ahead, would enable Campbell, Clark & Co. to make regular shipments and free the company from the risks inherent in speculative trading; the colony would have protection against shortages, and the officers' monopoly on retailing imported goods would be broken.

King followed Hunter's example by leaving the final decision to the home secretary, but he did not object to the company trading in the interim, although he stipulated that 'with respect to the article of spirituous liquors, any quantity beyond what may be permitted for the domestic purposes alone of the officers and a few deserving industrious settlers will, by His Majesty's commands, be absolutely prohibited from being landed or sold'. Two thousand gallons was the 'utmost' that King was willing to allow to be brought on shore from any single vessel, and even this permission was to be granted or withheld 'according to the number of vessels that may arrive with spirits for sale'.

For goods other than spirits, King made it clear that in return for its import concessions he expected 'fair-dealing' from the company with the objective of 'rescuing the settlers and other inhabitants from the oppressive monopolies that have hitherto existed here'.

While the company would try to get around the limits imposed by Governor King on the importation of spirits, Campbell stuck to his promise to trade on the 'most liberal' terms possible, offering credit and undercutting the mark-ups charged by the officers. Just four years after the company began trading, 200 settlers subscribed to a memorial that ended with the words, 'But for you, we had still been a prey to the Mercenary unsparing Hand of Avarice and Extortion.'

While the officers' trading monopoly was coming to an end, they were determined to maintain their economic power within the colony. In June 1800 King received information that 70 settlers on the Hawkesbury were being sued for unpaid debts. In the ten weeks since his arrival, most of the goodwill he had felt towards Governor Hunter had evaporated. He now sought Hunter's help to force the officers – 'these assassins of publick liberty and destroyers of individual industry' – to relinquish their demands against the settlers. At the same time, King wanted to limit their mark-up 'to about 100 per cent. profit on the goods brought here'.

Worn out and dispirited by the 'deceptions . . . practised upon me' and the 'very imperfect assistance' he had received in his attempts to curb the grog trade, Hunter offered King only tepid support.

The tone of their correspondence became increasingly irritable. King wanted Hunter gone and made little effort to disguise his impatience. 'I have now been here eleven weeks,' he told Under-Secretary

John King. 'The *Buffalo* is still and will in all appearance remain some weeks longer in fitting, so that I do not expect to have the government given up to me before September . . . I am here enduring the cold indifference of one, and the approaching hatred of all.'

More than 20 years younger than Hunter, King had proved himself a capable and imaginative lieutenant-governor of Norfolk Island. Taking over from the cantankerous Major Ross, King had found 'discord and strife on every person's countenance'. By the end of his 20 months in command, Ross had alienated just about everyone: convicts, settlers, officials and marines. Skilled labour was short and there were not enough tools to go round. King worked hard to win over the convicts and to improve the lives of the settlers. During his five years on the island, the settlement became self-sufficient in grain and was able to export pigs to Sydney. All of this helped to reduce the burden on the British Treasury.

In what must have felt to Hunter very much like a calculated affront, King suggested that he consider adopting an ordinance 'similar to one I fixed at Norfolk Island', holding the price of rum at 20 shillings per gallon and 'invalidating all claims for a greater price'. While acknowledging that the final decision 'must rest with your Excellency', King assured Hunter that he would 'have no hesitation on that head' when he took over command.

The pair exchanged increasingly acrimonious letters in July, when the governor reproached King for 'those indirect insults which I have experienced since your arrival'.

There was another reason for the tension between the two men besides Hunter's tardiness in leaving the colony. King had brought instructions for Hunter from the British Government aimed at stamping out the traffic in liquor, but Hunter would not act on them. The traffic continued, seemingly with the governor's approval. Towards the end of August, an attempt was made 'at three o'clock in the afternoon, to land without a permit 1016 gallons of wine and spirits, which were seized at the wharf by the centinel'. The purpose of such an 'incautious and daring' act, Collins surmised, 'could only have been . . . to try the integrity of the centinels, or the vigilance of the police'.

Although Hunter was not due to depart the colony for another month, King had run out of patience. On 8 September he sent Colonel Paterson a copy of the instructions he had delivered to Governor Hunter. At the same time, King asked Paterson to convene a meeting of civil and military officers to hear the new orders. While he told Paterson that 'due regard to the character of an officer' prevented him from making the instructions public, he wanted the officers to be in no doubt that they were to be 'understood as a public order'.

King's 'instructions' were, in fact, anything but. He had arrived in the colony without a personal commission and with no formal instructions other than to succeed Governor Hunter after his departure. (He was not commissioned as governor in his own right until 1802.) King turned the absence of royal instructions to his advantage by framing his own, based largely on conversations with Under-Secretary King before he left London.

Writing on 26 June 1800 to Major Foveaux, who was preparing to assume command at Norfolk Island, King quoted paragraphs of what he haughtily referred to as 'His Majesty's commands' or 'His Majesty's Instructions', when in truth he had drawn them up himself. He had every intention of repeating the trick when addressing the civil and military officers in September.

'To effect the points gained,' he would later tell Under-Secretary King, 'I have throughout acted on my own responsibility without a single written instruction, except the copy of the King's Instructions left by Governor Hunter, which were very unequal to meet a hundredth part of the excesses I wanted to remove.'

The 'excesses' King wanted to remove were the same as those Hunter had tried and failed to remove. King began by condemning the involvement of officers in the trafficking of spirits with 'settlers and convicts' who, he said, had been induced to 'barter away their breeding stock, as well as mortgaging their growing crops, for the said spirits, to their particular detriment and consequent misery of their families'. More woundingly, King criticised the officers for having brought 'His Majesty's service' into disrepute. In future, he warned them, no spirits were to be landed 'from any vessel coming to Port Jackson or Norfolk Island' without a written permit being obtained from the governor. Where the governor should 'judge it necessary to allow of that indulgence to the officers and deserving settlers', the liquor was to be 'for their domestic purposes alone' and should never become 'an object of traffic'.

To remove the incentive for private importations, 'ten pipes of port wine' were to be sent out annually 'for the use of the officers, civil and military, to be divided among them as the Governor may judge proper, at such an advance on the prime cost as will cover freight and wastage'.

The assembled officers must have been flabbergasted by the words they were hearing. King's 'instructions' amounted to a comprehensive attack on the officer corps, which stood accused of 'disgracing His Majesty's service' by trafficking in spirits. Not only were the men's reputations at stake; some also stood to lose large amounts of money.

Two of the officers who attended the meeting, the surgeon William Balmain and his assistant D'Arcy Wentworth, were energetic traders who had stockpiled enormous quantities of spirits – '1,400 gallons or upwards' for Balmain and 3000 gallons for Wentworth. By the terms of Gidley King's instructions, they would be prohibited from selling any of it.

Balmain wrote immediately to King, assuring him that he would not dream of attempting to dispose of a single drop 'without your permission and approbation', while pointing out that 'my loss will be more than my circumstances can possibly sustain if every means of getting rid of them is utterly denied me'.

Anxious to negotiate a solution, Balmain suggested that the government take the spirits off his hands at a price that would give him a return on his investment. 'Twenty shillings per gallon . . . is what I propose to ask,' he told King, 'and I trust it will not be deemed an extravagant demand, having regard to the various risques and losses on such articles, and when it is considered that the market price of them in general very far exceeds my demand.'

Balmain admitted to having bought around three-quarters of his stock at 'ten shillings the gallon', so the mark-up he demanded was around 100 per cent. With Hunter refusing to relinquish command, King did not have the power to authorise such a purchase on behalf of the government. Instead, he agreed to let the two men sell off whatever spirits they had accumulated before his arrival, on the strict proviso that King himself had to approve the purchaser (unless it was a 'commissioned officer, for his domestic purposes') and that the price could not be higher than 20 shillings a gallon.

The relationship between King and Hunter had reached rock bottom by the time Hunter finally embarked on the *Buffalo* on 28 September 1800. His last days were spent scribbling anguished letters to the home secretary and to Under-Secretary King defending his record as governor and denouncing the 'vile hireling writer' whose 'private and treacherous whispers' had poisoned Portland's opinion of him. Hurt and humiliated, Hunter would spend the rest of his life trying to rescue his reputation from the 'odium which I consider is cast upon it by the manner of my recall'.

For all his awareness of the social and economic harm caused by the grog trade, Hunter had found himself powerless to stop it. He neither broke the officers' monopoly nor curbed the traffic in spirits within the colony. His repeated public orders forbidding the landing of spirits had little or no effect.

Collins's remark that '[t]he governor's embarkation was attended with every mark of respect, attachment, and regret' cannot be trusted, since his source was Hunter himself. Perhaps they should be read as the benevolent words of an old friend who understood the humiliations Hunter had suffered and couldn't bring himself to twist the knife.

16

Half to the informer and half to the Orphan Fund

King's first priority as lieutenant-governor (his official title before being sworn in as governor) was to suppress the traffic in spirits, a necessary step towards reforming the economy and reducing the drain on the British Treasury. The perennial shortage of human resources, along with the desire of many farm labourers to be paid (at least partly) in rum, had pushed the cost of labour beyond the reach of farmers whose crops were already mortgaged to pay their debts. '[T]he misery of the greater part of the settlers is the present consequence,' King told the Duke of Portland, 'and . . . the total ruin of the colony at large must be the eventual end if a stop is not soon put to the unwarrantable price of labour and the hitherto existing monopolies and extortionate demands of usurious dealers and their dependent retailers.'

Although spirits never comprised more than a portion of the 'wages' demanded by ex-convict labourers, they were a prized luxury, along with tobacco, tea and sugar (although more desirable than all three). Hunter indicated as much when he told Portland in August 1796, 'Much work will be done by labourers, artificers and others for a small reward in this article [spirits] . . . which money could not purchase.' King himself acknowledged its usefulness by sending 'a quantity of spirits and wine' to Major Foveaux, then acting lieutenant-governor of Norfolk Island, to be used 'in payment for such free people as you may judge necessary to employ'.

Hard physical labour under the Australian sun could hardly be performed on rum alone, but 'extra labour' – work done by convicts in their own time, after they had spent all day building roads or carting bricks, or 'overtime' done by free labourers – could be obtained more easily by the promise of spirits than by the offer of money (or tea). Collins noted that under Lieutenant-Governor Grose, 'those who did any extra labour refused to be paid in money, or any other article than spirits'.

King knew that the rum traders would do everything they could to frustrate his reforms. He realised that his initial popularity could not last. 'My arrival here gives general satisfaction,' he had written to Sir Joseph Banks five months before taking over from Hunter, 'but I believe many will change their tone when their nefarious proceedings are arrested.'

The warm welcome he received from the officers derived in part from their belief that King could be persuaded not to interfere in their business activities. Having ruthlessly seen off his predecessor, the officers saw little reason to fear his replacement.

At first, King tried to maintain friendly relations with the New South Wales Corps even as he undertook to force the officers out of the rum trade. He petitioned the government for extra furniture and rations on the grounds that the soldiers were 'destitute of any kind of bedding or utensils whatever'. He asked for more troops to guard against rebellion by the Irish. And he went out of his way to praise the 'exactness and soldier-like behaviour of the regiment, which would do credit to the oldest regiment in His Majesty's service'. All these gestures were appreciated. But the cordiality could not last.

On 1 October 1800 King published an order declaring war on the 'unwarranted and scandalous monopolies that have existed in this colony' and which had been the cause of 'much distress and ruin to the settlers'. In future the government would decide what goods, if any, it wished to buy from visiting ships and how much the settlers would pay for them at the public store. Anything left over could be bought privately, but the government would set the retail price 'and in no case will private retailers be allowed to charge more than 20 per cent on the purchase from the ship'.

On the vexed subject of grog, 'no person whatever' was to be 'allowed to sell or retail any spirituous liquors', and anyone caught landing spirits or wines from any ship 'without the Governor's OWN PERMIT in writing' would forfeit the liquor to the Crown and be prosecuted 'as the law directs for selling spirits without a licence'.

To prevent further bankruptcies among the settlers, King also ordered that '[n]o greater price than twenty shillings per gallon for spirits' was to be admitted in any civil or criminal prosecution.

Acting on instructions given to Hunter rather than to himself, King achieved what Hunter could not: introducing government control of prices and wages; making it an offence for officers to traffic in rum; and imposing a cap on the profits that could be made from selling goods to the settlers.

In the same month, King announced tough new licence conditions for the sale of liquor. Any retailer caught selling spirits without a licence would be fined ten pounds or sentenced to two months' hard labour on the *Supply* hulk. Second offenders would get three months on the hulk. Constables were empowered 'to enter and search houses, and other places, occupied by those guilty thereof, and seize all such strong drinks as they find'. In the great tradition of colonial justice, the informant would be rewarded with half of the confiscated liquor (the other half was to go to the Orphan Fund).

As well as restricting the importation of spirits and licensing its distribution, King issued orders aimed at reducing drunkenness and the anti-social behaviour that went with it. There was to be no 'gambling, drunkenness, or other disorders' on licensed premises. Opening hours would be limited and any publican or retailer caught 'entertaining any person from the beating of the taptoo [the evening signal recalling soldiers to their barracks] until the following noon, or during Divine Service' would lose their licence and be fined five pounds, 'half to the informer and half to the Orphan Fund'.

King realised, however, that all his efforts to prevent the lawful importation of grog from visiting ships would be in vain if he could not stop the cargoes from being smuggled ashore and moved clandestinely around the settlement. After the discovery of a large haul of illegally landed spirits at Farm Cove, he gave orders forbidding the movement of more than half a gallon of spirits or wine 'from any one place or house to another' without a permit signed by himself, a magistrate or the officer in command at Sydney. He raised the stakes by promising two-thirds of the spirits seized to the person making the seizure (the rest, as usual, to the Orphan Fund).

But however determined he was to control the grog trade, King could not govern without the support of the New South Wales Corps, and the price of its allegiance was a ready supply of liquor.

When the *Royal Admiral* arrived in December 1800 with 7000 gallons of spirits, King bought 2000 gallons on behalf of the government at four shillings a gallon. By government order, 1171 gallons were to be distributed among civil and military officers at five shillings a gallon, with the rest to non-commissioned officers and soldiers at four shillings a gallon, and settlers at five shillings and sixpence. A remission for officers and soldiers of one shilling a gallon 'for 40 gallons per annum each' gave both groups a large incentive to re-sell their allocation to the settlers at a profit of between 30 and 40 per cent. Instead of putting a stop to rum trafficking by the military, King seemed to be encouraging it.

Like Hunter, King issued a series of orders against illegal stills. In August 1805, after 'a Still and Utensils, with a quantity of bad Spirits' were found at the home of a settler at Prospect Hill, King called again on 'the aid and Exertions of the Officers Civil and Military, and particularly those of the Magistracy' to seize and destroy the stills that he knew to be operating in the outlying settlements.

Aware that many of the bootleggers were supported by wealthy backers furnishing 'sugar and other Materials . . . for the purpose of such Distilling', King offered rewards for information leading to the conviction of 'any Settler, Dealer, or other Person of Property'. The rewards were substantial: for a convict, 'an Absolute Pardon, and a reward of Ten Pounds from the Gaol Fund'; and for a free man 'a Reward in Stock equal to Fifty six Pounds'.

Stills continued to be found in the settlements, usually well guarded and often concealed in remote and hard-to-reach places. Two soldiers, James Martin and John Hinder, received information about an illicit still belonging to the Irish rebel Joseph Holt. Fearing that the pair of them would not be strong enough to make the arrest, they sought the help of a constable, John Milton. An hour after sunset the men went looking for the still at the head of a creek behind a place known as 'Barrington's old Farm'. According to a lively report in the *Sydney Gazette*, they 'perceived a fire; and cautiously approaching, beheld two white men sitting by it, and a third procuring fuel at a short distance. Upon a nearer view they were satisfied that a still was then actually at work; and while consulting upon the most proper steps to be pursued for surprising and apprehending the workmen, J. Holt and a man named Healey coming accidently upon them, were instantly secured; the party levelling their pistols at the others, compelled two to surrender themselves, the third effecting his escape. The still . . . was knocked to pieces, and the head and worm taken into Parramatta with the prisoners.' A 'stricter' search later revealed 'seven casks of cyder, containing numerpous ingredients to promote fermentation, &c., together with a few quarts of pernicious spirits, concealed in the cavity of a rock'.

In his report on the incident, Captain Abbott told the governor, 'Never was a place better selected and more secret than it . . . the whole of the apparatus I have got . . . Holt has ackn'ged the material &c., to be his. He has given me information where there are several others, and this night promised to put me in possession of one which he thinks is now at work.'

The quality of Joseph Holt's moonshine must have been better than the *Gazette* implied, because Abbott finished his report by promising to 'send your Excellency a pint of the liquor'.

Meanwhile the grog ships kept coming. Remote as it was, New South Wales remained a lucrative port of call for any ship's master prepared to undertake the arduous voyage with a cargo of liquor. To King, it seemed that 'all the nations of the earth agreed to inundate the colony with spirits'. Britain was as guilty as the rest. 'There is not a ship that comes from England with convicts that does not bring . . . 8,000 gallons,' King told Portland in March 1801. 'One vessel has had the audacity to bring a quantity of spirits and water instead of spirits.'

Such was the 'certainty in America of any quantity of spirits being purchased here' that when Captain Parry arrived from Rhode Island in the *Follensby* with 13,000 gallons of spirits and 15,000 gallons of wine, he expected to sell every drop. King, however, refused Parry permission to land anything except tobacco. Parry begged to be allowed to sell his cargo, pleading 'the assurances of those who had been here before that he could not fail of getting an unheard-of profit'. But his pleas cut no ice with King, who forced the *Follensby* to sail away with its cargo of wine and spirits unsold.

To save other investors from the same fate, Parry persuaded King to write a letter to the American consul in London stating that in future American ships would not be allowed to land spirits at Sydney without the governor's permission in writing. The penalty for smuggling would be the seizure of both ship and cargo. King did as he was asked. He also wrote to the British consul in America, advising him that 'no greater quantity than 300 gallons of spirits will ever be allowed to be imported here from any one vessel'.

By refusing permission for unwanted spirits to be landed, King succeeded, at least temporarily, in reducing the amount of grog coming into the colony. In 1801, according to figures sent by King to the new secretary of state for war and the colonies, Lord Hobart, a total of 39,851 gallons of spirits were landed at Port Jackson and 32,320 gallons were sent away; during the first ten months of 1802, 5115 gallons were landed and 5511 sent away. 'I hope from the quantities sent away in the America and East India ships . . . that further supplies of that poison which has ruined this colony will soon be at an end,' the governor told Lord Hobart.

As well as sending away large quantities of grog, King attempted to deter cargoes from India and America by imposing a duty of 5 per cent on 'spirits and wines, goods of all kinds, except of British manufacture, brought from any part of the world'.

For a time, King was convinced that he had the rum traders on the run. In a letter to Portland, he scoffed at the doomsayers who warned that agriculture would collapse as a result of his decision to send away three ships carrying 58,000 gallons of wine and spirits, and expressed his confidence that 'labour can be carried on without spirituous liquors as well as with'.

By building up the government stores, King broke the officers' stranglehold over the economy. Writing to Lord Hobart, he boasted of the 'great advantage' to the settlers of 'being able to purchase necessaries from the stores at 25 and 50 per cent advance, instead of satisfying their domestic wants from monopolizing individuals, often at 400 or 500 per cent between the ship and the shore'. He told Sir Joseph Banks, 'The former systems of monopoly and extortion I hope are now eradicated. Of spirits I think the inundation is going off, and industry begins to know her produce will not be sacrificed to the infamous wretches that have preyed on the vitals of this colony.'

But King knew the rum traders were not beaten. In a letter marked 'private', he described to Under-Secretary King in London how his enemies 'set their wits to work, not only to thwart my exertions, but also to use every measure that art, cunning, and fraud could suggest to impede my efforts'.

The most dangerous of King's adversaries was Captain John Macarthur. 'I need not inform you who or what Captain McArthur is,' King told the under-secretary. 'He came here in 1790 more than £500 in debt, and is now worth at least $20,000 . . . His employment during the eleven years he has been here has been that of making a large fortune, helping his brother officers to make small ones (mostly at the publick expence), and sewing discord and strife.'

King's problems with Macarthur began soon after he became governor. Macarthur wanted to resign his post as commandant at Parramatta and return to England. Unable to sell his animals privately, except in small lots for slaughter, he proposed selling to the government, telling King that he would be 'very happy to dispose of the whole, with my farms, for the sum of four thousand pounds, which is what the cattle and sheep amount to at the very lowest prices that either species has ever been sold at in this settlement'.

Aware that Macarthur had been a thorn in Hunter's side (it was rumoured that Hunter had challenged Macarthur to a duel, although no such duel took place), King did his best to smooth his exit from the colony, advising the Treasury commissioners in London that the merino-crossed sheep 'would be a great acquisition for Government, from the very great advantage that will hereafter be derived from the Spanish wool, samples of which . . . are sent to the President of the Royal Society'.

The cattle, too, were 'generally of a very superior breed to those belonging to the Government', while the grass farm was 'the best in the colony'. Eager to promote the breeding of livestock in order to end the colony's reliance on imported salt pork and beef, King requested permission to make the deal.

The Duke of Portland took several months to reply before finally giving his approval for the public to buy the 'English cattle and Spanish sheep' (but not the horses and mares). He felt Macarthur's farm would do better in the hands of an 'industrious and thriving settler' than by belonging to the government.

The scale of Macarthur's agricultural activities took the home secretary by surprise. 'I can by no means account for his being a farmer to the extent he appears to be,' he told King. A copy of his letter was shown to the commander-in-chief of the army, the Duke of York, who reiterated that 'the officers be not permitted on any account whatever, to engage in the cultivation of farms, or in any occupations that are to detach them from their military duties'.

While the nature of Macarthur's involvement in the rum trade (unlike that of his fellow officers, Balmain and Wentworth) was ambiguous, King had no doubt that he was in it up to his neck. Macarthur's political power was equally shadowy, with King portraying him in a letter to Under-Secretary King as 'the master worker of the puppets he has set in motion'.

The falling out between the two men was as dramatic as it was inevitable. It arose from a clumsy attempt by Macarthur to turn his commanding officer, Colonel Paterson, against the governor. Paterson and King were old friends, having served together on Norfolk Island a decade earlier. Challenged by Paterson to a duel, Macarthur almost blew off his commanding officer's shoulder. Forced to intervene to protect his own authority, King had Macarthur arrested. Since there was little chance of a court martial in New South Wales finding against Macarthur, King sent him to be tried in England. '[I]f Captain McArthur returns here in any official character it should be that of Governor,' King told his namesake in London, 'as one-half of the colony already belongs to him, and it will not be long before he gets the other half.'

Expelling his adversary might have seemed like a good idea at the time, but the authorities in London had no interest in trying Macarthur, who saved them the trouble of ordering him back to face a court martial in Sydney by resigning his commission.

Macarthur brought with him to England some high-quality fleeces from his growing flock of almost pure merinos and soon set about spruiking his vision of an Australian fine-wool industry – an industry in which he would be the dominant player. Sir Joseph Banks, initially a cautious supporter, later changed his mind and intervened more than once to frustrate Macarthur's efforts, but he was outsmarted on each occasion. With his knack of hitching himself to influential patrons, the sheep baron was able to win support in the Privy Council for his scheme of colonial wool production.

Among those who spoke on his behalf before the Committee on Trade and Foreign Plantations was none other than his former nemesis, ex-governor Hunter. Asked whether he foresaw 'any great objection to making grants of land to persons disposed to increase the flocks of sheep and cattle', Hunter replied, 'There is so much land that I can conceive there can be no objection to such grants', adding that as governor he had 'made some [grants] larger than usual upon applications of that nature, and for that purpose'.

Thanks in part to Hunter's testimony, Macarthur got what he was after. After helping himself to the pick of the royal merinos (including a '4-tooth ram' for 27 guineas) to strengthen the bloodline and quality of his own flock, he set sail for New South Wales on 29 November

1804 with a grant for another 5000 acres of rich pasture, plus 5000 more if his scheme proved successful.

The *Argo*, with Macarthur and his merinos on board, sailed into Port Jackson on 7 June 1805. He returned a wealthy man. His Australian flock was now almost 3000 strong; King estimated that within a year the fleeces would be worth £3600. He had the patronage of Lord Camden, a Privy Counsellor, and had brought with him the nephew of another influential supporter, the royal physician, Sir Walter Farquhar.

During the three and a half years Macarthur was away, King had expanded the colony, reformed the economy and put down a major revolt by Irish convicts. As well as encouraging emancipists and increasing the number of pardons, King had persuaded the British Government to lift the proportion of free settlers to convicts and to improve selection procedures to attract migrants who were more likely to succeed.

King's achievements, however, had come at a cost. His battle with the rum traders had taken a toll on his health and his reputation. After his refusal to allow a cargo of spirits to be landed from the *Atlas*, a series of defamatory poems began to circulate around the colony. Convinced that they were the work of the officers, King had written to London asking for leave of absence while an inquiry was held into the allegations made against him by the 'dark and concealed assassins of my reputation'. His request was interpreted by the home secretary (perhaps at Macarthur's prompting) as an offer of resignation and immediately accepted.

Governor King had taken on the New South Wales Corps and lost. While he had succeeded to a large extent in containing the traffic in spirits, he could not stop it. The weaknesses he had criticised in Hunter were those of which he was all too often guilty himself. The government orders he issued were inconsistent and sometimes contradictory. On his instructions, large cargoes of spirits had been sent away, but vast amounts had been landed.

Philip Gidley King died in England on 3 September 1808, still waiting for the pension he was certain he deserved but that the government could not bring itself to give him.

The rum traders had seen off two governors, Hunter and King, but they would face an altogether tougher opponent in William Bligh.

17

The cultivation of the vine

King's governorship coincided with the first concerted attempt to dilute the 'pernicious' effects of spirits with home-grown wine.

In April 1800, two French prisoners of war, Francois de Riveau and his cousin Antoine L'Andre (or Landrin), were languishing in a prison ship at Portsmouth. The pair, natives of the Loire, had convinced their captors that they possessed 'a perfect knowledge of the cultivation of a vineyard and the whole process of making wine'. Such expertise was in short supply in New South Wales, and when Riveau and L'Andre offered to travel to the colony 'for the purpose of superintending the cultivation of the vine, and the making of wine there', the Duke of Portland jumped at the proposal. He ordered the

Admiralty to release the two Frenchmen and to put them on board the convict ship *Royal Admiral*, bound for Port Jackson.

In return for their freedom, Riveau and L'Andre agreed to work in the colony for three years. In a letter addressed to 'the Governor of New South Wales' (he was unsure whether Hunter or King would be in charge when the letter arrived), Portland expressed his hope that 'the employment of these men will enable you in a very short period to cultivate a vineyard for the Crown of such an extent as to allow of your producing, on the spot, whatever wine may be wanted on the public account'. Gingerly, he added, 'One of the men is also a cooper, a circumstance which will render him very useful to the colony.'

The dream of making wine in Australia had been fermenting for a long time. On 24 January 1791 Watkin Tench wrote in his journal, '[T]wo bunches of grapes were cut in the governor's garden, from cuttings of vines brought three years before from the Cape of Good Hope. The bunches were handsome, the fruit of a moderate size, but well filled out and the flavour high and delicious.' By early December Tench was admiring 'eight thousand vines . . . all of which in another season are expected to bear grapes'.

So well suited were the Australian soil and climate to grape-growing that Tench was convinced 'the grapes of New South Wales will, in a few years, equal those of any other country' and 'their juice will probably hereafter furnish an indispensable article of luxury at European tables'.

Tench was right in his assessment of Australian wine, although a couple of centuries out in his prediction. King, meanwhile, was impressed by the two Frenchmen and had no hesitation in ordering the commissary to pay them 'Sixty Pounds per year each, for a term of three years'.

The early results of their labours were mixed. On 1 March 1802 King told Portland that the Frenchmen had established a vineyard of about 7000 plants 'in as favourable a situation as can be found'. The young plants were doing very well, King assured the home secretary, 'but unfortunately those [older] vines . . . have been entirely blighted'.

If all went well, it would be two to three years before any wine could be produced from the young vines. Only one of the pair was needed to manage the vineyard, so L'Andre, the cooper, was employed making casks. By October 1802 King was able to inform Lord Hobart that 'upwards of 12000 vine cuttings are planted on the side of a hill at Parramatta, formed like a crescent, facing the north which is the best exposition'.

King hoped to persuade free settlers and time-expired convicts to try their hands at wine-making. To this end, part of an English translation of J. B. Laideau's *Method of Preparing a Piece of Land for the Purpose of Forming a Vineyard*, which had been brought out from England along with the two prisoners of war, was published in the first issue of the colony's first newspaper, the *Sydney Gazette*, on 5 March 1803.

Further instalments of Laideau's guide appeared on 12 and 26 March, when the *Gazette* also published a recipe for making brandy:

A copper must be erected over a furnace, the cover to be hermetically screwed on, so that the steam may be forced to pass through a pipe fixed near the cover, and joined to a spiral worm, which passes through a vessel of cold water, and the liquor drawn from a brass cock at the extremity thereof; the copper being charged with wine, the vessel through which the worm passes must be kept continually supplied with cold water, as otherwise the worm being heated would instead of producing a liquid, fly off in smoke. A constant regular fire should be kept up with billets of wood, as should it be too brisk, the worm would drip wine instead of brandy. The first liquid produced immediately after the still being set to work, not being perfect brandy, is returned into the copper whenever it may be replenished with fresh wine, for further distillation; as finally every particle of the wine is distilled into brandy, and nothing but pure water left.

That the colony's first newspaper could, under the governor's nose, publish a how-to guide for an activity he was bent on stamping out was evidence of the contradictions that plagued King's efforts to control the grog trade. The same subscribers who had learnt the art of distilling by reading the *Gazette* would soon read a General Order reiterating the 'Orders and Interdictions that have been given by every Governor of this Territory . . . Forbidding Individuals using Stills for making a destructive Spirit' and calling on civil and military officers to seize the 'Engines of destruction' whose use had been explained in the fourth issue of the *Gazette*.

King, meanwhile, understood that settlers would be unwilling to take the risk of making wine until they had seen whether the government could make a success of it.

Within a year, King's hopes of a flourishing Australian wine industry had begun to unravel. The French vignerons were found to be frauds. In 1804 the governor informed Lord Hobart:

'The two Frenchmen, natives of Nantes, who came out in 1800 to manage this object . . . knew very little of the business. They attempted last year to make wine from some of the best grapes that could be collected, but it turned out so bad, that I shall not trouble Your Lordship with the sample I intended sending.

By the terms of their agreement, Riveau and L'Andre were entitled, after three years' service, either to settle in the colony or be given a passage to England. While he considered that 'their conduct has not merited that indulgence', King grudgingly allowed Riveau to leave. He convinced L'Andre to stay another year 'to see if his progress when left to himself, is better, as he last year made some very good cyder, from peaches, which are now getting very plentiful'.

Partly redeemed, L'Andre remained in the colony, receiving a grant of land in Prospect before moving to Parramatta. On 8 October 1809 the *Sydney Gazette* reported, 'On Tuesday last Mr. Landrin, of Parramatta, was stung on one of the fingers of the right hand by a centipede . . . the whole hand is now covered with an open wound, and the patient is in a most agonizing condition.'

L'Andre survived the centipede sting but died two years later at the age of 40, taking his wine-making skills with him.

By then others, such as George Suttor and Gregory Blaxland, had begun to experiment with wine-growing, using vines brought out from Europe. In 1816 Macquarie was reputedly impressed by a wine made by Blaxland, prompting Blaxland to consider putting all his money into viticulture, provided the governor agreed to supply him with free convict labour and forgive him the usual levy on brandy. Macquarie refused the offer. Six years later, Blaxland became the first person to export Australian wine to London.

18

Dearer than life

To the colony's opponents in England, the grog problem – luridly described in letters home – was evidence of its moral failure. Few were more savage in their criticism than Jeremy Bentham who, in 1802, set out his views in two long letters to Lord Pelham under the heading 'Panopticon versus New South Wales: or, the Panopticon Penitentiary System, and the Penal Colonization System, Compared'.

A political radical with a keen interest in penal reform, Bentham – the son and grandson of attorneys – was scarcely a disinterested commentator on the merits of transportation. With his brother, Samuel, Bentham was the designer of the panopticon, a model prison based on the idea of round-the-clock supervision: individual cells radiated around a central point from which the gaolers could see everything the prisoners were doing.

Bentham had spent a fortune developing and refining the panopticon as a solution to Britain's crime problem. For a while, it was seen as a viable alternative to establishing a penal colony in the Pacific, but problems involved in building it led the government to opt instead for transportation.

Transportation fulfilled none of Bentham's requirements for an ideal penal system: it was expensive; it was of dubious and inconsistent punishment value; it took place too far away to deter crime at home; and its capacity to reform was compromised by the self-interest and corruption of the non-convict population.

After the settlement's difficult early years, the government's interest in the panopticon cooled further due to the supposedly 'improved' state of the colony. It was this alleged improvement that goaded Bentham to write his damning assessment.

Inconveniently for Bentham, official information about the colony was difficult to obtain. The House of Commons itself had heard little about the colony's progress since the early 1790s – a fact that Bentham attributed to the government's desire to cover up the failings of its far-flung penal settlement. Bentham needed a whistleblower, or at least an insider not afraid to report what he had seen. 'Happily a more competent, a more instructive, a more authentic source . . . could scarce have been wished for, than . . . the professed moral historiographer of the colony, the late judge advocate, *Captain Collins*.'

The two volumes of Collins's *Account of the English Colony in New South Wales* (the second, written in response to the 'very flattering reception' given to the first, had just been published) gave Bentham all the evidence he needed to argue his case. They confirmed his grim predictions, he told the penal reformer Sir Charles Bunbury, 'to a degree astonishing even to myself'. Collins, Bentham pointed out, was not merely 'the historiographer, but the panegyrist' of the colony – his observations on the development of the settlement were therefore doubly damning.

If transportation to America had been bad, Bentham asserted, then transportation to New South Wales was worse – much worse. There was no established community for convicts to enter, as there had been in America; the men in charge of the convicts were as immoral as the convicts themselves; once in the colony, convicts had endless opportunity and incentive to commit further crimes; and the place was awash with grog.

Collins himself had been disgusted by the effects of liquor on the colony. His *Account* (especially the second volume) was full of tales of grog-induced sloth, crime and debauchery, dutifully quoted (and slyly italicised) by Bentham, often with his 'observations' alongside:

No. 4, p. 467. *March* 1796. – 'At the Hawkesbury, *where alone any prospect of agricultural advantages was to be found*, the settlers were immersed in intoxication: riot and madness marked their conduct; and this was to be attributed to the spirits that, in defiance of every precaution, found their way thither.

No. 8, p. 203. *March* 1799. – '*To this pernicious practice of drinking to excess, more of the crimes which disgraced the colony, were to be ascribed, than to any other cause;* and more lives were lost through this than through any other circumstance . . . How much, then, was the importation of spirits to be lamented! *How much was it to be regretted, that it had become the interest of any set of people to vend them!'* [It might have been added . . . of *every* set of people without exception. As to its being *become,* so it always was from the first, and so it must be to the last.]

Bentham's intentions (and, not surprisingly, his conclusions) were exactly the opposite of those of Collins. Collins set out to celebrate the colony's progress, Bentham to denounce its very existence. Not even Collins could pretend that reform of convicts was universal, but he was keen to show that it was at least possible. Bentham, on the other hand, was determined to prove that under the conditions that existed in New South Wales – with its rivers of grog endlessly replenished from within and without – reform was *impossible*.

In the preface to volume one, Collins mentioned his desire to give the reader 'some account of the gradual reformation of such flagitious characters as had by many . . . persons in this country been considered as past the probability of amendment'. Bentham's riposte to Lord Pelham was withering. 'So far the magistrate historian,' he quipped. '[A]s to the flagitious characters, there is no want of them; but as to any evidence of their reformation, here and there a white blackamoor excepted, it is all of it in his wishes – there is none of it in his book.'

The purpose of Bentham's extensive quotations from Collins was twofold: to show the immorality of both the convicts *and* of the time-expired convicts who constituted the majority of the colony's free population. The evidence, as far as Bentham was concerned, was not so much their predisposition to crime as their addiction to grog:

> *Improvidence—Indolence—Helplessness*—all *extensive* as well as
> *intense*, to a degree scarce conceivable in this country, were the
> prominent features of this reformation colony, down to the
> time when its historiographer took his leave of it. But of all
> these weaknesses, *drunkenness* was the principal and perennial
> source.

To Bentham, the failure to control the traffic in spirits was proof of the system's inability to achieve reform. On the contrary, he argued, the rum trade seemed to bring out (and even reward) the very worst characteristics of everyone involved in it. The economic and agricultural 'improvements' that so impressed the British Government encouraged both smuggling and illegal distilling, while the steady expansion of the settled areas made these activities harder to detect. As Bentham saw it, grog was the lubricant that kept the wheels of an immoral society turning:

> Whatever regulations can ever be made for . . . preventing the
> introduction of spirits into the colony – be it by manufacture,
> be it by importation – there is scarcely a human being in the
> colony, in or out of power, who has not a personal interest
> in the inefficacy of them. Among the convicts themselves –
> non-expirees, as well as expirees . . . there is scarcely a man
> to whom this liquid poison is not dearer than life. Among all

classes of persons – convicts – military officers – civil officers – not a master that, so long as any of it is to be had anywhere, or from anybody, can get a servant to work for him on any other terms.

The only way to mend such a thoroughly depraved society was to ensure that 'not so much as a single master had so much as a single drop of the poison to give . . . But if *one* gives spirits *all* must.'

While Bentham conceded that it might be possible, by 'extraordinary exertions', to reduce the amount of spirits the colony consumed, the reduction could only be temporary, since it was in the interest of every employer to have more spirits than his neighbour in order to hire more labour. '[S]o long as the quantity of spirits in the colony is short of the full quantity which the convicts altogether are disposed to drink, so long must the . . . universal *competition* among the purchasers of the article . . . continue.'

From this miserable state of affairs Bentham gleefully deduced that 'the exclusion of the means of drunkenness out of the improved colony, presents itself . . . as an achievement, now and for everlasting morally impossible'.

By contrast, 'Not a drop of forbidden liquor can be either drunk in the [panopticon penitentiary] house, or so much as introduced into it, without being seen to be so by everybody: by officers – prisoners – visitors through curiosity – visitors upon business: therefore, were transgression ever so advantageous, detection and punishment would be inevitable'. The conclusion Bentham arrived at was hardly surprising: 'Drunkenness, in the "improved colony", universal: in a panopticon penitentiary house, impossible.'

But it was a false conclusion, based on a flawed and partisan reading of highly subjective data. In a penal settlement such as New South Wales, effective surveillance was impossible. Drunkenness was certainly widespread, but it was never, as Bentham insisted, 'universal'. By the time Bentham wrote 'Panopticon versus New South Wales', the colony was moving beyond agricultural self-sufficiency towards economic success, achieved through the efforts of hardworking soldiers and settlers, convicts and ex-convicts. Time-expired convicts were transforming themselves into men and women of business and property. Grog was the ruin of some, but it would be the making of others.

19

Beer will become common

Nobody gave the lie to Bentham's charge of 'universal' drunkenness better than James Squires, whose life and career were proof that not just reform but transformation was possible under the convict system. Far from the idle, debauched stereotype of Bentham's manifesto, Squires had shown himself to be a model of perseverance and ingenuity.

The chief obstacle to making beer in the colony had always been the difficulty of obtaining good quality hops. It was Squires's ability to overcome this problem that gave him an edge over his rivals.

In 1798 George Suttor (who would later try his hand at winemaking) was commissioned by Sir Joseph Banks to sail to New South Wales on the *Porpoise* with a cargo of plants to replace those lost in the wreck of the *Guardian*. Among them were some English hops. The *Porpoise* proved to be an unlucky ship and many of the plants, including the valuable hops, did not survive. Their loss caused Suttor to write an anguished letter to his patron, lamenting his failure to keep the precious plants alive. 'I now do and ever shall regret that I was not more successful,' he told Banks. 'As they have hops at the Cape, I have great hopes we shall soon receive some from thence.'

The loss of the hops was also felt by lieutenant-governor King, who wrote to Banks:

What a happy thing it would have been for this colony if the exertions made by you to give us the hop had not failed by the misfortunes . . . of the old *Porpoise* . . . While I am on this subject, I see by the [London] papers of October last year that hops are so plentiful in this colony that one of the clergymen has great plantations of them, and that the finest porter is made here. How this, among many other falsehoods, should get into the papers is to me astonishing . . . The truth is that nothing like the English hops exists in this colony.

Locked in battle with the rum traders, King confided his hope that '[w]hen the inundation of spirits is stopped, which must be the case in the course of this year . . . the brewing [of] beer will become common; but this has been much retarded for the want of hops'.

In August 1801 King wrote again to Banks, begging that 'the misfortunes of the *Porpoise* will not prevent you from making one more trial about the hops'. This time he suggested they be sent out with one of the whalers, perhaps inside the 'covered box' in which he was sending Banks some waratahs.

In August 1802 the secretary of state for war and the colonies, Lord Hobart, wrote warmly to King, applauding him for his efforts to 'prevent the improper importation of spirits' and musing on his plans for a government brewery. 'The introduction of beer into general use,' Hobart told him, 'would certainly tend in a great degree to lessen the consumption of spirituous liquors.' Full of optimism, he immediately took steps to send out 'ten tons of porter, six bags of hops, and two complete sets of brewing utensils'. Hobart also arranged for 'a further supply of porter' to be sent out in whaling ships and promised that 'a quantity of hop plants' would be sent 'at a proper season of the year'.

The success of Squires's brewery at Kissing Point had encouraged others to try their hand at brewing. On Christmas Day 1803 a man named Stabler at the 'Eating House in Pitts-row' advised the public that he had laid in 'a Stock of prime Strong BEER which he has had brewed of superior strength and quality, for the supply of his Customers'.

By early 1804 King was able to inform Lord Hobart that the brewing utensils and hops sent by the *Glatton* and *Cato* had arrived safely and were 'all fixed at Parramatta in a building appropriated for that purpose, with a kiln and every other requisite for malting barley and brewing under the same roof'. Of the hops:

142 pounds . . . were bartered with a settler [probably Squires] who has long brewed in small quantities. The remainder I

shall preserve for the purpose of brewing . . . which has always been an event much desired by me. A trial has been made in which we have succeeded in making a small quantity to begin with . . . That which is made is very good.

Although hampered by the lack of an experienced brewer in Sydney and by the 'indifferent kind of barley' grown in the colony, King was confident that 'we shall soon carry it on in a very large scale' and asked Lord Hobart to send 'some good seed barley and more hops . . . also another set of brewing utensils for Sydney and one for Norfolk Island'.

King's government brewery got off to an uncertain start. Thieves broke in before it was even ready for business, stealing iron bars embedded in the masonry for the malt kiln. King offered a reward of 30 pounds sterling 'and a further desirable Encouragement' for information leading to a conviction. The brewery opened on 16 September 1804. Thomas Rushton, a knowledgeable brewer brought over from Van Diemen's Land, was put in charge.

At the end of the month, the governor published a notice in the *Gazette* inviting 'licensed Persons' approved by him to submit orders for 'Thirty-two gallons of Beer, for which they will be charged One Shilling and Four-pence per gallon, on condition that they do not retail it at more than Six-pence each full Quart'. In addition, commissioned civil and military officers were to be allowed five gallons each weekly, 'Superintendants, Serjeants, &c.' three gallons and settlers 'such proportion as the Governor judges proper'. All customers were to be charged 'One shilling each gallon for both kinds of beer; Casks are to be furnished by those who receive the Beer at the Brewhouse in Parramatta, from whence they are to remove it at their own expence'. Payment was to be made in 'Wheat, Barley, Hops, Casks, or Iron Hoops delivered into His Majesty's Stores'.

The initial quantities were limited by the availability of ingredients, but King was confident that 'after a few weeks Brewing an overplus will remain to be disposed of'.

Five weeks after the opening, the *Gazette* reported that 'upwards of 2300 gallons of beer' had been produced and that 'the malt kilns and coppers . . . are capable of brewing 1800 gallons a week, and when some additional working tubs are made, upwards of 3000 gallons can be brewed weekly, provided the supply of barley and hops continues'. The supply of barley depended on the settlers, who were to be paid in beer.

The promise of beer for barley soon caused problems, as settlers at the Hawkesbury began reaping their barley before it was ripe, which made it useless for brewing beer since it could not produce malt. King had to issue another General Order in November 1804 that no barley was to be received into the store without a sample first being approved of by the superintendent of the brewery 'and in case the quantity turned in should not appear equal in quality to the Sample, or that it does not vegetate when Malted, One half of such Barley will be forfeited for the imposition'.

The difficulty of maintaining a reliable supply of barley and hops was proving a headache for all the colony's brewers. In July 1804 Squires offered to buy 'ANY quantity of BARLEY, from Ten to a

Thousand Bushels, for which a full price will be paid on delivery, in Cash or approved Bills'.

When barley was scarce, brewers had to make do with inferior substitutes. Apologising for not sending a sample of the government's beer, King told Lord Hobart, 'we have been obliged to use wheat lately instead of barley'. (He promised to send a sample by the next ship.)

In its first three months, the Parramatta brewery produced 4247 gallons of beer. King judged it to be a success. By keeping the price low, he claimed to have put beer 'within every person's reach'.

King was not alone in promoting the moral benefits of Australian beer. In December 1804, Patrick Larken's Colonial Brewery advertised 'Ales, Pale, Brown, and Amber; Two-penny, and London Porter, &c'. Larken expressed the hope that the 'general introduction of those wholesome, long and justly celebrated English Beverages' would 'supersede the too destructive use of ardent Spirits' and be conducive to 'Health, Sobriety, and Economy'.

The shortage of barley and hops would have made it difficult for Larken to live up to his claim to be making beer 'after the system of the British Breweries'; his advertisement in the *Gazette* did not appear again.

Governor King's buoyant prediction for the manufacture of 'peach cyder' also showed signs of paying off. The *Gazette* reported that several successful experiments had been made 'in such quantities as to promise real advantage'. Several of the settlers at Kissing Point had 'devoted much attention to the praise-worthy object'; one claimed to have produced 200 gallons that 'with a few months fermentation, he doubts not will be found equal to the apple-cyder in strength, and not inferior the taste'.

But, within 18 months, the government had given up brewing. Overstaffed and handicapped by a continuing shortage of barley, the brewery was simply too expensive to run. The employees, who were each allowed five gallons of beer a week, drank almost as much as they produced. On 1 March 1806 the Commissary's Office announced that the Parramatta brewery was to be 'discontinued' as a government concern, with the buildings, brewing utensils and cooperage to be rented to Thomas Rushton for a period of two years. The rent was to be paid in beer – 200 gallons a month to be given to convicts employed on public works.

In an attempt to keep the monopolists out, King instructed Rushton to supply 'Strong Beer at One Shilling sterling per Gallon; and not to dispose of the Beer so brewed to Individuals for the purpose of monopolizing its Sale by Retail: but its Distribution to be as general as possible'.

By then, James Squires had moved to safeguard his supply of hops by growing them on his property at Kissing Point. On 14 March 1806 Squires:

> waited on His Excellency at Government House, with 2
> vines of hops taken from his own grounds. On a vine from
> a last year's cutting were numbers of very fine bunches; and
> upon a two-year-old cutting the clusters, mostly ripe, were
> innumerable, in weight supposed to yield at least a pound and
> a half, and of a most exquisite flavour.

As a reward for his efforts in bringing the valuable plant to 'such a high degree of perfection', King gave orders for Squires to be given a cow from the government herd.

Thomas Rushton did not renew his lease on the Parramatta brewery, apparently finding the terms too onerous. In June 1808 he informed the public that he had begun brewing in the Brick-fields, Sydney. Free to set his own prices, Rushton promptly doubled them, offering 'good strong beer at 2s. per gallon' and fine table beer 'for private families' at 8d. per gallon, 'bittered with hops only'. Having bought all the hops recently imported in the *Fox*, Rushton promised to be able to continue brewing 'without interruption, and to comply with all the orders with which his numerous friends may favor him'.

Others followed Rushton's example. In 1809 a man named Kinsela advertised his 'strong, clear, wholesome and durable Beer' at two shillings a gallon and Absalom West offered '20 or 30 Hogsheads of the best Strong Beer [to be] sold by the Hogshead'. The following year, from his brewery at No. 5 Upper Pitt's Row, Kinsela was supplying 'excellent Beer in bottles . . . of a potent, wholesome, and excellent flavour . . . not inferior in strength to any beer imported in this Colony'.

The Parramatta brewery lay idle. It was advertised for rent in June 1809 and again the following year, but there were no takers. Not another pint of beer was ever squeezed out of Governor King's expensive investment.

James Squires's brewery, meanwhile, went from strength to strength. Unlike the officers, Squires was not a monopolist. Soon after being rewarded with a cow for his diligence in growing hops,

Squires offered for sale 'from 12 to 1500 Plants . . . the whole in a healthy state . . . to be disposed of at the rate of 6d. each.' Four years later the price had doubled, and Squires was asking a shilling each for '1000 perfect Plants'.

Within two years Squires was able to harvest 1500 pounds of hops from his five-acre plantation, but there would be no cows from Governor Bligh.

20

Two stills

Sir Joseph Banks had argued that Governor King's successor should be a man 'who had integrity unimpeached, a mind capable of providing its own resources in difficulties without leaning on others for advice, firm in discipline, civil in deportment and not subject to whimper and whine when severity of discipline is wanted to meet emergencies'. How far William Bligh fitted that description would soon become clear.

As governor of New South Wales, Bligh was to be paid £2000 a year, double the salary paid to King. In practice, Banks pointed out, he would be able to live on less than half this amount because he would have 'the whole of the Government power and stores' at his disposal.

Banks advised Bligh to take his family with him, as:

your daughters will have a better chance of marrying suitably than they can have here; for as the colony grows richer every year, and something of trade seems to improve, I can have no doubt but that in a few years there will be men there very capable of supporting wives in a creditable manner, and very desirous of taking them from a respectable and good family.

In Bligh, Banks believed the colony would have a governor who could be trusted not to bow to the interests of Macarthur and his military friends. 'King . . . is tired of his station; and well he may be so,' Banks had written to Bligh in March 1805. 'He has carried into effect a reform of great extent, which militated much with the interest of the soldiers and settlers there. He is consequently disliked and much opposed, and has asked leave to return.'

Bligh's ship, the *Sinclair*, sailed into Port Jackson on 6 August 1806 but, owing to 'some previous arrangements' made by King, it was another seven days before Bligh took over as the fourth governor of New South Wales.

Before he was sworn in, Bligh received three grants of land from Governor King that would prove fabulously lucrative to his heirs: 240 acres at Camperdown, near Sydney; 105 acres at Parramatta; and 1000 acres on the Hawkesbury Road near Rouse Hill. Soon after becoming governor, Bligh returned the favour by granting 790 acres to Mrs King. None of these grants was mentioned in official dispatches to London. (It was not King's first offence. A year earlier, he had illegally granted 2350 acres to his wife. The grant was cancelled before it could be executed and two years later the same land was divided among King's four children.)

Bligh's generosity towards Mrs King sat uneasily with his reluctance to grant land to others. During his 18 months in office, Bligh gave land grants totalling a mere 2180 acres, while King (over a longer period) had granted 73,337 acres. Settlers who came with recommendations from London for land grants were kept waiting while Bligh sought formal approval from the home secretary. His combination of miserliness and obstructionism would bring to a jarring halt the expansion of private farmland on which the colony's economic success had been built.

Bligh arrived to find the colony in crisis. Disastrous floods in March 1806 had almost wiped out the Hawkesbury settlement, its most important food-growing district. On 22 March the flood carried away 200 wheat stacks; as night fell, settlers clinging to trees or huddled on roofs fired muskets to attract the attention of rescuers. The *Sydney Gazette* reported that 'great numbers' were taken by boat to higher ground, but many more experienced 'a night of horror the most inexpressible'. The gunshots grew louder as desperate survivors dangerously overcharged their muskets 'to increase the noise of explosion'; dogs that had managed to swim to safety in the branches of trees howled piteously in the dark. William Leeson, his mother, wife and two children were carried away from his farm 'upon a barley mow' and driven nearly seven miles by the 'impetuous' current. More than 4000 animals – mostly pigs – were drowned, and 85,000 bushels of grain were destroyed.

'It is a calamity that threatens the very existence of the colony,' Macarthur wrote to Captain John Piper at Norfolk Island. 'What a scene for a new Governor and what a fine subject for panegyrick on the care, wisdom and foresight of *our friend* [Governor King].'

In the aftermath of the flood, there were acute food shortages and the price of grain reached unsustainable levels. Bread, which could be bought for fourpence a loaf before the floods, was changing hands for two or even five shillings. Finding 'the unfortunate settlers almost ruined and starved', Bligh organised relief supplies and boosted meat rations where they were needed. To the flooded Hawkesbury settlers, the new governor was a godsend, but in Sydney his fierce temper and foul language quickly made enemies.

'Our new Governor Bligh is a Cornishman by birth,' Elizabeth Macarthur reported to her friend Miss Kingdon. 'The Governor has already shown the inhabitants of Sydney that he is violent, rash, tyrannical. No very pleasing prospect at the beginning of his reign.'

The officer corps resented him from the start. By the time Bligh arrived in the colony, the trading power of the monopolists had been significantly eroded by competition from Robert Campbell and the emancipist merchants. Private enterprise was no longer confined to the officers but had caught on with other ranks: up to a third of Sydney's publicans were non-commissioned officers.

Like his predecessors, Bligh had firm orders from the home secretary to control the grog trade. A set of 'Additional Instructions from His Majesty', written by the secretary of state for war and the colonies, Viscount Castlereagh, on 20 November 1805, noted that 'the exertions of Gov. King have been productive of the most beneficial consequences' and urged Bligh to 'persevere in the system he has so wisely laid down of a rigorous prohibition in this pernicious beverage without a regular licence from you for the purpose'.

It soon became clear to Bligh, however, that King's regulations had not succeeded in ending the bartering and trafficking of spirits, which continued to distort the labour market while generating huge profits for the traffickers.

Writing in February 1807 to William Windham, Castlereagh's short-lived replacement as secretary of state for war and the colonies, Bligh explained how King had allowed individuals 'to receive certain quantities when a ship arrived, at the market price (about 8 or 9 shillings p'r gallon)' which they then 'bartered away at 20s. per gallon by General Orders', although the resale price could easily rise to three or five pounds, 'and even eight has been given by unfortunate people who will not do without it'. The extravagant value of spirits distorted the markets for both goods and labour:

> A sawyer will cut one hundred feet of timber for a bottle of spirits – value two shillings and sixpence – which he drinks in a few hours; when for the same labour he would charge two bushels of wheat, which would furnish bread for him for two months . . . A settler has been known often to give an acre of wheat for two gallons of spirits, to satisfy his labourer, or for his own use, which would maintain him a whole year.

While permitting a limited quantity of spirits to be imported and distributed among the settlers, Bligh was determined to 'put a total stop' to the practice of bartering spirits for goods or labour. He drew up a list of penalties for anyone caught in 'the exchange of spirits or other liquors for payment for grain, animal food, labour, wearing apparel or any other commodity whatever or for the hire of labourers'. The punishment for convicts was 100 lashes and/or 12 months' hard labour; for expirees and emancipists, three months and a fine of £20; and for free settlers, ships' masters and others, a fine of £50 and the loss of government privileges.

Set against the profits to be made from trafficking in spirits, the fines were not excessive, but they targeted all levels of society, upsetting everyone from officer-farmers to petty traders. As Major Foveaux argued in a letter dated 10 September 1808, anybody could discover 'in one week's observation of this colony' that such a system of punitive regulations against the importing and trafficking of spirits was futile. 'Three-fourths' of the amount of spirits imported into the colony was destined to fall into the hands of government employees and 'inhabitants of the town', who onsold it at a substantial mark-up to settlers and labourers living in the interior of the country:

> These people, sensible that a threefold proportion of the
> reward of their industry is extorted from them, eagerly engage
> in smuggling and distilling, and in nineteen cases out of
> twenty they do so with success . . . nor is it possible to prevent
> it in a country so thinly inhabited, and in which the whole of
> the population consider themselves oppress'd and injured by
> the existing regulations.

Bligh, however, considered his decrees effective, assuring William Windham that the 'barter of spirituous liquors is prohibited, by which means hired labour is become secured more equally to every man' and boasting to Viscount Castlereagh that 'these evils were now done away, to the great satisfaction of the people'.

Bligh's next target was illegal distilling, by now so widespread throughout the colony that any shortfall caused by the tighter regulation of imported spirits could be more than made up for with local moonshine.

At the beginning of March 1807, the whaler *Dart* sailed into Port Jackson carrying two stills, a 60-gallon one belonging to John Macarthur and a 40-gallon one belonging to Captain Abbott. Both men had apparently been led to believe that, subject to 'certain restrictions', some colonists would be allowed to set up private distilleries. (John Blaxland, who arrived in April 1807 to join his brother Gregory, was under the same impression, and offered Bligh shares in the firm in return for approval to open a distillery. Bligh refused.)

There was no attempt at subterfuge; the stills were openly included on the cargo list. Bligh, however, had no intention of permitting them to be imported and ordered them to be held in the bond store until a ship could take them back to England. Macarthur did not challenge Bligh's right, as governor, to impound the stills, although he insisted that he and Abbott were blameless.

As the copper boilers had been filled with 'a variety of small packages', making them awkward to carry to the bond store, the storekeeper removed the working parts (the worms and heads) and allowed the coppers to be transferred to a nearby warehouse co-owned by Macarthur and one of his cronies, a man named Garnham Blaxcell.

Macarthur's plan was to dispose of his now-unwanted still on the next ship to India or China, or, if Bligh objected, to strip out the working parts and keep the harmless boiler for 'some domestic purpose'. But before Macarthur could do either, Bligh's men raided the warehouse and carried off 'in an illegal manner, and contrary to the laws of the Realm . . . two copper boilers valued at £40'.

This time, Macarthur sued. To Bligh's fury, the court found in his favour. Macarthur's aggressive prosecution of his case made him a marked man. Bligh took immediate revenge on Richard Atkins, a member of the Bench that had taken Macarthur's side against his, writing a letter to London in which he accused Atkins of being a drunkard whose incompetence had made him 'the ridicule of the community'. (Macarthur, who was no friend of Atkins, had been saying virtually the same thing almost since Atkins's arrival in the colony.)

Before the end of the year, Bligh and Macarthur locked horns again, this time over the lease held by Macarthur for a property next to St Phillip's Church. Under Governor King's policy of offering secure leases to householders, Sydney had expanded rapidly to the south and east. In 1803 alone, the number of houses had doubled. Macarthur's lease now stood in the way of Bligh's scheme to create open space around Government House and St Phillip's Church. Bligh was determined to call in Macarthur's lease, as well as one held by

Major George Johnston of the New South Wales Corps – another man with whom he had recently quarrelled.

As well as calling in leases, Bligh ordered the arbitrary demolition of buildings of which he disapproved. One of these was a house belonging to Mr Mann, the chief commissary clerk and former personal secretary to Governor King, who had been granted a lease next to Government House for the purpose of being close to his employer. When the terrified Mann protested to Bligh that by English law the lease was legal and he was entitled to keep his house, Bligh exploded.

'Damn your laws of England!' Bligh was said to have shouted. 'Don't talk to me of your laws of England! I will make the laws of this Colony, and every wretch of you, son of a bitch, shall be governed by them.'

Mann was reported to have 'bowed to him and wished him good day' but later warned the commissary that 'unless steps were taken to conciliate the people, a revolution would shortly happen'.

Macarthur himself had been on the end of a tongue-lashing from Bligh over the 5000 acres granted to him by the Privy Council, which Bligh swore to confiscate. Dr Arnold – a former naval surgeon – described Bligh later as 'overpowering and affrighting every person that might have dealings with him, expecting from all a deference and submission that the proudest despot would covet'.

In short, Bligh's foul mouth, his vicious temper, his often arbitrary and tyrannical application of the law, his cronyism and his disregard for private property (not to mention his habit of enriching himself at the government's expense) had created an abundance of enemies, some of whom were already plotting against him.

In November 1807 Lieutenant Kemp was told that a cabal of wealthy traders had subscribed £1500 to send Macarthur to England to complain to the home secretary on their behalf about Governor Bligh. When told of this by Kemp, Bligh had damned the merchant conspirators, declaring himself 'as irremovable as Ararat'.

Bligh's relationship with the military was equally acrimonious. Major Johnston, the commanding officer of the New South Wales Corps while Paterson was establishing a new settlement in Van Diemen's Land, protested to the commander-in-chief of the army, the Duke of York, about Bligh's constant interfering in the corps' business – for instance, by assigning officers to serve as magistrates without consulting Johnston – and his abusive language towards the soldiers. '[H]is abusing and confining the soldiers without the smallest provocation . . . his casting the most undeserved and opprobrious censure on the Corps' were examples, Johnston said, of Bligh's 'indecorous' and 'oppressive' conduct towards the regiment.

'Governor Bligh,' Johnston concluded, 'seems ignorant of any instructions or rules whatever, but such as are dictated by the violent passion of the moment.'

Bligh's goal now was to rid the colony of the New South Wales Corps. Noting the high number of ex-convicts in the ranks and the habit of the rest of associating too closely with convicts, he warned Windham of the risk of a 'fixed corps becoming a dangerous militia'. The only remedy for such an 'evil tendency' was the 'removal of both officers and men' from the colony, to be replaced by other regiments on a rotating basis.

This amounted to a serious threat to soldiers who had put down roots in the colony and had no desire to go back to England, but it was scarcely grounds for mutiny.

The spark that led to rebellion, and to Bligh's overthrow as governor, came with the arrest of John Macarthur on 15 December 1807. Ostensibly, it had to do with the escape of an Irish convict, John Hoare – aka Gentleman John – who had skipped the colony as a stowaway on the *Parramatta*, a schooner owned by Macarthur. It was rumoured that Hoare sold grog for Macarthur and that 'by his iniquitous conduct and being supported by his employers [he] grew proud and independent, and his employers for fear of their wicked device being made manifest secreted him away in their vessel'.

Hoare absconded from a gaol gang and somehow – on a ship of just 102 tons – concealed himself 'among the firewood', where he eluded a search by customs before emerging from his hiding place to jump ship at Tahiti. The master, Captain Glen, made no attempt to drag Hoare back to Sydney. When the *Parramatta* sailed into Port Jackson on 15 November, with a cargo of pork but no Gentleman John, Macarthur and his co-owner, Blaxcell, found themselves liable for his escape to the tune of an £800 bond and personal securities of £50 each.

After the owners lodged an appeal – having apparently threatened not to pay the penalty if they lost – Bligh impounded the *Parramatta*, placing armed constables on board to stop her cargo from being landed. Macarthur took his protest to the deputy judge advocate – his old antagonist Atkins – who, after a few words with the governor, decided not to interfere. Macarthur's response was to wash his hands of Captain Glen and the ship, declaring himself no longer responsible for either their pay or provisions.

The hapless Captain Glen appealed to Bligh, only to be met with a volley of abuse as he stood at the back door: 'Begone, sir, for a scoundrel! . . . Damn you, sir, I will teach you to take away prisoners from this Colony, you scoundrel! If I ever catch you on these premises again –.'

Summoned to give their account of the affair, the ship's hungry crew ('deprived . . . of their usual allowance of provisions') came ashore and were promptly accused by Atkins of violating Colonial Regulations. The next evening, a constable was sent to Elizabeth Farm with a warrant for Macarthur's arrest, on the dubious grounds that he had failed to appear before Atkins that morning. Macarthur considered the warrant illegal and refused to go. Before sending the constable away, he handed him a note that he had signed and dated:

Mr Oakes, – You will inform the persons who sent you here with the warrant you have now shewn me, and given me a copy of, that I never will submit to the horrid tyranny that is attempted until I am forced; that I consider it with scorn and contempt, as I do the persons who have directed it to be executed.

To Governor Bligh, the note represented 'an overt act of high treason'. With Bligh telling him what to do, Atkins put together a list of charges against Macarthur. Some went back to the importation of the stills; the rest concerned Captain Glen and the *Parramatta,* and the hastily written note accusing Bligh of tyranny.

As Macarthur awaited trial, Bligh sent an order prohibiting him from building on the disputed plot beside St Phillip's Church. Macarthur, with bigger battles to fight, offered to 'make the sacrifice required of him' by exchanging his plot for the lease of an 'unoccupied piece of land . . . between the lease of Mr Jamison and one of Mr William Blake's' or, alternatively, a small piece of land on the western side of town.

Bligh shot down both suggestions. The only piece of land he was prepared to offer Macarthur was in Pitt's Row – a spot on the outskirts of Sydney 'where the common gallows had stood, and which was surrounded by all the vile and atrocious characters' of the settlement. It was a place that Macarthur 'could not possibly have inhabited, unless he had chosen to place his family in the centre of a nest of prostitutes'.

It could hardly have been clearer that Bligh had no intention of reaching a compromise, so Macarthur withdrew his offer and informed him that he was staying put. Not only that, but he defied Bligh's order forbidding him from building, directing his men to erect fence posts on the site, which were no sooner in the ground than Bligh sent a party of armed constables to pull them out.

Macarthur's trial was set for Monday 25 January 1808, with Atkins presiding as deputy judge advocate. Atkins's presence on the Bench was anathema to Macarthur, who petitioned Bligh to have him removed from the trial on the grounds that Atkins was 'deeply interested to obtain a verdict against me' and, if he could not obtain it, would inevitably be 'called upon to defend himself at the very bar to which he is about to drag me, for the false imprisonment I have suffered under the authority of his illegal warrant'.

Bligh turned him down.

When the criminal court gathered, Macarthur made a second attempt to oust Atkins. Claiming not to know the charges against him, he accused Atkins of being unfit to sit in judgment over him because he owed Macarthur money, and because Atkins had spread 'malignant falsehoods' and behaved with 'vindictive malice' towards him. Macarthur's allegations against the deputy judge advocate represented a deliberate attack not just against the judiciary but against Bligh's whole administration. 'You have the eyes of an anxious public upon you,' he advised the six officers of the New South Wales Corps who had been sworn in as judges, 'trembling for the safety of their property, their liberty, and their lives.'

According to Bligh's own account of the proceedings, Atkins leapt from his seat and cried, 'I will commit you to jail, sir!' only for one of the judges, Captain Kemp, to shout, 'You commit, sir! No, sir, I will commit you!'

Amid raucous applause from the soldiers in the courtroom, Atkins stormed out, convinced that the court could not function without him. Macarthur was released on bail – with a cluster of soldiers for his own protection – and the officers asked Bligh to appoint another deputy judge advocate in place of Atkins. Bligh again refused, and sent for the corps' commanding officer, Major Johnston, to come from his house in Annandale, four miles away. But Johnston had hurt his arm when falling out of his carriage the night before (allegedly while drunk) and sent back a message that he was 'dangerously ill, and it would endanger his life to come into camp'.

Egged on by his subservient magistrates, Bligh had Macarthur re-arrested the next morning and tossed in the common gaol, where it was rumoured there were plans to kill him.

Atkins, stewing on his public humiliation the day before, then drafted for Governor Bligh an embittered and inaccurate account of what had happened, noting the roles of the six officers in releasing Macarthur 'out of the hands of the civil power' and placing him 'under the protection of the military'. According to Atkins, the actions of the six officers – Anthony Fenn Kemp, John Brabyn, William Moore, Thomas Laycock, William Minchin and William Lawson – amounted to 'a usurpation of His Majesty's Government, and tend to incite or create rebellion or other outrageous treason in the people of this territory'.

News of Atkins's incendiary accusations spread quickly. Treason, as every soldier, settler and convict would have known, was a capital crime. Bligh immediately summoned the six officers to Government House. Three years later, at Major Johnston's court martial in London, Bligh insisted that he had never contemplated arresting the officers and wanted only to point out 'the illegality of their conduct' while 'hoping to bring them to a sense of their duty'. But this was not how the men themselves interpreted it, as a conversation overheard by another soldier made clear:

Laycock: By God we are all going to be hanged.

Unnamed: Why so?

Laycock: Old Bligh has summoned us to appear before him.

Minchin: If you are afraid I am not, and will find a way to
    cool him.

Laycock: How is that?

Minchin: By arresting him before he arrest us.

Bligh tried again to drag Major Johnston out of his sick bed in
Annandale, suggesting that if he was too sick he should consider
sending Captain Abbott 'to command the troops in your absence'.
This was the red rag that roused Johnston to action. Informed by
his doctor, Surgeon Harris, that 'an insurrection of the inhabitants
was to be feared', Johnston forgot his bruises and, in his own words,
'immediately set off in a carriage to the town'. He considered Bligh's
actions in summoning his fellow officers on a trumped-up charge of
treason to be 'illegal, outrageous, flagrant, and alarming'.

The case of the Irish rebel Michael Dwyer, who had been found
not guilty by a court, only to be re-tried and convicted by a Bench
of the governor's handpicked magistrates, proved that Bligh would
ride roughshod over the law when it suited him.

Clattering through the outskirts of Sydney on the evening of
26 January, Major Johnston noticed 'the common people . . . in
various groups in every street, murmuring and loudly complaining'.
Bligh was having dinner at Government House but Johnston did
not go there. He went instead to the barracks, where he spoke
to military officers and settlers, including the emancipist merchant
Simeon Lord (who was among those planning to send Macarthur to

London to protest about Bligh) and the physician rum trader D'Arcy Wentworth, whom Bligh had reprimanded for allegedly putting sick convicts to work for his own profit. The unanimous consensus among those advising him, Johnston would later testify, was that 'if I did not put the Governor in arrest, an insurrection and a massacre would ensue, and the blood of the inhabitants would be upon me'.

Macarthur was released from gaol. On the bail warrant, Johnston styled himself 'lieutenant-governor' – a title predicated on Bligh's removal from office. Something was needed from the settlers in writing to protect Johnston against any future prosecution, so Macarthur drafted the following letter:

Sir,

The present alarming state of this colony, in which every man's property, liberty, and life is endangered, induces us most earnestly to implore you instantly to place Governor Bligh under an arrest and to assume the command of the colony. We pledge ourselves, at a moment of less agitation, to come forward to support the measure with our fortunes and our lives.

The letter was signed first by Macarthur and later by 150 others – 'some of whom', Bligh commented bitterly, 'are the worst class of life'.

Convinced that, unless he took drastic action, 'nothing could limit the excess of the Governor's cruelties', Johnston set out at around six o'clock on the evening of 26 January 1808 to arrest Bligh. After a 'rigid search' that lasted two hours, the governor was eventually discovered – in Johnston's words – 'in a situation too disgraceful to be mentioned'. The soldiers who found him swore he was hiding under a bed in an attic room, 'the fore part of his coat, the lappels, were full of dust, and the back part full of feathers'. Johnston confiscated his public and private papers and his seal of office, and put Bligh under house arrest.

The governor had been deposed and his cronies scattered without a shot being fired. A scurrilous painting of Bligh being pulled out from under a bed was dashed off and put on display, no doubt with the intention of snuffing out support for the ousted governor by depicting him as a coward.

With Bligh safely under guard in Government House, Johnston declared martial law, revoking it the following day. 'When the officers and inhabitants found themselves relieved from the oppressions of Governor Bligh,' Johnston told Viscount Castlereagh, 'the general joy that was felt displayed itself in rejoicings, bonfires, and illuminations, and in a manifestation of the most perfect unanimity.'

Within days, Macarthur was acquitted of all charges against him. For the next six months, Major Johnston would rule the colony as lieutenant-governor. But the 'manifestation of . . . unanimity' that gave Johnston so much satisfaction was, he quickly discovered, 'not to be preserved without a sacrifice of His Majesty's interests'. If the officers were jumping for joy, it was because they expected the lieutenant-governor and his enterprising secretary to put an end to 'the regulations that have been made to check the importation of spirituous liquors into the colony'. The old tyrant was gone and the rum traders expected a swift return to business as usual.

21

A most troublesome, revengeful, unpleasant man

Nobody involved in the mutiny against Governor Bligh would have recognised it as a rum rebellion. The term wasn't even coined until nearly half a century later, when the Quaker William Howitt (a teetotaller) used it – in inverted commas – in his book *Land, Labour and Gold*. But that does not mean that the rum rebellion had nothing to do with rum.

Bligh had stirred up some of the most vengeful men in the colony by clamping down on the traffic in spirits. That these men expected to resume their grog trading – not to mention make up for profits lost during the 18 months Bligh was governor – was clear to Major Johnston almost from the day he took charge.

At the turn of the year, three ships loaded with grog had dropped anchor in Port Jackson. The captains of the *Jenny* and the *Eliza* had been allowed by Bligh to land cargoes of wine but had been forbidden to land their rum. Macarthur had bought some of the wine and offered to sell it to soldiers and non-commissioned officers of the New South Wales Corps for the 'very low price' of five shillings a gallon. The third ship, the *City of Edinburgh*, had arrived from the Cape of Good Hope in such a leaky state that the cargo would have spoilt had Bligh not relented and given permission for 7000 gallons to be taken into the government stores, where it remained.

No sooner had Major Johnston assumed command of the colony than he found himself besieged by friends and fellow officers eager to get their hands on the cargoes of the *Jenny* and the *Eliza*. Their demands were so relentless that Johnston was forced to issue a General Order forbidding 'any verbal request being made to him except on public affairs'. Torn between upholding the British Government's instructions to curb the traffic in spirits and his own need to conciliate the men who had supported his illegal grab for power, Johnston tried to do both. His General Order of 7 February was an artful attempt at compromise that was doomed to fail:

If the officers and respectable inhabitants are desirous to
purchase a moderate supply of spirits for their domestic uses,
the Lieutenant-Governor will readily grant them permission;
but it is at the same time to be understood that the former
orders respecting the importation and landing of spirits are still
in full force, and that a rigid observance of them is required.

Johnston expressed a cautious confidence that 'no officer will so far forget himself as to abuse the indulgence allowed him as to attempt to obtain spirits clandestinely'. At the same time, however, he made sure to offer the usual lavish rewards for finders and informers, promising that 'if any person in trust shall be detected by a soldier in illicit practices, the soldier shall be rewarded for the discovery with a discharge, a farm, and other indulgences; if by a prisoner, he shall receive an unconditional emancipation, and be provided with a passage to England'.

This was not the new, business-friendly regime that Johnston's backers had been expecting, and he soon found himself confronted by 'opposition from those persons from whom I had most reason to expect support'.

The mutiny had put Johnston in an invidious position. Although it seems doubtful that he was an active rum trader himself, he was certainly on familiar terms with others who were. Robert Campbell, by now the colony's biggest trader in goods and liquor, witnessed a conversation between Johnston and some fellow officers of the New South Wales Corps in which it was said that in Grose's time as lieutenant-governor:

> the Officers were allowed to go on board of Ships when they pleased, and purchase a cask or two from the Americans from three to four Shillings per gallon, and sell it afterwards for two to three pounds, that in those times Officers could live, cultivate their farms, and make money, but at present they could do nothing but barely exist.

Unfortunately for Johnston, the American ship *Jenny* was still in port, complete with her cargo of grog. 'Many people were desirous to get permission to purchase this cargo,' Johnston told Viscount Castlereagh in his dispatch of 11 April, but 'I thought it my duty to resist every solicitation; and having received information that spirits were smuggling from the American, I ordered her to quit the port, and sent the Colonial schooner *Estramina* to escort her out of sight of land.'

His peremptory dismissal of the *Jenny* and her cargo caused predictable anguish to the rum traders, who were not slow to make their resentment felt. The *Jenny*, meanwhile, had not slid obediently over the horizon but had sailed a few miles up the coast and put in to Broken Bay, where smugglers were soon busy relieving her of her cargo. When word of this flagrant violation of his orders reached Johnston, boats were:

> at my request directly armed and sent from the *Porpoise* with orders to seize the ship if any proof could be obtained of her smuggling. When the boats reached the *Jenny* they found a man from the shore preparing to take a cask of spirits, and as there were other strong corroborative proofs that spirits had been or were prepared to be landed, the ship was seized and brought back to the port.

Accused of having broken the law by allowing spirits to be smuggled, Captain Dorr of the *Jenny* stood to lose his ship. Evidence was given in court that 1209 gallons of spirits – around a quarter of the amount listed when she arrived in the colony – was missing. But neither that 'nor many other strong proofs that an illicit trade had been carried on' were enough to convince the court of Captain Dorr's connivance with the smugglers. The court's failure to convict, despite the evidence of the missing grog, would be enough (so Johnston thought) to convince London that 'the condemnation of a ship for smuggling will not easily be accomplished in New South Wales'.

The *Jenny* and her load of unsold spirits were again sent away, this time for good. The ship's departure, Johnston noted darkly, 'was highly disapproved of by many'. The rum traders' fury at the disappearance of a lucrative cargo was compounded by the growing realisation that Johnston was not going to be the creature of private enterprise that most had imagined when putting their signatures to the document calling on him to seize power.

Adding to their resentment over the spirits was the discovery of Johnston's determination to 'reduce the expenditure of public money and stores', to be 'extremely circumspect' in the allocation of livestock and convict labour, and not to grant any land without the direct approval of the British Government. It was dawning on private traders such as the emancipist Simeon Lord that while they had succeeded in getting rid of Bligh, they had failed to dismantle the policies they found so objectionable. Johnston now cut a beleaguered figure, deserted by the men who had pushed him to take power and conscious of the dubious legality of that power.

Explaining how these men had turned against him was 'the most painful part' of Johnston's task in making his report to Viscount Castlereagh, who was back in charge of war and the colonies. Increasingly isolated, the lieutenant-governor went to the one man in the colony he could count on to stare down his critics. 'Determined to persevere in this system,' he told Castlereagh, 'and finding I should require the aid of some gentleman in whose integrity I should have confidence, I requested Mr. McArthur to assist me in the arduous undertaking.' As there was no useful and vacant office to which Macarthur could be appointed, and as Johnston was anxious for his ally to have 'some public character', he made him secretary to the colony, a post that had never existed before (and for which, he pointed out, Macarthur would not be paid).

It would have been unlike William Bligh to submit meekly to his fate, and he showed no intention of doing so. He was kept under house arrest for a year, refusing to return to England until a lawfully appointed successor arrived in the colony. In March 1809 Bligh finally agreed to leave New South Wales on the *Porpoise*. However, instead of sailing back to England he went south to Hobart and tried in vain to enlist the support of the lieutenant-governor, David Collins, before returning to Sydney in January 1810 to find Lachlan Macquarie already installed as governor.

It was in Bligh's interest to make his suppression of the rum trade appear the primary cause of the mutiny, and to play down any wider dissatisfaction with his regime. This became clear at Johnston's court martial, which began on 7 May 1811 at Chelsea Hospital in London and sat for 13 days. (Since the mutiny, Johnston had been promoted to the rank of lieutenant colonel.)

The purpose of the court martial was to inquire into a charge that on 26 January 1808 Johnston did 'begin, excite, cause and join in a mutiny' that had seized, arrested and imprisoned the person of

William Bligh, then captain-general and governor-in-chief of New South Wales. Bligh's testimony, as chief witness for the prosecution, took up nearly a quarter of the sitting days. A transcript of the trial, commissioned by Bligh, was taken in shorthand by Mr Bartrum of Clement's Inn.

Bligh had hoped that the court martial would confine itself to inquiring into the immediate circumstances of the mutiny. Johnston's counsel, however, had other ideas. The basic outline of the night's events was not in dispute. Johnston's defence lay in demonstrating to the court that his actions were not only justified but unavoidable; that a state of emergency existed and that Johnston had taken the only course of action open to him to prevent bloodshed and save the colony from chaos. The result was to put Bligh's entire performance as governor under scrutiny. As Bligh himself observed in his closing address to the court, '[I]t is I, and not Col. Johnston, who for some days past have been on trial.'

The main drift of the prosecution's case was clear from the moment Bligh entered the witness stand:

In what state did you find the colony upon your arrival?
In a very miserable state.
Did you discover any, and what abuses, then existing with respect to spirits?
There was a barter of spirits for articles that were wanting of every description, by those persons who had spirits to purchase them with.
Were the officers or soldiers at all interested in that barter of spirits, and if so, how?

*The officers were very much interested in the barter of spirits; so much
so, as to be enabled to get whatever they wanted at a very cheap rate.*
What with respect to soldiers?
*The observation applies exactly the same to soldiers, provided they
could get it.*
Did you take any measures to prevent this barter of spirits?
Yes, sir.
What?
By prohibiting the barter of spirits altogether . . .
Did those measures of reform create any discontent in the
colony; and if so, mention who were discontented, and on
what account, and how they showed their discontent?
They did create discontent among a few.
Mention who were discontented.
*Those persons in particular who were connected with the mutiny, who
were connected with my arrest; M'Arthur, and a few others, whose
names are mentioned in my dispatches.*

Other witnesses – even those allied with Bligh – were far more
circumspect. Invited by the court to agree that suppression of
the traffic in spirits was 'the principal ground of all the mutiny',
Bligh's commissary, John Palmer, replied guardedly, 'I knew some
officers who had an interest in the sale of considerable quantities of
spirits and wine; but I cannot say that was the cause of the mutiny.'
Francis Oakes, the chief constable, identified the notorious rum
trader Captain Kemp as having bartered spirits both before and after
Governor Bligh was deposed. William Gore, the provost marshal,

noted that Bligh's order forbidding the barter of spirits 'gave extreme discontent'.

Macarthur, however, denied that Bligh's regulations on bartering spirits influenced his conduct 'in the smallest degree'. Asked whether the prohibition 'gave any dissatisfaction', Macarthur replied, 'I know of none,' insisting that the quantity of spirits imported under Bligh's administration was 'insignificant' and that the portions each person obtained 'so small' that the officers 'must have felt very little interest about it'.

Captain Kemp, one of the six officers Bligh had threatened with a charge of treason, was another who denied that his participation in the mutiny had been influenced by the ban on bartering spirits, despite his history as a rum trader. (Kemp was one of the officers said to have been involved in smuggling grog from the American ship *Jenny*.)

[D]id you mean to state that you were yourself not the least dissatisfied with Gov. Bligh for only permitting you to have five gallons of spirits during the four months you were in Sydney?
I certainly was not at all dissatisfied, because every body else was in the same situation with me . . .
Do you believe that the suppression of the barter of spirits under Gov. Bligh created no discontent?
I never heard any discontent among the officers in the colony.

Lieutenant Minchin, Johnston's adjutant and a close associate of Macarthur's, was even more adamant. Asked whether he believed the ban had 'operated materially in producing the general discontent against Governor Bligh', Minchin replied, 'I do not; I never heard any of the officers or respectable inhabitants say any thing about it, not one.'

None of these witnesses could be described as neutral; their contrasting evidence illustrates the determination of one side to portray the mutiny as a rum rebellion, and of the other to deny it.

Bligh's plan to stifle the grog trade went further than his order banning the barter of spirits. By allowing modest quantities of grog to be distributed widely from the public stores, he put the government in direct competition with private enterprise. A prosecution witness, Charles Walker, testified that he had 'always heard the settlers say that Gov. Bligh . . . was the only Governor who ever allowed the colonists any spirits, the officers having always that privilege to themselves; the other Governors only allowed the officers to have spirits'.

His evidence was supported by Robert Campbell, who as Bligh's naval officer effectively had control over all ships entering the harbour. Campbell was no friend of Macarthur's and had played a significant role in the events that led to Macarthur's trial. Under questioning by the prosecution, Campbell strongly hinted that the cause of the mutiny was the officers' discontent over his rum regulations:

What alteration did Gov. Bligh make in the distribution of spirits, and what effect did it produce in the colony?
He ordered a more general distribution to be made. I arrived in the ship Albion *from England about ten days after Gov. Bligh took the*

command, and he ordered from 1500 to 2000 gallons of the spirits
that formed part of the investment to be distributed among the settlers.
What effect did that produce?
More satisfaction among the settlers and the people at large of their
class of the inhabitants.
Were any persons dissatisfied?
I presume the officers were dissatisfied, because they did not receive
such large quantities as they had done formerly.
Do you know of any persons being dissatisfied of your own
knowledge?
It was notorious throughout the whole colony.
Why were they dissatisfied?
Because there was a more general distribution, I suppose; the settlers
had not been accustomed to receive spirits so generally.

Cross-examined by Johnston, Campbell was unable to substantiate
his claims of widespread opposition among the officers, conceding,
'I was not much in the habit of conversing with them on public
affairs; I cannot call to my remembrance that I did ever hear any of
them complain after the proclamation was issued.'

There was, however, plenty of evidence to support the claim that
Bligh's regulations were welcomed by the settlers as much as they
were resented by the rum traders. Two years before Johnston's court
martial, Viscount Castlereagh had received a petition from settlers
purporting to explain 'the cause and effects' of the mutiny. Among
other things, the 'memorialists' praised Governor Bligh for having
'put a stop to the bartering of spirits, and the stroling dealers who

were generally employ'd by our trading officers', and for introducing regulations that 'struck at the vitals of that monopoly and extortion which had so long reign'd in the colony, by which many of the officers and leading men had inriched themselves to the ruin of the inhabitants in general'.

Against this, Captain Kemp claimed to have heard '[Lieutenant] Hobby and several of the [Hawkesbury] settlers express themselves very much dissatisfied with the suppression of the barter of spirits'.

Johnston's court martial reflected the divisiveness of the incident that had brought it about: witnesses were partisan, evasive and self-interested; evidence was incomplete, inaccurate and sometimes contradictory. In his efforts to polish his own record, Bligh was not above slandering his predecessors, as when he told the court, 'The barter of spirits, a source of emolument to other Governors, I prohibited.'

In his closing address to the court, Bligh painted himself as a disinterested seeker after justice, claiming to have 'no vindictive feeling towards Col. Johnston' and promising to be 'the first to rejoice' at Johnston's acquittal, provided his own honour and reputation were vindicated. In reality, bitterness and animosity towards the mutineers bubbled out of everything he said.

The verdict was never in doubt. However abusive, arbitrary and even tyrannical Bligh had been in his governorship, however much he had enriched himself at the public's expense, there could be no legal justification for Johnston's having led an armed insurrection to remove him from office.

On 5 June 1811 Johnston was found guilty of 'the act of mutiny' and sentenced to be cashiered. No action was to be taken against any other officer involved in the mutiny. The manifestly lenient punishment imposed on Johnston was 'actuated by a consideration of the novel and extraordinary circumstances, which . . . may have appeared . . . to have existed during the administration of Gov. Bligh, both as affecting the tranquillity of the colony, and calling for some immediate decision'.

The light sentence – and the fact that the Prince Regent publicly stated his acquiescence – mortified Bligh, who raged against it for the remaining six years of his life. By the time the sentence was handed down, New South Wales had a new governor, Lachlan Macquarie, whose dispatches confirmed the court's view that Bligh's administration had been 'extremely unpopular, particularly among the higher orders of the people' and that Bligh himself was a 'most troublesome, revengeful, unpleasant man'.

Under Lieutenant-Governor Johnston, there was no abrupt reversal of Bligh's regulations against importing and bartering spirits. The capitalists who had rebelled against Bligh and later hounded Johnston for trading privileges were essentially the same men who had tormented Governor King when he tried to restrain their business activities. The mutiny against Governor Bligh was not a 'rum rebellion', but if it had been, it would have been judged a failure.

22

Spirits must be had

During Johnston's six months in charge, he had been careful not to invite further criticism of his actions either by meddling with the deposed governor's policies or showing favouritism towards those who had encouraged his grab for power. On 28 July 1808 Johnston's superior officer, Lieutenant Colonel Joseph Foveaux, arrived from England. Faced with the dilemma of whether to reinstate Bligh or to take charge himself, Foveaux took the diplomatic option of writing to London for guidance while leaving Bligh to stew. It wasn't until January 1809 that the senior military officer in the colony, Colonel Paterson, arrived from Van Diemen's Land to take over from Foveaux. Less than six weeks later, chronic ill-health forced Paterson to relinquish his duties and leave the running of the settlement to Foveaux.

Bligh's continued presence was both an embarrassment and an annoyance to the interim commanders. After returning to Sydney from Hobart, he made himself 'a great plague' to Macquarie before departing the colony for good on 13 May 1810.

By the time Macquarie took up office, Johnston and Macarthur had already sailed for England, saving him from a potentially awkward confrontation. The new governor brought with him the 73rd Regiment to replace the discredited and mutinous New South Wales Corps.

Privately, Macquarie claimed to have found the colony thriving and 'in a perfect state of tranquillity', but he was under no illusion about the discord that had brought him to New South Wales. At his swearing in, on New Year's Day 1810, Macquarie declared his intention to rule with strict justice and impartiality, and urged his listeners to put the past behind them. Officers dismissed in the aftermath of the uprising were reinstated; questionable land grants were revoked; and Acts passed by the 'revolutionary' regimes were annulled.

Macquarie's commission had come with the usual instructions from London relating to the present circumstances of the colony. 'The Great Objects of attention,' Viscount Castlereagh advised the new governor, 'are to improve the Morals of the Colonists, to encourage marriage, to provide for education, to prohibit the use of spirituous liquors, to increase the agriculture and stock, so as to ensure the Certainty of a full supply to the Inhabitants under all circumstances.'

Prohibiting the 'use of spirituous liquors' would be as unachievable for Governor Macquarie as it had been for all four governors before him. During the two years that followed the insurrection, the *Sydney Gazette* continued to report the discovery of illegal stills all over the colony. Some were found in surprising places. In September 1808 'John Drake was . . . sentenced to 200 lashes, for stealing a still from the house of the Chief Constable'. In December 1809 'a cart conveying wheat was searched for spirits of colonial distillation, three kegs, containing six gallons each, were found concealed in the bags; in consequence of which the whole property was seized, including the cart and a bullock by which it was drawn . . . as well as the spirits'.

On 30 April 1810, Governor Macquarie wrote bluntly to Viscount Castlereagh:

As . . . the Various Measures that have been taken hitherto to Check the Importation and regulate the Sale of Spirits have invariably failed, and as it is impossible totally to suppress the Use of them, a certain Quantity being essentially Necessary for the Accommodation of the Inhabitants, it appears to me that it would be good and sound Policy to sanction the free Importation of good Spirits under a high Duty of not less than three or four Shillings per Gallon . . . it would put an End to all further Attempts at Monopoly, and bartering Spirits for Corn and Necessaries, as likewise to Private Stills, which, in defiance of every Precaution, are still very Numerous in this Colony.

Macquarie's proposal was contrary to the policies followed by every governor since Phillip, all of whom had attempted to curb the trafficking of spirits inside the colony by limiting the quantity brought in. Anticipating criticism from those who believed that the more grog imported into the colony, the more it would be abused, Macquarie assured Castlereagh that 'this Measure, instead of promoting Drunkenness & Idleness, would tend rather to lessen both, for it has generally been observed that the Avidity of the lower orders of the people is in inverse ratio to the Quantity of Spirits imported'. Allowing the free importation of spirits, Macquarie believed, would stop the proliferation of illegal stills, since 'private Distillers would be Undersold by the fair Licensed Trader'.

The new secretary of state for war and the colonies, the Earl of Liverpool, did not share Macquarie's optimism. 'Inveterate habits of drunkenness and dissipation among the lower orders of the people,' he lectured Macquarie, 'are more likely to be increased than checked by the facility of indulgence.'

Before the British Government could reply formally to Macquarie's recommendation for 'free importation', Macquarie received an audacious proposition that caused him to rethink his strategy. On his arrival in the colony, Macquarie had been shocked by the dilapidated state of its public buildings – especially the hospital, which he considered to be 'in so wretched a State of Decay as to threaten tumbling down'. Macquarie chose an 'airy and elevated Situation' on the western edge of the governor's Domain as the site for a new hospital. Designs were drawn up, but the British Government – anxious as ever to reduce the drain on the Treasury – refused to pay for it. As a result, Macquarie entered into a contract with D'Arcy Wentworth, the principal surgeon, and two associates, Garnham

Blaxcell and Alexander Riley, for 'Erecting a General Hospital at Sydney' on terms which he considered 'highly advantageous to Government'.

The terms proposed by Wentworth, Blaxcell and Riley were bold to say the least: they demanded a three-year monopoly on the importation of spirits. In return for the 'Exclusive Privilege' of importing 45,000 gallons of spirits – 'no other Spirits being permitted within that time to be Imported into the Colony by private Individuals' – the consortium agreed to build a hospital to a plan approved by the governor.

(It was not only Sydney that owed its hospital to the grog trade. At Windsor, Macquarie bought a brewery belonging to the wealthy emancipist – and alleged bootlegger – Andrew Thompson and turned it into a hospital with space for 20 patients.)

The rum imported by the consortium was for general sale and did not include supplies imported for the garrison and for the private use of civil and military officers. The contractors had to pay duty of three shillings per gallon on the whole 45,000 gallons (calculated by Macquarie at 'Six thousand Seven Hundred and fifty Pounds in three Years'). It was a pragmatic deal to obtain an urgently needed public building, but it went against Macquarie's own argument in favour of free importation.

'The Building is to be elegant and Commodious, and sufficiently large to accommodate, comfortably, at least Two Hundred Sick persons,' Macquarie told the Earl of Liverpool in a letter dated 18 October 1811. 'The Terms of the Contract having appeared to me so very advantageous, and the Necessity for a New Building of this kind so imperious that I flatter Myself the Measure I have adopted will meet Your Lordship's fullest concurrence and approbation.'

He was mistaken.

Still under the impression that Macquarie intended to allow the free importation of spirits, Liverpool suggested in a letter dated 5 May 1812, 'A Short trial . . . will not only enable you to form a more correct opinion as to the rate of Duty which is ultimately to be fixed, but will afford ground for ascertaining how far an uncontrouled Importation of Spirits . . . may affect the morals and Industry of the Colonists.'

Before the ship due to carry Liverpool's letter could set sail, the secretary of state received Macquarie's letter of 18 October. He was horrified. 'Many objections might be urged to an Engagement of this nature under any circumstances,' Liverpool protested. 'But I am Surprized that you did not foresee the Embarrassment which would inevitably be occasioned in the Execution of this Contract by the adoption of the Suggestions contained in your Despatch of 30th April 1810.'

The cause of the expected 'embarrassment' was that, on the basis of Macquarie's argument for free importation, several ships laden with grog had already left England bound for New South Wales. Now the masters of those ships were sailing straight into the teeth of a new (and this time legally constituted) monopoly.

'It would have been adviseable that an Engagement of this kind had not been entered into, until you had an opportunity of learning the Sentiments of His Majesty's Government upon the Propriety of adopting the measures which you had proposed and had So Strongly recommended,' Liverpool told Macquarie. 'It must be left to your own discretion to take Such measures as may appear to you the best calculated under all circumstances to do justice to the several parties whose Interests are affected by the arrangements which have been made in New South Wales and in this Country.'

Macquarie did his best to be fair to both sides, giving permission for the spirits to be imported and compensating the hospital consortium by extending their monopoly for another 12 months. In his own defence, he pointed out that at the time he recommended free importation he 'had no idea of the restriction being taken off by the Government at home. I expected instructions from Your Lordship, authorising me to open the Port here when I conceived it best to do so.'

The whole fiasco demonstrated that, more than two decades after settlement, the unreliability of communications between New South Wales and London made it impossible to efficiently coordinate policies between the two administrations. Macquarie himself complained of the 'Circuitous Mode of transmitting My public Despatches by Way of India, or by South Sea Whalers, which Occasionally touch here for Repairs and Refreshments', declaring it 'so . . . precarious, that I have not hitherto deemed it Safe or Adviseable to trust my Despatches to such Conveyances'.

But Macquarie's plans to reform the colony's drinking habits were not finished. Convinced of the 'Great Improvement' that had taken place in the first three years of his rule (during which time, he told Liverpool, the colonists had become 'daily more regular in their Conduct, More temperate in their Habits, and infinitely More

Moral and religious than they Were on my Arrival'), Macquarie proposed a scheme that was arguably even more audacious than the free importation of spirits:

> I am now about to recommend a Measure to Your Lordship which I Consider as so Essential to the Interests and Prosperity of this Colony that I shall be much disappointed if it does Not Meet With Your Lordship's Approbation. What I mean to propose is, that Permission may be granted by Government for Establishing a Distillery in this Country as soon as possible on an extensive Scale.

A distillery, Macquarie argued, would provide a market for the colony's surplus grain, which would otherwise be left to rot; it would encourage farmers to grow more, alleviating the risk of famine; and it would keep wealth from being sucked out of the colony to pay for imported grog. 'The Nature of the Inhabitants of this Country,' he told Liverpool, 'is such that Spirits Must be had . . . The many Advantages to be Obtained on this Account must be too obvious to require any farther Explanation from Me.'

Macquarie's idea was for the distillery to be privately owned by 'Opulent and respectable Persons, already settled in the Colony: as Persons, Newly Arrived, have many Difficulties to Struggle with, and would find much opposition thrown in their Way by the Monied People here, Who Would Naturally Consider them as *Intruders*, running away with a profitable Branch of Business Which they might Consider themselves exclusively entitled to.'

The 1812 House of Commons Select Committee on Transportation leapt at Macquarie's suggestion of a distillery – but only at the expense of his plan for free importation. (Macquarie wanted both.) It hardly mattered, since the new secretary of state, Earl Bathurst, did not share Macquarie's belief in the moral improvement of the lower orders. On the contrary, Bathurst remarked in a letter dated 23 November 1812, 'From the avidity with which spirits have uniformly been sought after, there is some reason to think that the eagerness on the part of the distilleries to meet the demand, might therefore produce so improvident a consumption of grain as to lay the foundation of a scarcity the ensuing year.'

It was to be another seven years before the government re-examined the idea of a 'colonial' distillery. In 1819 John Thomas Bigge was sent out to New South Wales with the authority to investigate 'all the laws, regulations and usages of the settlements'. As a priority, Bigge was instructed by Bathurst to discover 'whether a Distillation of Spirits in the Colony could be so checked and controlled as to prevent the indiscriminate and unrestrained Dissemination of Ardent Spirits throughout a Population, too much inclined already to an immoderate use of them, and too likely to be excited by the use of them to Acts of Lawless Violence'.

The Bigge inquiry was ostensibly a royal commission into the state of the colony and the effectiveness of transportation as a deterrent to crime. It soon became clear to Macquarie, however, that its real purpose was to find fault with his regime, especially his perceived leniency towards convicts and his alleged extravagance in public works.

Since his arrival in the colony, Macquarie had shown a genuine interest in rehabilitating – rather than simply punishing – convicts. Unlike his predecessors, he was also prepared to accept that a convict could attain social respectability after serving his or her sentence. Emancipation, he told Viscount Castlereagh, was 'the greatest Inducement that Can be held out to the Reformation of the manners of the Inhabitants . . . [W]hen United with Rectitude and long tried Good Conduct, [it] should lead a man back to that Rank in Society which he had forfeited and do away, as far as the case will admit, with All Retrospect of former Bad Conduct.'

Such enlightened views did not go down well with the capitalists, who saw convicts primarily as a source of cheap labour, or with their patrons and allies in England, or with the conservative Earl Bathurst, who believed that transportation had to be made 'an Object of real Terror' in order to deter crime at home.

Bigge came to New South Wales under clear instructions from Bathurst to reverse Macquarie's policies, and he conducted his inquiry accordingly. When interrogating witnesses, he did not distinguish between sworn and unsworn testimony, or between fact and opinion. Evidence was often taken in private. To Macquarie, it smacked of a witch-hunt.

The results of Bigge's Commission of Inquiry were compiled in a three-volume report. By the time the three volumes were tabled to the House of Commons in 1822 and 1823, Macquarie had left the colony. The sweeping criticisms contained in Bigge's report undermined Macquarie's legacy and signalled a shift away from the policies he had pursued. Under the next governor, life for the convicts would become harsher; emancipists would be held down, and the grand building project begun by Macquarie would be cut short.

Barely a decade after the first brick was laid, Governor Macquarie's Rum Hospital was already in need of major repairs. Those who had criticised it for being too complicated for the rudimentary skills of the convict workforce were proved right. Asked for his opinion of the workmanship, the convict architect Francis Greenaway remarked scornfully that the new hospital 'must soon fall into ruin'. Before passing the governorship to Sir Thomas Brisbane on 1 December 1821, Macquarie ordered the consortium to remedy the defects – which included inadequate foundations, decaying stonework and rotten timbers – but some faults would remain uncorrected for another 170 years.

The hospital was also too big for the colony's needs. Bigge noted in his report that, three years after it was opened, no more than three of its eight wards were being used by patients. For a time, 'Mr Lewen, an artist,' occupied one of the hospital's empty wards 'for the purpose of painting several large pictures'.

During the period of its rum monopoly, the consortium tested Macquarie's faith in the improved morals of the colonists. According to one estimate, the contractors imported as much as 40,000 gallons on top of the 60,000 gallons allowed under the revised four-year contract. As both the colony's principal surgeon and its superintendent of police, D'Arcy Wentworth oversaw the licensing and conduct of public houses throughout the settlement. In 1810, the year before the contract came into force, 31 annual licences were issued. According to Bigge's report, during the four years of the monopoly, the number of licences issued was 60, 117, 93 and 110. For the next five years, the number remained constant at about 85.

Bigge chastised Governor Macquarie for his 'disposition . . . to increase, rather than diminish, the number of houses licensed for the sale of spirits in Sydney and the other towns'. In fact, one of Macquarie's first acts as governor had been to *cut* the number of public houses by almost three-quarters. At the same time, he raised the licence fee and increased the penalty for unlicensed vending. These measures failed to stop illicit trafficking. In 1817 Macquarie raised the penalty for unlicensed taverns to £30, all of it to go to the informer, but few landlords were ever convicted – perhaps because the superintendent of police was himself active in the wholesale liquor business.

Macquarie's efforts to control the liquor trade – ineffective and inconsistent as they were – did not impress Bigge, who criticised the governor for his failure to recognise 'the great evil of placing strong temptation in the way of men whose previous habits, and whose present occupations and local employments, were calculated to render them easy victims of . . . dissipation'.

The commissioner's words echoed Governor Phillip's prediction, made 30 years earlier, that 'permitting of spirits amongst the civil & military may be necessary, but it will certainly be a great evil'.

Bigge's travels around the colony had convinced him that where spirits were available for purchase, it was impossible to prevent convicts from buying them. D'Arcy Wentworth, whose twin roles as police magistrate and authorised rum monopolist had given him 'considerable experience on this subject', considered the desire of 'spirituous liquors' to be 'the principal incentive to crime amongst the convicts'. As far as Wentworth was concerned, the 'greatest and only chance' of improving the convicts lay in the 'absolute privation' of grog.

Absolute privation – as Wentworth knew better than anyone – had been impossible to enforce from the moment the officers of the New South Wales Corps entered the rum trade.

The colony eventually won approval for its own distilleries, although Macquarie did not stay long enough to see them. On 3 February 1821 regulations governing colonial distillation were published in the *Sydney Gazette*. From 1 August 1822 it would be lawful to distil within the colony, and in stills licensed by the governor, spirit of '7 per cent above hydrometer proof' from grain grown in the colony 'and from no other grain whatever'. The governor would have the power to suspend the distillation of spirit from grain whenever the price of wheat rose above 10 shillings a bushel in the Sydney market for two consecutive days, although during this time 'distillation from fruit might be permitted'. Nobody with an interest in a licensed distillery would be allowed to retail spirits and licensed distilleries were barred from selling quantities of less than 100 gallons.

In his report on the state of agriculture and trade, Bigge was sceptical of the appeal of 'colonial' spirits, commenting 'I think it probable that the long-established use of the Bengal spirit in the colony will secure it a preference in the market [over locally distilled spirits]'. He was confident, however, that 'means will be found to improve the quality of the latter, and to accommodate it gradually to the taste of the inhabitants'.

One man fiercely opposed to the idea of a colonial distillery was John Macarthur, who told Bigge, 'The establishment of a Distillery from grain in this Colony with its present unfortunate population would, I fear, be an exceedingly dangerous undertaking.'

In his reports to the House of Commons, Commissioner Bigge gave the total population of New South Wales at the end of 1820 (not counting its Aboriginal inhabitants, of course) as 23,939, of whom 1307 were free settlers, 3255 were free 'by servitude and expiration of sentence' and 9451 were convicts under sentence. Most of the remainder were children, ticket-of-leave and pardoned convicts, or people born in the colony. Just 3707 were women.

Lord Bathurst's instructions to Bigge had noted the dangers of 'ill considered Compassion for Convicts', as a result of which the penalty of transportation to New South Wales risked being 'divested of all Salutary Terror'. Bathurst was mortified to find that fear of transportation had so diminished since the early days under Phillip that 'numerous applications' were being made by those sentenced to imprisonment for 'Minor Transgressions' to be transported instead!

The express purpose of Bigge's inquiry was to review the system for the purpose of making life tougher for convicts and restricting the opportunities for emancipists. The rogues and drunkards and bludgers Bigge portrayed as taking advantage of Governor Macquarie's leniency differed little from the incorrigible felons who haunted the pages of Lieutenant Ralph Clark's handwritten journal. But the colony was changing, and so was the role of grog.

Sentenced to 350 lashes in 1789 for 'feloniously stealing a certain quantity of medicines . . . and one pound of pepper', Squires had spent the rest of his life accumulating his 900-acre estate at Kissing Point. His rise to prosperity and respectability was emblematic of Governor Macquarie's doctrine of convict rehabilitation.

Squires did not share the fear and contempt felt by many colonists towards the first Australians. One of the regular visitors to his estate was Baneelon, the once-powerful warrior who had travelled to England with Governor Phillip and returned, nearly three years later, with Governor Hunter. Sometime after his return, Baneelon abandoned the settlement and went to live with his people on the banks of the Parramatta River, not far from Kissing Point. Perhaps that is how the two men met.

In his book *The Present Picture of New South Wales*, published in London in 1811, David Dickinson Mann reported that Baneelon had:

> taken to the woods again, returned to his old habits, and now lives in the same manner as those who have never mixed with the civilized world. Sometimes . . . he holds intercourse with the colony; but every effort uniformly fails to draw him once again into the circle of polished society, since he prefers to taste of liberty amongst his native scenes.

James Squires and Baneelon formed some kind of friendship, although it seems unlikely that Mann, who left the colony in 1809, would have considered Squires part of the 'circle of polished society'.

Joseph Holt, the self-styled 'general of the Irish rebels', claimed it was his custom to 'take in the chief [Baneelon] and his Gin [wife], and give them their breakfast and a glass of grog'.

Baneelon died in January 1813 and was buried in the garden of Squires's estate. His liking for (and tolerance of) alcohol, which had once won him the admiration of Watkin Tench, now provoked only condescension and contempt. His death was noted by the *Sydney Gazette*, which found little in his life worth commemorating:

Bennelong died on Sunday morning last at Kissing Point.
Of this veteran champion of the native tribe little favourable
can be said. His voyage to, and benevolent treatment in Great
Britain produced no change whatever in his manners and
inclinations, which were naturally barbarous and ferocious.
The principal Officers of Government had for many years
endeavoured, by the kindest of usage, to wean him from his
original habits, and draw him into a relish for civilized life;
but every effort was in vain exerted, and for the last few years
he has been little noticed. His propensity to drunkenness was
inordinate; and when in that state he was insolent, menacing
and overbearing. In fact, he was a thorough savage, not to be
warped from the form and character that nature gave him, by
all the efforts that mankind could use.

The colony's master brewer, James Squire (his name had by now lost the final 's'), outlived Baneelon by nine years. He died on 16 May

1822 and was buried two days later at the Old Sydney Burial Ground. His funeral was said to have been the largest the colony had ever seen.

Squire's son, another James, would manage the brewery for three years until his death in 1826. Afterwards it was taken over by his son-in-law, Thomas Farnell, who promised to 'spare no pains or expence, in order to supply his Friends with good wholesome Beer, not to be excelled by any House in the Colony'.

One of the last First Fleeters, James Squire died not just respectable, but respected. 'As one of the primary inhabitants of the Colony . . . none ever more exerted himself for the benefit of the inhabitants than the deceased,' said his obituary in the *Gazette*. 'He might . . . be styled the *Patriarch of Kissing Point*; as he had lived, where he died, 26 years.'

Between them, the warrior Baneelon and the brewer James Squire embodied opposing sides of the developing Australian story. The unusual and mostly undocumented relationship between the pair – the Aboriginal man a tolerated and perhaps awkwardly welcome guest on land that had once been exclusively his – can be seen as a symbol of the ideal of friendly coexistence that had already been renounced by other settlers.

Squire's death at the age of 67 signalled the looming end of the colony's first era. The 'old hands', the *Gazette* remarked solemnly, were becoming 'thinned in their ranks'. The one-time London chicken thief had outlasted five governors as well as the military pretenders who came between them; he had lived (and prospered) through the years when the monopolists of the New South Wales Corps held a stranglehold on trade; he had watched the colony grow from a bedraggled camp on the edge of the harbour into a cluster of settlements spreading gradually but relentlessly across the continent.

The forger, artist and ex-convict Joseph Lycett, who knew Squire and drew a picture of his property, said of his old friend:

> He was . . . universally respected and beloved for his amiable
> and useful qualities as a member of society, and more espe-
> cially as the friend and protector of the lower class of settlers.
> Had he been less liberal, he might have died more wealthy;
> but his assistance always accompanied his advice to the poor
> and unfortunate.

Another contemporary, Peter Cunningham, described the brewer as 'jocose' and recalled how Squire 'took pleasure in quoting' the words he found on a headstone belonging to one of his regulars at the Malting Shovel. With a larrikin Australian humour that echoes down the centuries, the long-lost inscription is supposed to have read:

> Ye who wish to lie here
> Drink Squire's beer!

Afterword

Before New South Wales was a colony, it was a vision. To those who never set foot in it, it remained a vision, clouded by idealism as much as by prejudice.

The stories recounted by David Collins of drunken settlers running amok in the Hawkesbury in his *Account of the English Colony in New South Wales* tended to confirm scathing observations found in letters, journals and sermons. By the time the *Penny Cyclopaedia of the Society for the Diffusion of Useful Knowledge* was published in 27 volumes between 1828 and 1843, the colony's reputation for drunkenness was fixed. Under the entry for 'Transportation', the *Cyclopaedia* reported that:

[S]hortly after the commencement of the present century, the colony had become one scene of brutal dissipation and

licentiousness, of lawless violence and rapine. It was no
uncommon occurrence for men to sit down round a bucket
of spirits, and drink it with great quart pots, until they were
unable to stir from the spot.

When John Dunmore Lang, Sydney's first Presbyterian minister,
gave evidence to the House of Commons Select Committee on
Transportation in 1838, he did not hesitate to name grog as the
cause of all the colony's moral failings:

Do you mean that opportunities exist of gaining an honest
livelihood, but the temptations to a dishonest course are too
great to be withstood?
Unquestionably.
Does that arise from the peculiar state of society and moral
feeling that prevails?
*It arises chiefly from the facility of getting ardent spirits; this is the
bane of the colony.*

Along with the idea that the colonists were perpetually intoxicated
went the perception that the colonial economy was itself 'addicted
to rum' through its dependence on a bartering system in which the
most desirable commodity was grog. According to this theory, the
economy ran on rum, which functioned as the colony's de facto
currency (a problematic term, since currencies need to circulate,
and much of the rum was drunk before it could be circulated).
Lurid generalisations such as the following, from Robert Hughes's

The Fatal Shore, have only cemented the reputation for wholesale inebriation: 'Colonial Sydney was a drunken society, from top to bottom. Men and women drank with a desperate, addicted, quarrelsome single-mindedness.'

Some recent historians have sought to play down the significance of grog. Alan Atkinson, in the first volume of *The Europeans in Australia*, showed scant interest in the role of rum in the colony's evolution. On the subject of Bligh's overthrow, Atkinson offhandedly informed his readers, 'I say very little about the usual explanations, Bligh's prohibition of the barter of spirits and his attempt to suppress trading monopolies.'

If everybody had been as drunk as Hughes and others have claimed, the colony would not have been able to feed itself, let alone grow surpluses and prosper. If, on the other hand, rum played such a minor part in the life of the settlement, why did successive governors spend so much time worrying about it? Between these two extremes, a more nuanced story is possible, one that recognises the importance of eye-witnesses such as David Collins, Richard Atkins and the *Britannia*'s log-keeper, Robert Murray, without being seduced by the arguments of the colony's ideological enemies.

To reduce grog to a mere economic footnote in the history of Australia is to ignore its role in the seismic changes the colony underwent in the first 30 years of its existence – a role that was sometimes central and was rarely less than significant. Among other things, grog was a political tool; a key component in a system of bartering; a reward for labour and an enticement to informants; an important factor in a revolution; and a source of funding for public works, including a hospital that, for all its shoddy workmanship, still stands today.

To the marines on the *Scarborough*, a continuing supply of grog after the fleet landed at Botany Bay was 'indispensably requisite for the preservation of our lives'. Should their allowance be withdrawn, they told their commanding officer, 'we cannot expect to survive'. A few of those marines decided to settle in the colony; others died of sickness or were executed – some for crimes involving grog. They were not the last Australians to consider life unimaginable without a drink.

A note on sources

I t is easy to immerse oneself in Australia's colonial history; electri-
fying eyewitness accounts by Watkin Tench, David Collins, John
Hunter, William Bradley, Philip Gidley King, Surgeon John
White, Governor Phillip and others can all be read in modern print
or facsimile editions, and most are accessible online. The eccentric
spelling and bare-faced misogyny of a diarist such as Ralph Clark,
whose journal was not intended for publication, cannot diminish
the raw immediacy of his observations.

The multi-volume *Historical Records of New South Wales* and
Historical Records of Australia gathers up correspondence between the
colony's early governors and the authorities in London, as well as
private letters, statistical data, petitions, Government and General
Orders and a lot more. Together with Dr John Cobley's idiosyncratic

but groundbreaking *Sydney Cove* books, which drew on contemporary sources to provide a daily record of the settlement's early years, they offer the modern reader a window on the colony as it was in the process of forming.

Australia's first newspaper, the *Sydney Gazette and New South Wales Advertise*r, began publication in 1803 under the editorship of George Howe, who had worked on *The Times* in London before being transported for life for shoplifting. A series of facsimile reproductions covers the first nine years of its existence, and every edition is available online. The words 'Published by Authority' beneath the masthead betray who was ultimately in control, but its pages breathe with the pungent goings-on of the colony at all levels of society.

Bibliography

Primary sources

Bentham, Jeremy, *The Works of Jeremy Bentham, vol. 4 (Panopticon, Constitution, Colonies, Codification)*, Edinburgh, William Tait, 1843.

Bowes Smyth, Arthur, *The Journal of Arthur Bowes Smyth: Surgeon, Lady Penrhyn 1787–1789*, Sydney, Australian Documents Library, 1979.

Bradley, William, *A Voyage to New South Wales: The Journal of Lieutenant William Bradley R.N. of HMS* Sirius, *1786–1792,* facsimile reproduction, 2 vols, Sydney, Trustees of the Public Library of New South Wales, 1969.

Clark, Ralph, *Journal and Letters of Lt. Ralph Clark 1787–1792*, Sydney, Australian Documents Library, 1969.

Collins, David, *An Account of the English Colony in New South Wales*, 2 vols, London, 1798, 1802, reprinted Sydney, A.H. & A.W. Reed, 1975.

Cook, James, *The Journals, vol. 1, The Voyage of the Endeavour, 1768–1771*, ed. J. C. Beaglehole, Cambridge, Cambridge University Press, 1967.

Cunningham, Peter, *Two Years in New South Wales, Comprising Sketches of the Actual State of Society in that Colony, of Its Peculiar Advantages to Emigrants, of Its Topography, Natural History, &c &c*, London, 1828, reprinted Sydney, Angus & Robertson, 1966.

Easty, John, *Memorandum of the Transactions of a Voyage from England to Botany Bay, 1787–1793: A First Fleet Journal by John Easty, Private Marine*, Sydney, Public Library of New South Wales, 1965.

Historical Records of Australia, vols 1–10.

Historical Records of New South Wales, vols 1–7.

Holt, Joseph, *Memoirs of Joseph Holt, General of the Irish Rebels, in 1798*, London, Henry Colburn, 1838.

Hunter, John, *An Historical Journal of the Transactions at Port Jackson and Norfolk Island*, London, 1793, reprinted Sydney, Angus and Robertson, 1968.

King, Philip Gidley, *The Journal of Philip Gidley King, Lieutenant, R.N., 1787–1790*, Sydney, Australian Documents Library, 1980.

Lang, John Dunmore, *An Historical and Statistical Account of New South Wales: From the Founding of the Colony in 1788 to the Present Day*, 2 vols, London, 1837, reprinted London, Sampson Low, Marston, Low & Searle, 1875.

Mann, David Dickinson, *The Present Picture of New South Wales*, London, 1811, digital text reproduced by University of Sydney Library, Sydney, 2003.

Phillip, Arthur, *The Voyage of Governor Phillip to Botany Bay*, London, 1789, reprinted Sydney, Angus & Robertson, 1970.

Report from the Select Committee on Transportation, ordered by the House of Commons to be printed, 1812.

Tench, Watkin, *Sydney's First Four Years, being a reprint of A Narrative of the Expedition to Botany Bay and a Complete Account of the Settlement at Port Jackson by Captain Watkin Tench of the Marines*, with an introduction and annotations by L. F. Fitzhardinge, Sydney, Library of Australian History, 1979.

White, John, *Journal of a Voyage to New South Wales by John White Esq*, London, 1790, reprinted Sydney, Angus & Robertson, 1962.

Worgan, George, *Journal of a First Fleet Surgeon*, Sydney, Library of Australian History, 1978.

Secondary sources

Allen, Matthew, 'Alcohol and Authority in Early New South Wales: The Symbolic Significance of the Spirit Trade, 1788–1808', *History Australia*, vol. 9, no. 3, December 2012.

Atkinson, Alan, *The Europeans in Australia: a History, vol. 1*, Melbourne, Oxford University Press, 1997.

Barton, George Burnett, *History of New South Wales From the Records, Governor Phillip, 1783–1789*, Sydney, Charles Potter, Government Printer, 1889.

Britton, Alexander, *History of New South Wales From the Records, vol. II, Phillip and Grose, 1789–1794*, Sydney, Charles Potter, Government Printer, 1894.

Butlin, S. J., *Foundations of the Australian Monetary System 1788–1851*, Melbourne, 1953, digital text reproduced by University of Sydney Library, Sydney, 2002.

Champion, Shelagh & Champion, George, 'Illicit Stills and Smuggling in Manly, Warringah and Pittwater to 1850', article, privately published, 1992, 1993.

Clark, Manning, *A History of Australia, vol. 1, From the Earliest Times to the Age of Macquarie*, Melbourne, Melbourne University Press, 1962.

Clendinnen, Inga, *Dancing with Strangers*, Melbourne, Text, 2003.

Clune, David & Ken Turner (eds), *The Governors of New South Wales 1788–2010*, Sydney, Federation Press, 2010.

Cobley, John, *Sydney Cove 1788*, Sydney, Hodder & Stoughton, 1962.

——*Sydney Cove 1789–1790*, Sydney, Angus & Robertson, 1963.

——*Sydney Cove 1791–1792*, Sydney, Angus & Robertson, 1965.

——*Sydney Cove 1793–1795: The Spread of Settlement*, Sydney, Angus & Robertson, 1983.

——*Sydney Cove 1795–1800: The Second Governor*, Sydney, Angus & Robertson, 1986.

Deutscher, Keith, *Breweries of Australia: A History*, Melbourne, Lothian, 1999.

Dortins, Emma, 'The Many Truths of Bennelong's Tragedy', *Aboriginal History*, vol. 33, 2009, pp. 53–75.

Duffy, Michael, *Man of Honour: John Macarthur – Duellist, Rebel, Founding Father*, Sydney, Pan Macmillan, 2003.

Ellis, M. H., *John Macarthur*, Sydney, Angus & Robertson, 1967.

Evatt, H.V., *Rum Rebellion: A Study of the Overthrow of Governor Bligh*, Sydney, Angus & Robertson, 1944.

Frost, Alan, *Arthur Phillip 1738–1814: His Voyaging*, Melbourne, Oxford University Press, 1987.

——*Botany Bay: The Real Story*, Melbourne, Black Inc., 2011.

——*The First Fleet: The Real Story*, Melbourne, Black Inc., 2011.

Gillen, Mollie, *The Founders of Australia: A Biographical Dictionary of the First Fleet*, Sydney, Library of Australian History, 1989.

Hughes, David, 'Australia's First Brewer', *Journal of the Royal Australian Historical Society*, vol. 82, no. 2, 1996, pp. 153–67.

Hughes, Robert, *The Fatal Shore*, London, Collins Harvill, 1987.

Levi, Werner, *American–Australian Relations*, Minneapolis, University of Minnesota Press, 1947.

Lisle, Phillip, 'Rum Beginnings: Towards a New Perspective of the Grose Years', *Journal of the Royal Australian Historical Society*, vol. 91, no. 1, 2005, pp. 15–28.

Mackaness, George (ed.), *Some Private Correspondence of the Rev. Samuel Marsden and Family 1794–1824*, Dubbo, Australian Historical Monographs, 1976.

Nagle, John Flood, *Collins, the Courts & the Colony: Law & Society in Colonial New South Wales 1788–1796*, Sydney, UNSW Press, 1996.

Nicol, John, *Life and Adventures, 1776–1801*, Melbourne, Text, 1997.

Norval, Morris & David Rothman (ed.), *The Oxford History of the Prison: The Practice of Punishment in Western Society*, New York, Oxford University Press, 1995.

Parsonson, Ian, *The Australian Ark: A History of Domesticated Animals in Australia*, Melbourne, CSIRO, 1998.

Ritchie, John, *The Evidence to the Bigge Reports*, 2 vols, Melbourne, Heinemann, 1971.

——*Punishment and Profit: The Report of Commissioner John Bigge on the Colonies of New South Wales and Van Diemen's Land, 1822, Their Origins, Nature and Significance*, Melbourne, Heinemann, 1970.

Robinson, Portia, *The Women of Botany Bay: A Reinterpretation of the Role of Women in the Origins of Australian Society*, Ringwood, Penguin, 1993.

Spigelman, J. J., 'The Macquarie Bicentennial: A Reappraisal of the Bigge Reports', The Annual History Lecture, History Council of NSW, 4 September 2009.

State Library of New South Wales, *The Governor: Lachlan Macquarie 1810–1821* (exhibition catalogue).

Wentworth, William Charles, *Description of the Colony of New South Wales*, London, 1819, reprinted Sydney, Doubleday Australia, 1978.

Index

Phillip, Governor Arthur (*continued*)
  health of 136–7
  kidney pain 137
  leniency 66
  Macarthur's antipathy to 167–8
  money 62
  powers 56
  return to England 138, 143
  self-sufficiency, goal of 136
  Sirius, wreck of 125
  South Head, at 112
  spear injury to 116
  Sydney Cove, at 52
  water, needing 43
  whale as gift to 113
Pinchgut Island 60, 184
Piper, Captain John 249
Pitt 144
Pitt's Row 258
Point Solander 41
Ponds, The 183
Porpoise 237–8, 267, 269
Port Jackson 47, 49, 103, 117, 127, 131,
    140, 142, 148, 197, 225, 247, 252,
    256, 265
  gallons landed at 217
  people landing at 51
  Third Fleet reaching 134
Port Royal 12
'porter' 141, 239
  licence for sale of 141
  prices 157
Portsmouth 224
Powers, John 23
*The Present Picture of New South
    Wales* 293
Price, Mary 131
prices, government control of 213
Prince of Wales 21, 34, 50, 59, 109
private enterprise/trade 180, 186
prohibition 183
Prospect 228

Prospect Hill 183, 214
public houses 287, 288
  licensing laws 291
  publication of list of licensed 291
Pugh, Elizabeth 28
punishment
  military, imposed by 156
  theft, for 104

Raven, Mr 165
Raven, Simon 184
Reliance 175
The Revenge 177
Rhode Island 148, 165–6, 216
Richmond Hill 173
Riley, Alexander 281
Rio de Janeiro 23, 24–8, 29, 175
  liquor purchased at 32
River Thames 3
Roberts, William 132–3
Rose, Thomas 179
Rose Hill 131
  productive land at 136
Ross, Major 7, 8, 10–11, 14, 31, 43, 53,
    54, 56, 65, 66, 72, 74, 108, 205
  return to England 136
Rouse Hill 247
Rowe, William 173
Royal Admiral 141, 214, 225
Royal Navy 6, 11–12
  drunkenness 12
rum
  addiction to 298
  Barsby blaming actions on 60
  cargoes of 150, 198, 199, 265
  de facto currency, as 298
  economy, in 171, 298
  First Fleet marines rations 11
  Jamaican 11, 177
  prices 157
  Rio de Janeiro, in 25, 28
  sailors' rations 11–12